DATE DUE			

30408000005153

327.1273
ESP

Espionage and
intelligence

Woodland High School
HENRY COUNTY PUBLIC SCHOOLS

Current
CONTROVERSIES

Espionage
and Intelligence

Other Books in the Current Controversies Series

Espionage and Intelligence

Debra A. Miller, Book Editor

GREENHAVEN PRESS

An imprint of Thomson Gale, a part of The Thomson Corporation

Detroit • New York • San Francisco • New Haven, Conn. • Waterville, Maine • London

Christine Nasso, *Publisher*
Elizabeth Des Chenes, *Managing Editor*

© 2007 The Gale Group.

Star logo is a trademark and Gale and Greenhaven Press are registered trademarks used herein under license.

For more information, contact:
Greenhaven Press
27500 Drake Rd.
Farmington Hills, MI 48331-3535
Or you can visit our Internet site at http://www.gale.com

Articles in Greenhaven Press anthologies are often edited for length to meet page requirements. In addition, original titles of these works are changed to clearly present the main thesis and to explicitly indicate the author's opinion. Every effort is made to ensure that Greenhaven Press accurately reflects the original intent of the authors. Every effort has been made to trace the owners of copyrighted material.

Cover photograph © Sven Hagolani/zefa/Corbis.

ISBN-13: 978-0-7377-3719-6 (hardcover)
ISBN-10: 0-7377-3719-0 (hardcover)
ISBN-13: 978-0-7377-3720-2 (pbk.)
ISBN-10: 0-7377-3720-4 (pbk.)

Library of Congress Control Number: 2007931891

Printed in the United States of America
10 9 8 7 6 5 4 3 2 1

Contents

Chapter 2: Will Post-9/11 Reforms of the U.S. Intelligence System Be Effective?

Yes: Post-9/11 Reforms of the U.S. Intelligence System Will Be Effective

Chapter 3: Do Intelligence-Gathering Activities Threaten Civil or Human Rights?

Yes: Intelligence-Gathering Activities Threaten Civil or Human Rights

Chapter 4: What Can Be Done to Improve U.S. Intelligence-Gathering Abilities?

Foreword

By definition, controversies are "discussions of questions in which opposing opinions clash" (Webster's Twentieth Century Dictionary Unabridged). Few would deny that controversies are a pervasive part of the human condition and exist on virtually every level of human enterprise. Controversies transpire between individuals and among groups, within nations and between nations. Controversies supply the grist necessary for progress by providing challenges and challengers to the status quo. They also create atmospheres where strife and warfare can flourish. A world without controversies would be a peaceful world; but it also would be, by and large, static and prosaic.

The Series' Purpose

The purpose of the Current Controversies series is to explore many of the social, political, and economic controversies dominating the national and international scenes today. Titles selected for inclusion in the series are highly focused and specific. For example, from the larger category of criminal justice, Current Controversies deals with specific topics such as police brutality, gun control, white collar crime, and others. The debates in Current Controversies also are presented in a useful, timeless fashion. Articles and book excerpts included in each title are selected if they contribute valuable, long-range ideas to the overall debate. And wherever possible, current information is enhanced with historical documents and other relevant materials. Thus, while individual titles are current in focus, every effort is made to ensure that they will not become quickly outdated. Books in the Current Controversies series will remain important resources for librarians, teachers, and students for many years.

In addition to keeping the titles focused and specific, great care is taken in the editorial format of each book in the series. Book introductions and chapter prefaces are offered to provide background material for readers. Chapters are organized around several key questions that are answered with diverse opinions representing all points on the political spectrum. Materials in each chapter include opinions in which authors clearly disagree as well as alternative opinions in which authors may agree on a broader issue but disagree on the possible solutions. In this way, the content of each volume in Current Controversies mirrors the mosaic of opinions encountered in society. Readers will quickly realize that there are many viable answers to these complex issues. By questioning each author's conclusions, students and casual readers can begin to develop the critical thinking skills so important to evaluating opinionated material.

Current Controversies is also ideal for controlled research. Each anthology in the series is composed of primary sources taken from a wide gamut of informational categories including periodicals, newspapers, books, U.S. and foreign government documents, and the publications of private and public organizations. Readers will find factual support for reports, debates, and research papers covering all areas of important issues. In addition, an annotated table of contents, an index, a book and periodical bibliography, and a list of organizations to contact are included in each book to expedite further research.

Perhaps more than ever before in history, people are confronted with diverse and contradictory information. During the Persian Gulf War, for example, the public was not only treated to minute-to-minute coverage of the war, it was also inundated with critiques of the coverage and countless analyses of the factors motivating U.S. involvement. Being able to sort through the plethora of opinions accompanying today's major issues, and to draw one's own conclusions, can be a complicated and frustrating struggle. It is the editors' hope that Current Controversies will help readers with this struggle.

Introduction

> *"Intelligence . . . has always been used by the United States to support U.S. military operations, but much of what forms today's intelligence system was not created until after the December 7, 1941, Japanese attack on Pearl Harbor."*

Intelligence—information needed by the president and policy makers to conduct foreign policy and protect the United States from its enemies—has always been used by the United States to support U.S. military operations, but much of what forms today's intelligence system was not created until after the December 7, 1941, Japanese attack on Pearl Harbor. The surprise attack revealed major flaws in U.S. intelligence capabilities, brought the United States into World War II, and spurred the United States to develop a much larger and more coordinated intelligence community.

Indeed, even during the war, the United States moved to improve its intelligence system. The army, navy, and marines each conducted intelligence operations, and the United States created the Office of Strategic Services (OSS) under the Joint Chiefs of Staff, a military advisory group, to analyze all national security information. All of these intelligence efforts were successful during the war, producing critical intelligence that helped America win the conflict. After the war, President Harry S. Truman closed down the OSS, but the Soviet Union's postwar decision to expand its influence in Europe caused him to rethink the need for intelligence. Numerous independent and congressional investigations recommended a variety of approaches to intelligence. One of the major issues considered was whether the military should retain control of intelligence or whether a civilian intelligence agency should be created.

The end result of these investigations was the passing of the National Security Act of 1947, a law that created the framework for today's national security and intelligence system. Under the act, a civilian Central Intelligence Agency (CIA), headed by a director of central intelligence, was established to handle all national intelligence gathering and to advise the president. In addition, a National Security Council (NSC) was created to coordinate national security policy; the army, the navy, and the newly created air force were unified under a new cabinet position, the secretary of defense; and the Joint Chiefs of Staff were charged solely with providing military advice to the president and the secretary of defense.

This CIA-run intelligence system became one of the key features of the Cold War—the decades-long period of tension and threats between the United States and the Soviet Union that ended only with the economic and political collapse of the latter in 1991. During the Cold War, all of the CIA's operations were designed to counteract Soviet activities that U.S. officials believed constituted a threat to the United States and world security. As a result, the CIA focused on sending spies to various locations to extract secrets about the Soviet military buildup and on protecting the U.S. military establishment from Soviet espionage efforts. This period also witnessed a large escalation in the use of satellites and other technological devices for detecting Soviet military intentions and activities. Many intelligence analysts and employees became experts on the Soviet Union, with little knowledge of other parts of the world.

When the Cold War ended, however, this intelligence system suddenly seemed obsolete. The system's failure to predict or prevent the terrorist attacks on September 11, 2001, together with the lack of weapons of mass destruction (WMDs) found in Iraq after the George W. Bush administration used the threat of WMDs as the underpinning for the Iraq war, led to calls for intelligence reform. These events caused many policy makers and intelligence experts to conclude that the

U.S. intelligence community was not properly configured to develop accurate information about terrorism, nuclear weapons proliferation, and other modern threats. This conclusion was bolstered by the findings of two independent commissions created by the government—the National Commission on Terrorist Attacks upon the United States (the "9/11 Commission") and the Commission on the Intelligence Capabilities of the United States Regarding Weapons of Mass Destruction (the "WMD Commission"). In 2004, Congress passed legislation that, together with some previous reforms, provided for a series of major changes in the organization of the U.S. intelligence system.

Today's U.S. intelligence community is composed of a group of sixteen federal agencies and organizations under the control of the executive branch. The CIA continues to be a principal intelligence agency, together with the Federal Bureau of Investigation (FBI), two components of the Department of Homeland Security (DHS), and a growing number of intelligence entities within the Department of Defense (such as the Defense Intelligence Agency (DIA), the National Security Agency (NSA) and the National Reconnaissance Office (NRO)). Recent reforms, however, created the position of Director of National Intelligence (DNI) to oversee all intelligence activities throughout the government, taking this responsibility away from the director of the CIA. Reforms also added the Drug Enforcement Administration (DEA) to the list of intelligence agencies, and established two new national centers—the National Counterterrorism Center (NCTC) and the Weapons Intelligence, Nonproliferation, and Arms Control Center (WINPAC)—to encourage collaboration among intelligence agencies on these specific national security concerns. As these reforms suggest, the work of the intelligence community now includes collecting information not only on the activities of foreign governments and their agents, but also on weapons proliferation around the globe, international narcotics activities, and potential terrorist threats.

Making this transition into the twenty-first century of intelligence gathering is the focus of many of the selections in *Current Controversies: Espionage and Intelligence*. The authors in this volume discuss a variety of issues, including the severity and nature of the intelligence failures relating to 9/11 and Iraq, the effectiveness of recent reforms, and suggestions for additional improvements. In addition, authors provide their perspectives on whether recent intelligence activities may be impinging on important civil and human rights. As all of these selections suggest, creating an intelligence system that fits America's needs in the post–Cold War period is one of the nation's biggest challenges.

CHAPTER 1

Current
CONTROVERSIES

Has the U.S. Espionage and Intelligence-Gathering System Been Successful?

Chapter Preface

Although the country is focused on allegations of recent intelligence failures, many intelligence experts say the United States has experienced intelligence failures throughout its history. Commentators point to several times in the nation's past when the U.S. government relied on intelligence information that was later considered to be questionable, inaccurate, misunderstood, or misused.

In 1898, for example, incorrect information about the sinking of an American warship, the USS *Maine*, helped to push the United States into the Spanish-American War. The ship exploded while anchored in a harbor in Havana, Cuba—an incident that destroyed the ship and killed 266 crew members. The U.S. Navy concluded that the explosion was caused by an enemy mine, and the American press sensationalized the story, creating a fervor that led to war with Spain. Later, however, an investigation found that the explosion was caused by an accident—a spontaneous combustion of coal that was used as the ship's fuel.

Questionable intelligence also formed the basis for U.S. involvement in both world wars. In 1917, a telegram from German foreign minister Arthur Zimmerman to Mexico, proposing an alliance between the two countries against the United States, was intercepted by British intelligence. The telegram was leaked to the press, and it caused a public uproar that quickly brought America into World War I. Although the German ambassador confirmed the telegram's authenticity, rumors circulated at the time and since then about whether the telegram may have been just a hoax designed to force America into the war.

Of course, one of the most well-known U.S. intelligence failures was the U.S. military's failure to predict or prevent Japan's surprise attack on U.S. forces stationed in Pearl Harbor, Hawaii—the event that propelled the United States into World War II. Launched on December 7, 1941, the Japanese attack killed 2,403 U.S. service members, wounded another 1,178 Americans, and destroyed five battleships, three destroyers, three cruisers, and 188 American planes. Before the attack, a number of commentators had warned of such a scenario, and on December 6, 1941, the U.S. military actually cracked encrypted Japanese diplomatic communications suggesting the possibility of an attack, but no warning reached Pearl Harbor in time because of radio interference. A warning was sent in a Western Union telegram to U.S. commanders in Hawaii, but it was not marked "urgent" and was never read. The Pearl Harbor attack brought a reluctant nation into the war and launched a major reform of the U.S. intelligence system.

Despite improvements in U.S. intelligence-gathering and analysis, however, the intelligence system remained far from perfect and the United States has continued to justify military decisions based on questionable information. During the Vietnam War, for example, a controversial incident involving an American destroyer, the USS *Maddox*, was used by President Lyndon Johnson to justify increasing American forces in the region. In 1964, the *Maddox* was monitoring North Vietnamese radar signals in the region, and U.S. officials claimed that one particular message threatened an attack on the ship and that the attack soon materialized. The *Maddox* sank several North Vietnamese torpedo boats, but the North Vietnamese have always claimed that they never approached or attacked the ship. Nevertheless, the incident provided justification for Congress to pass the Gulf of Tonkin Resolution, authorizing a buildup of American forces on the side of the South Vietnamese.

Another relatively recent incident occurred in 1975, when President Gerald Ford sent U.S. Marines to rescue the crew of an American merchant ship, the *Mayaguez*, which was held captive by Cambodian troops for supposedly entering Cambodian territorial waters. Because of faulty intelligence, however, U.S. forces attacked the wrong island in Cambodia, resulting in forty-one American combat deaths even as the Cambodians were returning the crew members to U.S. custody. A few years later, in 1983, President Ronald Reagan staged a similarly unnecessary rescue effort to free American medical students said to be held hostage during a coup attempt against the government of Grenada, a small island country in the Caribbean. The military attack resulted in the death of twenty-three American soldiers as well as hundreds of Grenadians, but the students were never in any real danger; instead, U.S. intelligence about the incident was simply wrong.

Although some commentators see these historical examples and more recent incidents as evidence to support reform of U.S. intelligence-gathering, other experts suggest that no intelligence system can ever be free from error. These authorities argue that the very nature of intelligence work requires the collection of vast amounts of information through both human and technological means. Most of this information is trivial and meaningless. The task of finding bits and pieces of useful information amid this massive pile of data, and putting those pieces together to formulate a clear picture soon enough to protect the United States from impending attacks or justify military action, is almost impossible. Despite these difficult odds, U.S. intelligence agencies have succeeded in providing accurate and helpful intelligence analyses on many occasions. The fact that intelligence failures sometimes occur, some experts conclude, must be expected.

Yet the desire to improve intelligence is a natural reaction when the United States is surprised by a deadly attack or politicians rely on imperfect intelligence to justify sending out American troops. The following selections highlight the differing assessments of U.S. intelligence capabilities following two recent events—the 9/11 terrorist attacks and the U.S. invasion of Iraq.

U.S. Intelligence Agencies Failed to Prevent the September 11, 2001, Terrorist Attacks

The National Commission on Terrorist Attacks upon the United States

The National Commission on Terrorist Attacks upon the United States was an independent, bipartisan commission created by congressional legislation and the signature of President George W. Bush in late 2002 to investigate the September 11, 2001, terrorist attacks and make recommendations to guard against future attacks.

September 11, 2001, was a day of unprecedented shock and suffering in the history of the United States. The nation was unprepared.

A Nation Transformed

At 8:46 on the morning of September 11, 2001, the United States became a nation transformed. An airliner traveling at hundreds of miles per hour and carrying some 10,000 gallons of jet fuel plowed into the North Tower of the World Trade Center in Lower Manhattan. At 9:03, a second airliner hit the South Tower. Fire and smoke billowed upward. Steel, glass, ash, and bodies fell below. The Twin Towers, where up to 50,000 people worked each day, both collapsed less than 90 minutes later.

At 9:37 that same morning, a third airliner slammed into the western face of the Pentagon. At 10:03, a fourth airliner crashed in a field in southern Pennsylvania. It had been aimed

The National Commission on Terrorist Attacks upon the United States, executive summary, in *The 9/11 Commission Report*, National Archives and Records Administration, July 22, 2004, pp. 1–16.

at the United States Capitol or the White House, and was forced down by heroic passengers armed with the knowledge that America was under attack.

More than 2,600 people died at the World Trade Center; 125 died at the Pentagon; 256 died on the four planes. The death toll surpassed that at Pearl Harbor in December 1941.

This immeasurable pain was inflicted by 19 young Arabs acting at the behest of Islamist extremists headquartered in distant Afghanistan. Some had been in the United States for more than a year, mixing with the rest of the population. Though four had training as pilots, most were not well-educated. Most spoke English poorly, some hardly at all. In groups of four or five, carrying with them only small knives, box cutters, and cans of Mace or pepper spray, they had hijacked the four planes and turned them into deadly guided missiles.

The 9/11 attacks were a shock, but they should not have come as a surprise.

Why did they do this? How was the attack planned and conceived? How did the U.S. government fail to anticipate and prevent it? What can we do in the future to prevent similar acts of terrorism?

A Shock, Not a Surprise

The 9/11 attacks were a shock, but they should not have come as a surprise. Islamist extremists had given plenty of warning that they meant to kill Americans indiscriminately and in large numbers. Although Usama Bin Ladin [the founder of al Qaeda terrorist organization] himself would not emerge as a signal threat until the late 1990s, the threat of Islamist terrorism grew over the decade.

In February 1993, a group led by Ramzi Yousef [a Kuwaiti member of al Qaeda] tried to bring down the World Trade

Center with a truck bomb. They killed six and wounded a thousand. Plans by Omar Abdel Rahman [an Egyptian Muslim cleric and leader of the militant Islamic Group] and others to blow up the Holland and Lincoln tunnels and other New York City landmarks were frustrated when the plotters were arrested. In October 1993, Somali tribesmen shot down U.S. helicopters, killing 18 and wounding 73 in an incident that came to be known as "Black Hawk down." Years later it would be learned that those Somali tribesmen had received help from al Qaeda.

In early 1995, police in Manila [the Philippines] uncovered a plot by Ramzi Yousef to blow up a dozen U.S. airliners while they were flying over the Pacific. In November 1995, a car bomb exploded outside the office of the U.S. program manager for the Saudi National Guard in Riyadh, [Saudi Arabia,] killing five Americans and two others. In June 1996, a truck bomb demolished the Khobar Towers apartment complex in Dhahran, Saudi Arabia, killing 19 U.S. servicemen and wounding hundreds. The attack was carried out primarily by Saudi Hezbollah, an organization that had received help from the government of Iran.

Until 1997, the U.S. intelligence community viewed Bin Ladin as a financier of terrorism, not as a terrorist leader. In February 1998, Usama Bin Ladin and four others issued a self-styled fatwa [Muslim decree], publicly declaring that it was God's decree that every Muslim should try his utmost to kill any American, military or civilian, anywhere in the world, because of American "occupation" of Islam's holy places and aggression against Muslims.

In August 1998, Bin Ladin's group, al Qaeda, carried out near-simultaneous truck bomb attacks on the U.S. embassies in Nairobi, Kenya, and Dar es Salaam, Tanzania. The attacks killed 224 people, including 12 Americans, and wounded thousands more.

In December 1999, Jordanian police foiled a plot to bomb hotels and other sites frequented by American tourists, and a U.S. Customs agent arrested Ahmed Ressam at the U.S.-Canadian border as he was smuggling in explosives intended for an attack on Los Angeles International Airport.

By September 2001, the ... U.S. government ... had received clear warning that Islamist terrorists meant to kill Americans in high numbers.

In October 2000, an al Qaeda team in Aden, Yemen, used a motorboat filled with explosives to blow a hole in the side of a destroyer, the USS *Cole*, almost sinking the vessel and killing 17 American sailors.

The 9/11 attacks on the World Trade Center and the Pentagon were far more elaborate, precise, and destructive than any of these earlier assaults. But by September 2001, the executive branch of the U.S. government, the Congress, the news media, and the American public had received clear warning that Islamist terrorists meant to kill Americans in high numbers.

Who Is the Enemy?

Who is this enemy that created an organization capable of inflicting such horrific damage on the United States? We now know that these attacks were carried out by various groups of Islamist extremists. The 9/11 attack was driven by Usama Bin Ladin.

In the 1980s, young Muslims from around the world went to Afghanistan to join as volunteers in a jihad (or holy struggle) against the Soviet Union. A wealthy Saudi, Usama Bin Ladin, was one of them. Following the defeat of the Soviets in the late 1980s, Bin Ladin and others formed al Qaeda to mobilize jihads elsewhere.

The history, culture, and body of beliefs from which Bin Ladin shapes and spreads his message are largely unknown to many Americans. Seizing on symbols of Islam's past greatness, he promises to restore pride to people who consider themselves the victims of successive foreign masters. He uses cultural and religious allusions to the holy Qur'an [Islam's holy book] and some of its interpreters. He appeals to people disoriented by cyclonic change as they confront modernity and globalization. His rhetoric selectively draws from multiple sources—Islam, history, and the region's political and economic malaise.

Bin Ladin also stresses grievances against the United States widely shared in the Muslim world. He inveighed against the presence of U.S. troops in Saudi Arabia, which is the home of Islam's holiest sites, and against other U.S. policies in the Middle East.

None of the measures adopted by the U.S. government from 1998 to 2001 disturbed or even delayed the progress of the al Qaeda plot.

Upon this political and ideological foundation, Bin Ladin built over the course of a decade a dynamic and lethal organization. He built an infrastructure and organization in Afghanistan that could attract, train, and use recruits against ever more ambitious targets. He rallied new zealots and new money with each demonstration of al Qaeda's capability. He had forged a close alliance with the Taliban, a regime providing sanctuary for al Qaeda.

By September 11, 2001, al Qaeda possessed:

- leaders able to evaluate, approve, and supervise the planning and direction of a major operation;

- a personnel system that could recruit candidates, indoctrinate them, vet them, and give them the necessary training;

- communications sufficient to enable planning and direction of operatives and those who would be helping them;

- an intelligence effort to gather required information and form assessments of enemy strengths and weaknesses;

- the ability to move people great distances; and

- the ability to raise and move the money necessary to finance an attack. . . .

Failures of Imagination and Policy

Since the plotters were flexible and resourceful, we cannot know whether any single step or series of steps would have defeated them. What we can say with confidence is that none of the measures adopted by the U.S. government from 1998 to 2001 disturbed or even delayed the progress of the al Qaeda plot. Across the government, there were failures of imagination, policy, capabilities, and management. . . .

Terrorism was not the overriding national security concern for the U.S. government under either the [Bill] Clinton or the pre-9/11 Bush administration.

The most important failure was one of imagination. We do not believe leaders understood the gravity of the threat. The terrorist danger from Bin Ladin and al Qaeda was not a major topic for policy debate among the public, the media, or in the Congress. Indeed, it barely came up during the 2000 presidential campaign.

Al Qaeda's new brand of terrorism presented challenges to U.S. governmental institutions that they were not well-designed to meet. Though top officials all told us that they understood the danger, we believe there was uncertainty among them as to whether this was just a new and especially venomous version of the ordinary terrorist threat the United States had lived with for decades, or it was indeed radically new, posing a threat beyond any yet experienced.

As late as September 4, 2001, Richard Clarke, the White House staffer long responsible for counterterrorism policy coordination, asserted that the government had not yet made up its mind how to answer the question: "Is al Qaeda a big deal?" A week later came the answer. . . .

Terrorism was not the overriding national security concern for the U.S. government under either the [Bill] Clinton or the pre-9/11 Bush administration. The policy challenges were linked to this failure of imagination. Officials in both the Clinton and Bush administrations regarded a full U.S. invasion of Afghanistan as practically inconceivable before 9/11.

The most serious weaknesses in agency capabilities were in the domestic arena.

Capabilities Failures

Before 9/11, the United States tried to solve the al Qaeda problem with the capabilities it had used in the last stages of the Cold War and its immediate aftermath. These capabilities were insufficient. Little was done to expand or reform them. The CIA [Central Intelligence Agency] had minimal capacity to conduct paramilitary operations with its own personnel, and it did not seek a large-scale expansion of these capabilities before 9/11. The CIA also needed to improve its capability to collect intelligence from human agents.

At no point before 9/11 was the Department of Defense fully engaged in the mission of countering al Qaeda, even though this was perhaps the most dangerous foreign enemy threatening the United States.

America's homeland defenders faced outward. NORAD [North American Aerospace Defense Command, a U.S.-Canada organization that provides aerospace warnings for North America] itself was barely able to retain any alert bases at all. Its planning scenarios occasionally considered the danger of hijacked aircraft being guided to American targets, but only aircraft that were coming from overseas.

The most serious weaknesses in agency capabilities were in the domestic arena. The FBI [Federal Bureau of Investigation] did not have the capability to link the collective knowledge of agents in the field to national priorities. Other domestic agencies deferred to the FBI.

The U.S. government did not find a way of pooling intelligence . . . to guide . . . the CIA, the FBI, the State Department, the military and the [homeland security] agencies.

FAA [Federal Aviation Administration, a federal agency responsible for civil aviation safety] capabilities were weak. Any serious examination of the possibility of a suicide hijacking could have suggested changes to fix glaring vulnerabilities—expanding no-fly lists, searching passengers identified by the CAPPS [Computer Assisted Passenger Pre-Screening System] screening system, deploying federal air marshals domestically, hardening cockpit doors, alerting air crews to a different kind of hijacking possibility than they had been trained to expect. Yet the FAA did not adjust either its own training or training with NORAD to take account of threats other than those experienced in the past.

Management Failures

The missed opportunities to thwart the 9/11 plot were also symptoms of a broader inability to adapt the way government manages problems to the new challenges of the twenty-first century. Action officers should have been able to draw on all available knowledge about al Qaeda in the government. Management should have ensured that information was shared and duties were clearly assigned across agencies, and across the foreign-domestic divide.

There were also broader management issues with respect to how top leaders set priorities and allocated resources. For instance, on December 4, 1998, DCI [director of central intelligence George] Tenet issued a directive to several CIA officials and the DDCI [deputy director of central intelligence] for Community Management, stating: "We are at war. I want no resources or people spared in this effort, either inside CIA or the Community." The memorandum had little overall effect on mobilizing the CIA or the intelligence community. This episode indicates the limitations of the DCI's authority over the direction of the intelligence community, including agencies within the Department of Defense.

The U.S. government did not find a way of pooling intelligence and using it to guide the planning and assignment of responsibilities for joint operations involving entities as disparate as the CIA, the FBI, the State Department, the military, and the agencies involved in homeland security. . . .

Because of offensive actions against al Qaeda, and defensive actions to improve homeland security, we believe we are safer today. But we are not safe.

Are We Safer?

Since 9/11, the United States and its allies have killed or captured a majority of al Qaeda's leadership; toppled the Taliban [government], which gave al Qaeda sanctuary in Afghanistan; and severely damaged the organization. Yet terrorist attacks continue. Even as we have thwarted attacks, nearly everyone expects they will come. How can this be?

The problem is that al Qaeda represents an ideological movement, not a finite group of people. It initiates and inspires, even if it no longer directs. In this way it has transformed itself into a decentralized force. Bin Ladin may be limited in his ability to organize major attacks from his hideouts. Yet killing or capturing him, while extremely important, would not end terror. His message of inspiration to a new generation of terrorists would continue.

Because of offensive actions against al Qaeda since 9/11, and defensive actions to improve homeland security, we believe we are safer today. But we are not safe.

U.S. Intelligence on Iraq's Possession of Weapons of Mass Destruction Was Dead Wrong

The Commission on the Intelligence Capabilities of the United States Regarding Weapons of Mass Destruction

The Commission on the Intelligence Capabilities of the United States Regarding Weapons of Mass Destruction was established by President George W. Bush on February 6, 2004, to assess whether the U.S. intelligence community is adequately authorized, organized, equipped, trained, and resourced to identify and warn the U.S. government about the proliferation of weapons of mass destruction and other threats of the twenty-first century.

On the brink of war, and in front of the whole world, the United States government asserted that Saddam Hussein had reconstituted his nuclear weapons program, had biological weapons and mobile biological weapon production facilities, and had stockpiled and was producing chemical weapons. All of this was based on the assessments of the U.S. Intelligence Community. And not one bit of it could be confirmed when the war was over.

While the intelligence services of many other nations also thought that Iraq had weapons of mass destruction, in the end it was the United States that put its credibility on the line, making this one of the most public—and most damaging—intelligence failures in recent American history.

The Nature of Intelligence Failures

This failure was in large part the result of analytical shortcomings; intelligence analysts were too wedded to their as-

The Commission on the Intelligence Capabilities of the United States Regarding Weapons of Mass Destruction, "Overview of the Report: Introduction," in *Report to the President*, March 31, 2005, pp. 3-8. www.wmd.gov/report.

sumptions about Saddam's intentions. But it was also a failure on the part of those who collect intelligence—CIA's [Central Intelligence Agency] and the Defense Intelligence Agency's (DIA) spies, the National Security Agency's (NSA) eavesdroppers, and the National Geospatial-Intelligence Agency's (NGA) imagery experts. In the end, those agencies collected precious little intelligence for the analysts to analyze, and much of what they did collect was either worthless or misleading. Finally, it was a failure to communicate effectively with policymakers; the Intelligence Community didn't adequately explain just how little good intelligence it had—or how much its assessments were driven by assumptions and inferences rather than concrete evidence.

Was the failure in Iraq typical of the Community's performance? Or was Iraq, as one senior intelligence official told the Commission, a sort of "perfect storm"—one-time breakdown caused by a rare confluence of events that conspired to create a bad result? In our view, it was neither.

Across the board, the Intelligence Community knows disturbingly little about the nuclear programs of many of the world's most dangerous actors.

The failures we found in Iraq are not repeated everywhere. The Intelligence Community played a key role, for example. in getting Libya to renounce weapons of mass destruction and in exposing the long-running [rogue Pakistani nuclear engineer] A.Q. Khan nuclear proliferation network. It is engaged in imaginative, successful (and highly classified) operations in many parts of the world. Tactical support to counterterrorism efforts is excellent, and there are signs of a boldness that would have been unimaginable before September 11, 2001.

But neither was Iraq a "perfect storm." The flaws we found in the Intelligence Community's Iraq performance are still all too common. Across the board, the Intelligence Community knows disturbingly little about the nuclear programs of many of the world's most dangerous actors. In some cases, it knows less now than it did five or ten years ago. As for biological weapons, despite years of Presidential concern, the Intelligence Community has struggled to address this threat.

To be sure, the Intelligence Community is full of talented, dedicated people. But they seem to be working harder and harder just to maintain a status quo that is increasingly irrelevant to the new challenges presented by weapons of mass destruction. Our collection agencies are often unable to gather intelligence on the very things we care the most about. Too often, analysts simply accept these gaps; they do little to help collectors identify new opportunities, and they do not always tell decisionmakers just how limited their knowledge really is.

The Intelligence Community is also fragmented, loosely managed, and poorly coordinated; the 15 intelligence organizations are a "Community" in name only.

Taken together, these shortcomings reflect the Intelligence Community's struggle to confront an environment that has changed radically over the past decade. For almost 50 years after the passage of the National Security Act of 1947, the Intelligence Community's resources were overwhelmingly trained on a single threat—the Soviet Union, its nuclear arsenal, its massive conventional forces, and its activities around the world. By comparison, today's priority intelligence targets are greater in number (there are dozens of entities that could strike a devastating blow against the United States) and are often more diffuse in character (they include not only states but also nebulous transnational terror and proliferation networks). What's more, some of the weapons that would be most dangerous in the hands of terrorists or rogue nations are difficult to detect. Much of the technology, equipment, and materials necessary to develop biological and chemical weapons, for example, also has legitimate commercial applications. Biological weapons themselves can be built in small-scale facilities that are easy to conceal, and weapons-grade uranium can be effectively shielded from traditional detection techniques. At the same time, advances in technology have made the job of technical intelligence collection exceedingly difficult.

Major Change Needed

The demands of this new environment can only be met by broad and deep change in the Intelligence Community. The Intelligence Community we have today is buried beneath an avalanche of demands for "current intelligence"—the pressing need to meet the tactical requirements of the day. Current intelligence in support of military and other action is necessary, of course. But we also need an Intelligence Community with strategic capabilities: it must be equipped to develop long-term plans for penetrating today's difficult targets, and to identify political and social trends shaping the threats that lie over the horizon. We can imagine no threat that demands greater strategic focus from the Intelligence Community than that posed by nuclear, biological, and chemical weapons.

The Intelligence Community is also fragmented, loosely managed, and poorly coordinated; the 15 intelligence organizations are a "Community" in name only and rarely act with a unity of purpose. What we need is an Intelligence Community that is integrated: the Community's leadership must be capable of allocating and directing the Community's resources in a coordinated way. The strengths of our distinct collection agencies must be brought to bear together on the most difficult intelligence problems. At the same time we need a Community that preserves diversity of analysis, and that encourages structured debate among agencies and analysts over the interpretation of information.

Perhaps above all, the Intelligence Community is too slow to change the way it does business. It is reluctant to use new human and technical collection methods; it is behind the curve in applying cutting-edge technologies; and it has not adapted its personnel practices and incentives structures to fit the needs of a new job market. What we need is an Intelligence Community that is flexible—able to respond nimbly to an ever-shifting threat environment and to the rapid pace of today's technological changes.

In short, to succeed in confronting today's and tomorrow's threats, the Intelligence Community must be transformed—a goal that would be difficult to meet even in the best of all possible worlds. And we do not live in the best of worlds. The CIA and NSA may be sleek and omniscient in the movies, but in real life they and other intelligence agencies are vast government bureaucracies. They are bureaucracies filled with talented people and armed with sophisticated technological tools, but talent and tools do not suspend the iron laws of bureaucratic behavior. Like government bodies everywhere, intelligence agencies are prone to develop self-reinforcing, risk averse cultures that take outside advice badly. While laudable steps were taken to improve our intelligence agencies after September 11, 2001, the agencies have done less in response to the failures over Iraq, and we believe that many within those agencies do not accept the conclusion that we reached after our year of study: that the Community needs fundamental change if it is to successfully confront the threats of the 21st century.

We are not the first to say this. Indeed, commission after commission has identified some of the same fundamental failings we see in the Intelligence Community, usually to little effect. The Intelligence Community is a closed world, and many insiders admitted to us that it has an almost perfect record of resisting external recommendations.

But the present moment offers an unprecedented opportunity to overcome this resistance. . . .

[However,] no matter how much we improve the intelligence Community, weapons of mass destruction will continue to pose an enormous threat. Intelligence will always be imperfect and, as history persuades us, surprise can never be completely prevented. Moreover, we cannot expect spies, satellites, and analysts to constitute our only defense. As our biological weapons recommendations make abundantly clear, all national capabilities—regulatory, military, and diplomatic—must be used to combat proliferation. . . .

The U.S. Intelligence Community Is Bureaucratic, Obsolete, and Ill-Equipped to Counter Twenty-First-Century Threats

Richard L. Russell

Richard L. Russell is a professor of national security affairs at the National Defense University's Near East–South Asia Center for Strategic Studies. He previously served as a political-military analyst at the Central Intelligence Agency (CIA).

The controversy surrounding the American pre-war intelligence assessment of Iraq's weapons of mass destruction programs dominates the airwaves and print media. Behind-the-scenes investigations spawned by the Iraq performance as well as the tragedies of September 11, 2001 offer a fleeting window of opportunity to chart and implement much-needed reforms of a beleaguered intelligence community.

Antiquated Capabilities

The intelligence community's failure to warn with the clarity needed to disrupt the conspiracy of September 11 and its less-than-stellar performance in assessing Iraqi WMD [weapons of mass destruction] programs highlight both the dangers to security and the demands for strategic intelligence in the twenty-first century. The community can hardly be trusted to do an honest and balanced critique of its performance in the wake of these events. It comprises numerous intelligence agencies, each with its own set of entrenched interests. As it stands today, the intelligence agencies are bureaucratically modeled after management layers and hierarchies of the blue-chip companies of old, such as IBM. But while the market weeds out noncompetitive companies that are too rigid and inflexible to be successful in the private sector, noncompetitive organizations are perpetuated by inertia in the public sector. As Richard K. Betts insightfully noted in *Foreign Affairs* ("Fixing Intelligence," January–February 2002), "The current crisis presents the opportunity to override entrenched and outdated interests, to crack heads and force the sorts of consolidation and cooperation that have been inhibited by bureaucratic constipation."

The intelligence community's antiquated capabilities are devoted to exploitation of clandestinely acquired information that collectively sheds only a narrow light on the broad array of national security threats. Intelligence—in its boiled-down essence—is information, and information is critical to the power of competitive businesses as well as to the power of terrorists and nation-states. But in the United States, the intelligence community has profoundly lost its competitive advantage over the private sector for the collection and analysis of publicly available information. In order to gain greater access to the secrets that transnational organizations and nation-states seek to deny the U.S. as well as to exploit the explosion in public information, the community must sharpen its collection and analytic tools. Reforms instigated by independent reviews and implemented either by executive order or by congressional legislation need to be aimed at transforming the intelligence community from failed top-down institutions based on obsolete business models of the 1950s to the nimble, bottom-up, flat, and networked organizations that thrive in the age of information technology revolution. The United States needs to reforge its obsolescent intelligence community if it is to match wits with transnational threats to American security such as al Qaeda and traditional threats stemming from nation-states with the political intent and military means to challenge American interests and power. . . .

CIA Bureaucracy

The Central Intelligence Agency is the "first among equals" in the intelligence community and deserves particularly close independent scrutiny. The agency benefits from a bureaucratic position that separates it from the pressures of policy interests to a far greater degree than its brother intelligence agencies. The CIA also uniquely benefits from its traditional privileged access to the president and his key national security lieutenants. Yet the CIA's support to the commander-in-chief over the past decade in major armed conflicts reveals a consistent pattern of shortcomings, particularly in regard to human intelligence collection. One of the starkest lessons to be gleaned from looking at past CIA performance is that it has consistently failed to produce top-quality human intelligence against the greatest threats to the United States.

The [CIA] today operates on a top-down organizational model rather than the bottom-up model that succeeds in the private information-technology sector.

The CIA suffers from a ponderous bureaucratic structure that makes it sluggish in response to events, impedes intellectual and analytic initiative, and diverts resources from nurturing and keeping analytic talent. . . . Analysis moves painstakingly slowly through the bureaucratic structure, and iconoclastic views that challenge conventional wisdom are very likely to have their edges substantially smoothed in the laborious review process. Analysts suffer considerable frustration. Their charge is to write analyses for the senior levels of the national security policymaking community. Even uncontroversial analysis suffers from pronounced dumbing-down effects as it passes up and through the chain of command. More often than not, policymakers are substantially more conversant with international issues than CIA managers, who in the review act more as overpaid editors—without the technical expertise of professional editors—to make analysis more understandable for themselves rather than the far more expert consumers in the policy community.

A Top-Down Model

The production of intelligence analysis takes the form of an inverted pyramid. One or a few junior analysts, for example, might draft a piece of intelligence analysis. It then passes through a chain of command loaded with GS-15 [high-salaried] and Senior Intelligence Service (SIS) managers, who typically impose more stylistic than substantive changes. The piece of analysis then passes to a current intelligence staff stuffed with GS-15 or higher individuals, who further massage the analysis into stale and boring prose before publication in the President's Daily Brief or the more widely disseminated Senior Executive Intelligence Brief. . . .

The agency today operates on a top-down organizational model rather than the bottom-up model that succeeds in the private information-technology sector. Agency analytic managers frequently push down orders for intelligence analyses. Such orders often force analysts to produce analyses whether or not there is a critical mass of classified intelligence that fills knowledge gaps in publicly available information and assessments for policymakers. The analysis produced by this top-down approach often strikes policymaker consumers as shoddy, incompetent, or simply inconsequential. It is no wonder that the 1996 Brown Commission [on the roles and capabilities of the United States intelligence community] found that "often what they [policymakers] receive fails to meet their needs by being too late or too unfocused, or by adding little to what they already know."

This top-down cultural ethos has grown stronger over the years, in part because the agency does poorly in training, nurturing, and retaining experts. As the working-level analytic workforce becomes younger and more inexperienced, the aging ranks of agency managers are increasingly insecure about the quality, timeliness, and policy relevance of analysis. They compensate by micromanaging the production cycle. Micromanagement, in turn, discourages analysts and stifles intellectual innovation among inexperienced and more seasoned analysts alike.

Security Barriers

Onerous security procedures are also formidable barriers to expertise in the DI [Directorate of Intelligence, the CIA's analytical arm]. The United States is blessed with an enormously diverse population, but the CIA and the intelligence community at large have failed miserably at tapping this wealth of cultural talent and harnessing it for intelligence collection and analysis to defend the country. Security background investigations are loaded with ethnocentric biases that collectively border on xenophobia. Job candidates who are naturalized or first-generation American citizens are assumed to be spies for hostile foreign powers until proven otherwise. Those job candidates with relatives or close friends overseas and extensive travel abroad have high chances of being precluded from intelligence service out of concern that they would be too vulnerable to foreign influences.

Security barriers are contributing substantially to chronic linguistic skill shortages in the CIA and increasing American vulnerability to attack.

These are unacceptable cases of the security and administrative tail wagging the operational and analytic dog. What American citizen is going to be fluent in languages such as

Arabic or Chinese unless he or she has close friends or family abroad or has lived overseas for extended periods of time? Despite the CIA security restrictions and expectations, one simply does not become fluent in difficult languages by living like a vestal virgin. These overly burdensome security considerations prevent the intelligence community from making full and wise use of the National Security Education Program, which is designed to give scholarships to undergraduate and graduate students studying hard languages, frequently abroad. Recipients are required to pay off their scholarships with postgraduation service in the government, but security concerns often prevent scholarship recipients from serving in intelligence agencies.

These security barriers are contributing substantially to chronic linguistic skill shortages in the CIA and increasing American vulnerability to attack. As the Congressional Joint Inquiry into the September 11 attack and the intelligence community's performance determined, "the Intelligence Community was not prepared to handle the challenge it faced in translating the volumes of foreign language counterterrorism intelligence it collected. Agencies within the Intelligence Community experienced backlogs in material awaiting translation, a shortage of language specialists and language-qualified field officers, and a readiness level of only 30 percent in the most critical terrorism-related languages." . . .

These security requirements [also] act as concrete barriers to the nourishing of CIA analytic contacts with outside experts. As the Brown Commission rightly judged, "The failure to make greater use of outside expertise at the CIA appears to result in part from a lack of financial resources and in part from onerous security requirements—particularly the polygraph examination and the requirement to submit subsequent publications for review—that discourages some outside experts from participating in intelligence work." CIA analysts might have occasion to chat with a foreign scholar over substantive issues at an academic conference in the United States, but the wrath of security officers would fall on an analyst's head if he or she had a one-on-one discussion with the same expert abroad.

A Lack of Experts

One of the most damning criticisms of the agency is that it fails miserably at recruiting, nurturing, and retaining experts of its own, while excelling at producing bureaucrats. The Brown Commission found that "while there are some analysts in the Intelligence Community who are nationally known experts in their respective fields, they are the exception rather than the rule." To underscore this point, few of this journal's readers, off the top of their heads, would be able to name a handful of agency analysts who are widely respected experts. Are the agency's "Team Leaders" or "Issue Managers" responsible for the multi-disciplinary teams that produce analysis on North Korea, China, Iraq, Iran, Russia, Pakistan, India, or Europe internationally or nationally recognized scholars or experts? In marked contrast, many readers would likely be able to identify numerous foreign affairs experts from the halls of academe or think tanks such as the Brookings Institution, the Council on Foreign Relations, and the Rand Corporation.

The tragedy of September 11 was only the most recent in a string of . . . [CIA] human intelligence collection failures.

The sorry state of affairs is such that while the CIA has few experts of national or international standing, guessing from the bureaucratic wire diagram of the analytic corps posted on the agency's website, the DI alone has managers numbering in the triple digits. The American policymaking community and the general public have the right to ask: What is the agency's contribution to national security—expert analysts who make sense of the world for our decision makers or bureaucrats who push paper? . . .

It is long past time for the White House or Congress to order CIA management to remodel DI business practices for recruiting, nurturing, and retaining analytic expertise.

Stilettos Inside the Beltway

While the quality of analysis is dull inside CIA headquarters, knife fights are underway over power relationships within the intelligence community writ large. The press has swirled with reports that the Pentagon established a small intelligence unit specifically to analyze defector reporting from Iraq. Leaks from anonymous community insiders are concerned that the Pentagon put a political spin on analysis to press the president into war. As the *New York Times* reported [in 2002], "Some officials say the creation of the team reflects frustration on the part of . . . senior officials that they are not receiving undiluted information on the capacities of President Saddam Hussein of Iraq and his suspected ties to terrorist organizations. But officials who disagree say the top civilian policy makers are intent on politicizing intelligence to fit their hawkish views on Iraq."

Charges of politicizing intelligence at this stage are probably overblown. The CIA is indeed best positioned bureaucratically to produce intelligence analysis that is divorced from policy interests, and as long as the DCI [Director of Central Intelligence, the head of the CIA] continues to have access to the president . . . it is not likely that Pentagon analysis will unduly straitjacket the president's policy deliberations. . . .

The Failure to Collect Human Intelligence

The DO [CIA Directorate of Operations] is still working according to business practices developed into standard operating procedure during the Cold War—namely, of actively recruiting agents and running them in place inside their governments to provide intelligence on an ongoing basis. Unfortunately, this model has consistently failed to give the United States access to our adversaries' decision-making councils. Our history of human penetrations against adversaries with whom we are at war is poor. We had no top-level penetrations of North Korea and China in the 1950s, of North Vietnam in the 1960s and early 1970s, of the Soviet Union during the entire Cold War, and of Iraq in the first Gulf War. Judging from the preliminary findings of the Senate-House Joint Inquiry the CIA had a variety of human sources reporting on al Qaeda operational planning against the United States, but obviously not the deep penetrations required to cut through the fog of gossip and speculation to gain sufficient clarity to stop a September 11 conspiracy. The jury is still out as to how bad the DO human intelligence was against Iraq, particularly on Baghdad's weapons of mass destruction and ballistic missile programs. The initial read does not look favorable.

CIA's persistent operational and analytic shortcomings elude quick and easy fixes.

The tragedy of September 11 was only the most recent in a string of DO human intelligence collection failures. As the Joint Inquiry determined, "Prior to September 11, 2001, the Intelligence Community did not effectively develop and use human sources to penetrate the al-Qa'ida inner circle. This lack of reliable and knowledgeable human sources significantly limited the Community's ability to acquire intelligence that could be acted upon before the September 11 attacks. In part, at least, the lack of unilateral (i.e., U.S.-recruited) counterterrorism sources was a product of an excessive reliance on foreign liaison services." Overreliance on foreign liaison services is in no small measure attributable to the dearth of Arabic language skills in the DO, for reasons discussed earlier.

This longstanding dismal performance of American human intelligence in wartime demands independent examination. . . .

Reforms Needed

Sharpening the dull intelligence blade will require a strong hand from outside the intelligence community. Left to their own devices, the CIA's DO and DI managements have no incentive to bring about reforms; they have clearly vested interests in the perpetuation of a system in which they benefit regardless of the worth of intelligence to American policymakers. CIA's persistent operational and analytic shortcomings elude quick and easy fixes. . . .

Experts are needed to conduct strategic analysis the likes of which the U.S. failed to produce before September 11. Given the analytic and operational shortcomings discussed in this article, it is no surprise that the CIA failed to foresee with sufficient clarity the events of that day. With the proliferation of weapons of mass destruction and their delivery systems, the U.S. can ill afford to fail to redress these profound shortcomings in strategic intelligence.

U.S. Intelligence Agencies Have Had More Successes than Failures in Countering Terrorism

Richard K. Betts

Richard K. Betts is director of the Institute of War and Peace Studies at Columbia University and was a member of the National Commission on Terrorism, a bipartisan commission created by Congress in 2000 to provide recommendations about the U.S. counterterrorism policy. Betts also is the author of the book Surprise Attack: Lessons for Defense Planning *(2001), from which this viewpoint is excerpted.*

As the dust from the attacks on the World Trade Center and the Pentagon was still settling, the chants began: The CIA was asleep at the switch! The intelligence system is broken! Reorganize top to bottom! The biggest intelligence system in the world, spending upward of $30 billion a year, could not prevent a group of fanatics from carrying out devastating terrorist attacks. Drastic change must be overdue. The new conventional wisdom was typified by Tim Weiner, writing in *The New York Times* on October 7, [2001]: "What will the nation's intelligence services have to change to fight this war? The short answer is: almost everything."

Yes and no. A lot must, can, and will be done to shore up U.S. intelligence collection and analysis. Reforms that should have been made long ago will now go through. New ideas will get more attention and good ones will be adopted more readily than in normal times. There is no shortage of proposals and initiatives to shake the system up. There is, however, a shortage of perspective on the limitations that we can expect from improved performance. Some of the changes will substitute new problems for old ones. The only thing worse than business as usual would be naive assumptions about what reform can accomplish.

The Limits of Intelligence

Paradoxically, the news is worse than the angriest critics think, because the intelligence community has worked much better than they assume. Contrary to the image left by the destruction of September 11, U.S. intelligence and associated services have generally done very well at protecting the country. In the aftermath of a catastrophe, great successes in thwarting previous terrorist attacks are too easily forgotten—successes such as the foiling of plots to bomb New York City's Lincoln and Holland tunnels in 1993, to bring down 11 American airliners in Asia in 1995, to mount attacks around the millennium on the West Coast and in Jordan, and to strike U.S. forces in the Middle East in the summer of 2001.

The awful truth is that even the best intelligence systems will have big failures. The terrorists that intelligence must uncover and track are not inert objects; they are living, conniving strategists. They, too, fail frequently and are sometimes caught before they can strike. But once in a while they will inevitably get through. Counterterrorism is a competitive game. Even Barry Bonds could be struck out at times by a minor-league pitcher, but when a strikeout means people die, a batting average of less than 1,000 looks very bad indeed.

It will take large investments to make even marginal reductions in the probability of future disasters.

It will be some time before the real story of the September 11 intelligence failure is known, and longer still before a reliable public account is available. Rather than recap the rumors and fragmentary evidence of exactly what intelligence did and did not do before September 11, at this point it is more appropriate to focus on the merits of proposals for reform and the larger question about what intelligence agencies can reasonably be expected to accomplish.

Spending Money for Marginal Returns

One way to improve intelligence is to raise the overall level of effort by throwing money at the problem. This means accepting additional waste, but that price is paid more easily in wartime than in peacetime. Unfortunately, although there have certainly been misallocations of effort in the past, there are no silver bullets that were left unused before September 11, no crucial area of intelligence that was neglected altogether and that a few well-targeted investments can conquer. There is no evidence, at least in public, that more spending on any particular program would have averted the September 11 attacks. The group that carried them out had formidable operational security, and the most critical deficiencies making their success possible were in airport security and in legal limitations on domestic surveillance. There are nevertheless several areas in which intelligence can be improved, areas in which previous efforts were extensive but spread too thinly or slowed down too much.

It will take large investments to make even marginal reductions in the probability of future disasters. Marginal improvements, however, can spell the difference between success and failure in some individual cases. If effective intelligence collection increases by only five percent a year, but the critical warning indicator of an attack turns up in that five percent, gaining a little information will yield a lot of protection. Streamlining intelligence operations and collection is a nice idea in principle but risky unless it is clear what is not needed.

When threats are numerous and complex, it is easier to know what additional capabilities we want than to know what we can safely cut. . . .

Improving Technology and Human Intelligence

Another way to improve intelligence is to do better at collecting important information. Here, what can be improved easily will help marginally, whereas what could help more than marginally cannot be improved easily. The National Security Agency (NSA), the National Imagery and Mapping Agency (NIMA), and associated organizations can increase "technical" collection—satellite and aerial reconnaissance, signals intelligence, communications monitoring—by buying more platforms, devices, and personnel to exploit them. But increasing useful human intelligence, which everyone agrees is the most critical ingredient for rooting out secretive terrorist groups, is not done easily or through quick infusions of money. . . .

More and better spies will help, but no one should expect breakthroughs if we get them. It is close to impossible to penetrate small, disciplined, alien organizations.

Human intelligence is key because the essence of the terrorist threat is the capacity to conspire. The best way to intercept attacks is to penetrate the organizations, learn their plans, and identify perpetrators so they can be taken out of action. Better human intelligence means bolstering the CIA's Directorate of Operations (DO), the main traditional espionage organization of the U.S. government. The DO has been troubled and periodically disrupted ever since the evaporation of the Cold War consensus in the late stage of the Vietnam War provoked more oversight and criticism than spies find congenial. Personnel turnover, tattered esprit, and a growing culture of risk aversion have constrained the DO's effectiveness. . . .

More and better spies will help, but no one should expect breakthroughs if we get them. It is close to impossible to penetrate small, disciplined, alien organizations like Osama bin Laden's al Qaeda, and especially hard to find reliable U.S. citizens who have even a remote chance of trying. Thus we usually rely on foreign agents of uncertain reliability. Despite our huge and educated population, the base of Americans on which to draw is small: there are very few genuinely bilingual, bicultural Americans capable of operating like natives in exotic reaches of the Middle East, Central and South Asia, or other places that shelter the bin Ladens of the world....

Sharpened Analysis

Money can buy additional competent people to analyze collected information more readily than it can buy spies who can pass for members of the Taliban—especially if multiplying job slots are accompanied by enhanced opportunities for career development within intelligence agencies to make long service attractive for analysts. Pumping up the ranks of analysts can make a difference within the relatively short time span of a few years. The U.S. intelligence community has hundreds of analysts, but also hundreds of countries and issues to cover. On many subjects the coverage is now only one analyst deep—and when that one goes on vacation, or quits, the account may be handled out of the back pocket of a specialist on something else. We usually do not know in advance which of the numerous low-priority accounts might turn into the highest priority overnight.

Hiring more analysts will be a good use of resources but could turn out to have a low payoff, and perhaps none at all, for much of what they do.... Postmortems of intelligence failures usually reveal that very bright analysts failed to predict the disaster in question, despite their great knowledge of the situation, or that they had warned that an eruption could happen but without any idea of when. In fact, expertise can get in the way of anticipating a radical departure from the norm, because the depth of expert knowledge of why and how things have gone as they have day after day for years naturally inclines the analyst to estimate that developments will continue along the same trajectory. It is always a safer bet to predict that the situation tomorrow will be like it has been for the past dozen years than to say that it will change abruptly. And of course, in the vast majority of cases predictions of continuity are absolutely correct; the trick is to figure out which case will be the exception to a powerful rule....

The Problem of Surprise Attacks

The issue for reform is whether any fixes at all can break a depressing historical pattern. After September 11, intelligence officials realized that fragmentary indicators of impending action by bin Laden's network had been recognized by the intelligence system but had not been sufficient to show what or where the action would be. A vague warning was reportedly issued, but not one that was a ringing alarm. This is, sadly, a very common occurrence.

There are often numerous false alarms before an attack, and they dull sensitivity to warnings of the attack that does occur.

What we know of intelligence in conventional warfare helps explain why powerful intelligence systems are often caught by surprise. The good news from history is that attackers often fail to win the wars that they start with stunning surprises: Germany was defeated after invading the Soviet Union, Japan after Pearl Harbor, North Korea after 1950, Argentina after taking the Falkland Islands, Iraq after swallowing Kuwait. The bad news is that those initial attacks almost always succeed in blindsiding the victims and inflicting terrible losses.

Once a war is underway, it becomes much harder to surprise the victim. The original surprise puts the victim on unambiguous notice. It shears away the many strong reasons that exist in peacetime to estimate that an adversary will not take the risk of attacking. It was easier for Japan to surprise the United States at Pearl Harbor than at Midway. But even in the midst of war, surprise attacks often succeed in doing real damage: recall the Battle of the Bulge or the Tet offensive. For Americans, September 11 was the Pearl Harbor of terrorism. The challenge now is to make the next attacks more like Midway than like Tet.

Surprise attacks often succeed despite the availability of warning indicators. This pattern leads many observers to blame derelict intelligence officials or irresponsible policymakers. The sad truth is that the fault lies more in natural organizational forces, and in the pure intractability of the problem, than in the skills of spies or statesmen.

After surprise attacks, intelligence postmortems usually discover indicators that existed in advance but that were obscured or contradicted by other evidence. Roberta Wohlstetter's classic study of Pearl Harbor identified this as the problem of signals (information hinting at the possibility of enemy attack) getting lost in a crescendo of "noise" (the voluminous clutter of irrelevant information that floods in, or other matters competing for attention). Other causes abound. Some have been partially overcome, such as technical limitations on timely communication, or organizational obstacles to sharing information. Others are deeply rooted in the complexity of threats, the ambiguity of partial warnings, and the ability of plotters to overcome obstacles, manipulate information, and deceive victims.

One reason surprise attacks can succeed is the "boy who cried wolf" problem, in which the very excellence of intelligence collection works against its success. There are often numerous false alarms before an attack, and they dull sensitivity to warnings of the attack that does occur. Sometimes the supposed false alarms were not false at all, but accurate warnings that prompted timely responses by the victim that in turn caused the attacker to cancel and reschedule the assault—thus generating a self-negating prophecy.

Attacks can also come as a surprise because of an overload of incomplete warnings, a particular problem for a superpower with world-spanning involvements. In the spring of 1950, for example, the CIA warned President Harry Truman that the North Koreans could attack at any time, but without indications of whether the attack was certain or when it would happen. "But this did not apply alone to Korea," Truman noted in his memoirs. The same reports also continually warned him of many other places in the world where communist forces had the capability to attack.

Intelligence can rarely be perfect and unambiguous, and there are always good reasons to misinterpret it.

Intelligence may correctly warn of an enemy's intention to strike and may even anticipate the timing but still guess wrong about where or how the attack will occur. U.S. intelligence was warning in late November 1941 that a Japanese strike could be imminent but expected it in Southeast Asia. Pearl Harbor seemed an impractical target because it was too shallow for torpedo attacks. That had indeed been true, but shortly before December the Japanese had adjusted their torpedoes so they could run in the shallows. Before September 11, similarly, attacks by al Qaeda were expected, but elsewhere in the world, and not by the technical means of kamikaze hijacking.

The list of common reasons why attacks often come as a surprise goes on and on. The point is that intelligence can rarely be perfect and unambiguous, and there are always good reasons to misinterpret it. Some problems of the past have been fixed by the technically sophisticated system we have now, and some may be reduced by adjustments to the system. But some can never be eliminated, with the result being that future unpleasant surprises are a certainty. . . .

Reforms that can be undertaken now will make the intelligence community a little better. Making it much better, however, will ultimately require revising educational norms and restoring the prestige of public service. Both are lofty goals and tall orders, involving general changes in society and professions outside government. Even if achieved, moreover, such fundamental reform would not bear fruit until far in the future.

But this is not a counsel of despair. To say that there is a limit to how high the intelligence batting average will get is not to say that it cannot get significantly better. It does mean, however, that no strategy for a war against terror can bank on prevention. Better intelligence may give us several more big successes like those of the 1990s, but even a .900 average will eventually yield another big failure. That means that equal emphasis must go to measures for civil defense, medical readiness, and "consequence management," in order to blunt the effects of the attacks that do manage to get through. Efforts at prevention and preparation for their failure must go hand in hand.

U.S. Intelligence on Iraqi WMDs Was Based on the Best Information Available

George Tenet

George Tenet was the director of central intelligence (DCI) at the Central Intelligence Agency (CIA) from 1997 to 2004 and is currently a professor of diplomacy at Georgetown University in Washington, D.C.

Editor's Note: The following viewpoint is taken from a speech delivered by the author in 2004 at Georgetown University.

I have come here today to talk to you and to the American people about something important to our nation and central to our future: how the United States intelligence community evaluated Iraq's weapons of mass destruction programs over the past decade, leading to a national intelligence estimate in October of 2002. I want to tell you about our information and how we reached our judgments. I want to tell you what I think, honestly and directly. . . .

Before talking about Iraq's weapons of mass destruction [WMDs], I want to set the stage with a few words about intelligence collection and analysis, how they actually happen in a real world. This context is completely missing from the current debate.

By definition, intelligence deals with the unclear, the unknown, the deliberately hidden. What the enemies of the United States hope to deny we work to reveal. The question being asked about Iraq in the starkest terms is, were we right or were we wrong? In the intelligence business, you are almost never completely wrong or completely right. That applies in

George Tenet, "Iraq and Weapons of Mass Destruction," remarks prepared for delivery at Georgetown University, February 5, 2004. www.cia.gov.

full to the question of [former Iraqi dictator Saddam Hussein's] weapons of mass destruction. And like many of the toughest intelligence challenges, when the facts of Iraq are all in, we will neither be completely right nor completely wrong. As intelligence professionals, we go to where the information takes us. We fear no fact or finding, whether it bears us out or not. Because we work for high goals—the protection of the American people—we must be judged by high standards.

The Basis for the CIA's Intelligence on Iraq

Let's turn to Iraq. Much of the current controversy centers on our prewar intelligence, summarized in the national intelligence estimate of October of 2002. National estimates are publications where the intelligence community as a whole seeks to sum up what we know about a subject, what we don't know, what we suspect may be happening and where we differ on key issues. This estimate asked if Iraq had chemical, biological and nuclear weapons and the means to deliver them. We concluded that in some of these categories Iraq had weapons, and that in others where it did not have them, it was trying to develop them.

To conclude before the war that Saddam had no interest in rebuilding his weapons of mass destruction programs, we would have had to ignore his long and brutal history of using them.

Let me be clear: Analysts differed on several important aspects of these programs and those debates were spelled out in the estimate. They never said there was an imminent threat. Rather, they painted an objective assessment for our policymakers of a brutal dictator who was continuing his efforts to deceive and build programs that might constantly surprise us and threaten our interests. No one told us what to say or how to say it.

How did we reach our conclusions? We had three streams of information; none perfect, but each important. First, Iraq's history. Everyone knew that Iraq had chemical and biological weapons in the 1980s and 1990s. Saddam Hussein used chemical weapons against Iran and his own people on at least 10 different occasions. He launched missiles against Iran, Saudi Arabia and Israel. And we couldn't forget that in the early 1990s, we saw that Iraq was just a few years away from a nuclear weapon. This was not a theoretical program. It turned out that we and other intelligence services of the world had significantly underestimated his progress. And finally, we could not forget that Iraq lied repeatedly about its unconventional weapons. To conclude before the war that Saddam had no interest in rebuilding his weapons of mass destruction programs, we would have had to ignore his long and brutal history of using them.

Our second stream of information was that the United Nations could not and Saddam would not account for all the weapons the Iraqis had: tons of chemical weapons precursors, hundreds of artillery shells and bombs filled with chemical or biological agents. We did not take this data on face value. We did take it seriously. We worked with the inspectors, giving them leads, helping them fight Saddam's deception strategy of cheat and retreat. Over eight years of inspections, Saddam's deceptions and the increasingly restrictive rules of engagement [that] U.N. inspectors were forced to negotiate with the regime undermined efforts to disarm him. To conclude before the war that Saddam had destroyed his existing weapons, we would have had to ignore what the United Nations and allied intelligence said they could not verify.

The third stream of information came after the U.N. inspectors left Iraq in 1998. We gathered intelligence through human agents, satellite photos and communications intercepts. Other foreign intelligence services were clearly focused on Iraq and assisted in the effort. In intercepts of conversations and other transactions, we heard Iraqis seeking to hide prohibited items, worrying about their cover stories and trying to procure items Iraq was not permitted to have. Satellite photos showed a pattern of activity designed to conceal movement of material from places where chemical weapons had been stored in the past. We also saw reconstruction of dual-purpose facilities previously used to make biological weapons or chemical precursors. And human sources told us of efforts to acquire and hide materials used in the production of such weapons. And to come to conclusions before the war other than those we reached, we would have had to ignore all the intelligence gathered from multiple sources after 1998.

We said that Saddam did not have a nuclear weapon and probably would have been unable to make one until 2007 or 2009.

Did these strands of information weave into a perfect picture? Could they answer every question? No, far from it. But taken together, this information provided a solid basis on which to estimate whether Iraq did or did not have weapons of mass destruction and the means to deliver them. . . .

The Nuclear Weapons Finding

So what did our estimate say? . . .

In the estimate, all agencies agree that Saddam Hussein wanted nuclear weapons. Most were convinced that he still had a program and if he obtained fissile material he could have a weapon within a year. But we detected no such acquisition. We made two judgments that get overlooked these days. We said that Saddam did not have a nuclear weapon and probably would have been unable to make one until 2007 to 2009. Most agencies believed that Saddam had begun to reconstitute his nuclear program, but they disagreed on a number of issues, such as which procurement activities were designed to support his nuclear program. But let me be clear: Where there are differences, the estimate laid out the disputes clearly.

So what do we know now? [Leading U.S. weapons inspector] David Kay told us that "the testimony we have obtained from Iraqi scientists and senior government officials should clear up any doubts about whether Saddam still wanted to obtain nuclear weapons." Keep in mind that no intelligence agency thought that Iraq's efforts had progressed to the point of building an enrichment facility or making fissile material. We said that such activities were a few years away. Therefore it's not surprising that the Iraq Survey Group has not . . . found evidence of uranium enrichment facilities.

Regarding prohibited aluminum tubes, a debate laid out extensively in the estimate and one that experts still argue over, were they for uranium enrichment or conventional weapons? We have additional data to collect and more sources to question. Moreover, none of the tubes found in Iraq so far match the high-specification tubes Baghdad sought and may never have received the amounts needed. Our aggressive interdiction efforts may have prevented Iraq from receiving all but a few of these prohibited items.

My provisional bottom line today: Saddam did not have a nuclear weapon, he still wanted one, and Iraq intended to reconstitute a nuclear program at some point. We have not yet found clear evidence that the dual-use items Iraq sought were for nuclear reconstitution. We do not yet know if any reconstitution efforts had begun. But we may have overestimated the progress Saddam was making.

The Biological Weapons Finding

Let me turn to biological weapons. The estimates said Baghdad had them and that all key aspects of an offensive program—research and development, production and weaponization—were still active and most elements were larger and more advanced than before the Gulf War. We believe that Iraq had lethal biological weapons agents, including anthrax, which it could quickly produce and weaponize for delivery by bombs, missiles, aerial sprayers and covert operatives. But we said we had no specific information on the types or quantities of weapons, agent or stockpiles at Baghdad's disposal.

Based on an assessment of the data we collected over the past 10 years, it would have been difficult for analysts to come to any different conclusions.

What do we know today? [In 2003] the Iraqi Survey Group uncovered, "significant information, including research and development of biological weapons, applicable organisms, the involvement of the Iraqi intelligence service in possible biological weapons activities and deliberate concealment activities." All of this suggests that Iraq, after 1996, further compartmentalized its program and focused on maintaining smaller covert capabilities that could be activated quickly to surge the production of biological weapons agents.

The Iraq Survey Group found a network of laboratories and safe houses controlled by Iraqi intelligence and security services that contained equipment for chemical and biological research and a prison laboratory complex possibly used in human testing for biological weapons agents that were not declared to the United Nations. It also appears that Iraq had the infrastructure and the talent to resume production, but we have yet to find that it actually did so, nor have we found weapons. . . .

My provisional bottom line today: Iraq intended to develop biological weapons. Clearly, research and development work was under way that would have permitted a rapid shift to agent production if seed stocks were available. But we do not yet know if production took place. And just as clearly, we have not yet found biological weapons. . . .

The Chemical Weapons Finding

Let me now turn to chemical weapons. We said in the estimate with high confidence that Iraq had them. We also believed, though with less certainty, that Saddam had stocked at least 100 metric tons of agent. That may sound like a lot, but it would fit in a few dorm rooms on this campus. And the last time I remember, they're not very big rooms. Initially, the community was skeptical about whether Iraq had started chemical weapons agent production. Sources had reported that Iraq had begun renewed production and imagery and intercepts gave us additional concerns. But only when analysts saw what they believed to be satellite photos of shipments of materials from ammunition sites did they believe that Iraq was again producing chemical weapons agents.

A blanket indictment of our human intelligence around the world is dead wrong. We have spent . . . years rebuilding our clandestine service.

What do we know today? The work done so far shows a story similar to that of his biological weapons program. Saddam had rebuilt a dual-use industry. David Kay reported that Saddam and his son Uday wanted to know how long it would take for Iraq to produce chemical weapons. However, while some sources indicate Iraq may have conducted some experiments related to developing chemical weapons, no physical evidence has yet been uncovered. We need more time.

My provisional bottom line today: Saddam had the intent and capability to quickly convert civilian industry to chemical weapons production. However, we have not yet found the weapons we expected. . . .

CIA Intelligence Is Reliable

So what do I think about all this today? Based on an assessment of the data we collected over the past 10 years, it would have been difficult for analysts to come to any different conclusions than the ones reached in October of 2002. However, in our business simply saying this is not good enough. We must constantly review the quality of our work. For example, the National Intelligence Council is reviewing the estimate line by line. [In August 2003], we also commissioned an internal review to examine the tradecraft of our work on Iraq's weapons of mass destruction. And through this effort we are finding ways to improve our processes. . . .

To be sure, we had difficulty penetrating the Iraqi regime with human sources. And I want to be very clear about something: A blanket indictment of our human intelligence around the world is dead wrong. We have spent the last seven years rebuilding our clandestine service. As director of central intelligence, this has been my highest priority. When I came to the CIA in the mid-'90s, our graduating class of case officers was unbelievably low. Now, after years of rebuilding, our training programs and putting our best efforts to recruit the most talented men and women, we are graduating more clandestine officers than at any time in the history of the Central Intelligence Agency. It will take an additional five years to finish the job of rebuilding our clandestine service, but the results so far have been obvious.

A CIA spy led us to Khalid Sheik Mohammed, the mastermind of the September 11th attacks. Al Qaeda's operational chief [Abd al-Rahimal-] Nashiri, the man who planned and executed the bombing of the USS *Cole*, was located and arrested because of our human reporting. Human sources were critical to the capture of Hambali, the chief terrorist in Southeast Asia, who organized and killed hundreds of people when they bombed a nightclub in Bali. So when you hear pundits say that we have no human intelligence capability, they don't know what they're talking about. It's important that I address these misstatements because the American people must know just how reliable American intelligence is on the threats that confront our nation.

Intelligence Successes

Let's talk about Libya, where a sitting regime has volunteered to dismantle its WMD program. Somebody on television said we completely missed it. Well, he completely missed it. This was an intelligence success. Why? Because American and British intelligence officers understood the Libyan programs. Only through intelligence did we know each of the major programs Libya had going. Only through intelligence did we know when Libya started its first nuclear weapons program and then put it on the back burner for years. Only through intelligence did we know when the nuclear program took off again. We knew because we had penetrated Libya's foreign supplier network. . . .

Let me briefly mention Iran, and I will not go into detail. I want to assure you of one thing: that recent Iranian admissions about their nuclear programs validate our intelligence assessments. It is flat wrong to say that we were surprised by reports from the Iranian opposition [in 2003].

And on North Korea, it was patient analysis of difficult-to-obtain information that allowed our diplomats to confront the North Korean regime about their pursuit of a different route to a nuclear weapon that violated international agreements.

Our analysts . . . have a duty to inform and warn. They did so honestly and with integrity when making judgments about the dangers posed by Saddam Hussein.

One final spy story. [In 2003,] in my annual worldwide threat testimony before Congress in open session, I talked about the emerging threat from private proliferators, especially nuclear brokers. I was cryptic about this in public, but I can tell you now that I was talking about A.Q. Khan [Paki-stani nuclear scientist who sold nuclear know-how on the black market]. His network was shaving years off the nuclear weapons development timelines of several states, including Libya. . . .

What did intelligence have to do with this? First, we dis-covered the extent of Khan's hidden network. We tagged the proliferators, we detected the networks stretching across four continents offering its wares to countries like North Korea and Iran. Working with our British colleagues, we pieced to-gether the picture of the network, revealing its subsidiaries, its scientists, its front agents, its finances and manufacturing plants on three continents. Our spies penetrated the network through a series of daring operations over several years. Through this unrelenting effort, we confirmed the network was delivering such things as illicit uranium enrichment cen-trifuges. And as you heard me say in the Libya case, we stopped deliveries of prohibited material. . . .

A Committed Intelligence Community

Our analysts, at the end of the day, have a duty to inform and warn. They did so honestly and with integrity when making judgments about the dangers posed by Saddam Hussein. Sim-ply assessing stacks of reports does not speak to the wisdom experienced analysts brought to bear on a difficult and decep-tive subject. But as all these reviews are under way we must take some care. We cannot afford an environment to develop where analysts are afraid to make a call, where judgments are held back because analysts fear they will be wrong. Their work and these judgments make vital contributions to the country's security.

I came here today to also tell the American people that they must know that they are served by dedicated, courageous professionals. It is evident on the battlefields of Afghanistan and Iraq. It is evident by their work against proliferators. It is evident by the fact that well over two-thirds of Al Qaeda's leaders can no longer hurt the American people.

We are a community that some thought would not be needed at the end of the Cold War. We have systematically been rebuilding all of our disciplines with a focused strategy and care. Our strategy for the future is based on achieving capabilities that will provide the kind of intelligence that the country deserves.

Policy Makers Misused Accurate Intelligence to Justify the Iraq War

Paul R. Pillar

Paul R. Pillar served as National Intelligence Officer for the Near East and South Asia at the Central Intelligence Agency (CIA) from 2000 to 2005, and is currently on the faculty of the Security Studies Program at Georgetown University in Washington, D.C.

The most serious problem with U.S. intelligence today is that its relationship with the policymaking process is broken and badly needs repair. In the wake of the Iraq war, it has become clear that official intelligence analysis was not relied on in making even the most significant national security decisions, that intelligence was misused publicly to justify decisions already made, that damaging ill will developed between policymakers and intelligence officers, and that the intelligence community's own work was politicized. As the national intelligence officer responsible for the Middle East from 2000 to 2005, I witnessed all of these disturbing developments.

Intelligence Not the Basis for War

Public discussion of prewar intelligence on Iraq has focused on the errors made in assessing Saddam Hussein's unconventional weapons programs. A commission chaired by Judge Laurence Silberman and former Senator Charles Robb usefully documented the intelligence community's mistakes in a solid and comprehensive report released in March 2005. Corrections were indeed in order, and the intelligence community has begun to make them.

At the same time, an acrimonious and highly partisan debate broke out over whether the Bush administration manipulated and misused intelligence in making its case for war. The administration defended itself by pointing out that it was not alone in its view that Saddam had weapons of mass destruction (WMD) and active weapons programs, however mistaken that view may have been.

In this regard, the Bush administration was quite right: its perception of Saddam's weapons capacities was shared by the [Bill] Clinton administration, congressional Democrats, and most other Western governments and intelligence services. But in making this defense, the White House also inadvertently pointed out the real problem: intelligence on Iraqi weapons programs did not drive its decision to go to war. A view broadly held in the United States and even moreso overseas was that deterrence of Iraq was working, that Saddam was being kept "in his box," and that the best way to deal with the weapons problem was through an aggressive inspections program to supplement the sanctions already in place. That the administration arrived at so different a policy solution indicates that its decision to topple Saddam was driven by other factors—namely, the desire to shake up the sclerotic power structures of the Middle East and hasten the spread of more liberal politics and economics in the region.

The proper relationship between intelligence gathering and policymaking sharply separates the two functions.

If the entire body of official intelligence analysis on Iraq had a policy implication, it was to avoid war—or, if war was going to be launched, to prepare for a messy aftermath. What is most remarkable about prewar U.S. intelligence on Iraq is not that it got things wrong and thereby misled policymakers; it is that it played so small a role in one of the most important U.S. policy decisions in recent decades. . . .

Intelligence As Justification for War

The proper relationship between intelligence gathering and policymaking sharply separates the two functions. The intelligence community collects information, evaluates its credibility, and combines it with other information to help make sense of situations abroad that could affect U.S. interests. Intelligence officers decide which topics should get their limited collection and analytic resources according to both their own judgments and the concerns of policymakers. Policymakers thus influence which topics intelligence agencies address but not the conclusions that they reach. The intelligence community, meanwhile, limits its judgments to what is happening or what might happen overseas, avoiding policy judgments about what the United States should do in response.

In practice, this distinction is often blurred, especially because analytic projections may have policy implications even if they are not explicitly stated. But the distinction is still important. National security abounds with problems that are clearer than the solutions to them; the case of Iraq is hardly a unique example of how similar perceptions of a threat can lead people to recommend very different policy responses. Accordingly, it is critical that the intelligence community not advocate policy, especially not openly. If it does, it loses the most important basis for its credibility and its claims to objectivity. When intelligence analysts critique one another's work, they use the phrase "policy prescriptive" as a pejorative, and rightly so.

The Bush administration's use of intelligence on Iraq did not just blur this distinction; it turned the entire model upside down. The administration used intelligence not to inform decision-making, but to justify a decision already made. It went to war without requesting—and evidently without being influenced by—any strategic-level intelligence assessments on any aspect of Iraq. Congress, not the administration, asked for the now-infamous October 2002 National Intelligence Estimate (NIE) on Iraq's unconventional weapons programs, although few members of Congress actually read it. . . .

Official intelligence on Iraqi weapons programs was flawed, but even with its flaws, it was not what led to the war. On the issue that mattered most, the intelligence community judged that Iraq probably was several years away from developing a nuclear weapon. The October 2002 NIE also judged that Saddam was unlikely to use WMD [weapons of mass destruction] against the United States unless his regime was placed in mortal danger.

The Bush administration . . . [used] intelligence to win public support for its decision to go to war.

Before the war, on its own initiative, the intelligence community considered the principal challenges that any postinvasion authority in Iraq would be likely to face. It presented a picture of a political culture that would not provide fertile ground for democracy and foretold a long, difficult, and turbulent transition. It projected that a Marshall Plan–type effort would be required to restore the Iraqi economy, despite Iraq's abundant oil resources. It forecast that in a deeply divided Iraqi society, with Sunnis resentful over the loss of their dominant position and Shiites seeking power commensurate with their majority status, there was a significant chance that the groups would engage in violent conflict unless an occupying power prevented it. And it anticipated that a foreign occupying force would itself be the target of resentment and attacks—including by guerrilla warfare—unless it established security and put Iraq on the road to prosperity in the first few weeks or months after the fall of Saddam.

In addition, the intelligence community offered its assessment of the likely regional repercussions of ousting Saddam. It argued that any value Iraq might have as a democratic exemplar would be minimal and would depend on the stability of a new Iraqi government and the extent to which democracy in Iraq was seen as developing from within rather than being imposed by an outside power. More likely, war and occupation would boost political Islam and increase sympathy for terrorists' objectives—and Iraq would become a magnet for extremists from elsewhere in the Middle East. . . .

Cherry-Picking Intelligence Information

The Bush administration deviated from the professional standard not only in using policy to drive intelligence, but also in aggressively using intelligence to win public support for its decision to go to war. This meant selectively adducing data— "cherry-picking"—rather than using the intelligence community's own analytic judgments. In fact, key portions of the administration's case explicitly rejected those judgments. In an August 2002 speech, for example, Vice President Dick Cheney observed that "intelligence is an uncertain business" and noted how intelligence analysts had underestimated how close Iraq had been to developing a nuclear weapon before the 1991 Persian Gulf War. His conclusion—at odds with that of the intelligence community—was that "many of us are convinced that Saddam will acquire nuclear weapons fairly soon."

In the upside-down relationship between intelligence and policy that prevailed in the case of Iraq, the administration selected pieces of raw intelligence to use in its public case for war, leaving the intelligence community to register varying degrees of private protest when such use started to go beyond what analysts deemed credible or reasonable. The best-known example was the assertion by President George W. Bush in his 2003 State of the Union address that Iraq was purchasing uranium ore in Africa. U.S. intelligence analysts had questioned the credibility of the report making this claim, had kept it out of their own unclassified products, and had advised the White House not to use it publicly. But the administration put the claim into the speech anyway, referring to it as information from British sources in order to make the point without explicitly vouching for the intelligence. . . .

No matter how much the process of intelligence gathering itself is fixed, the changes will do no good if the role of intelligence in the policymaking process is not also addressed.

But the greatest discrepancy between the administration's public statements and the intelligence community's judgments concerned not WMD (there was indeed a broad consensus that such programs existed), but the relationship between Saddam and al Qaeda. The enormous attention devoted to this subject did not reflect any judgment by intelligence officials that there was or was likely to be anything like the "alliance" the administration said existed. The reason the connection got so much attention was that the administration wanted to hitch the Iraq expedition to the "war on terror" and the threat the American public feared most, thereby capitalizing on the country's militant post-9/11 mood. . . .

Fixing the Policymaking Process

Although the Iraq war has provided a particularly stark illustration of the problems in the intelligence-policy relationship, such problems are not confined to this one issue or this specific administration. Four decades ago, the misuse of intelligence about an ambiguous encounter in the Gulf of Tonkin figured prominently in the [Lyndon] Johnson administration's justification for escalating the military effort in Vietnam. Over a century ago, the possible misinterpretation of an explosion on a U.S. warship in Havana harbor helped set off the chain of events that led to a war of choice against Spain. The Iraq case needs further examination and reflection on its own. But public discussion of how to foster a better relationship between intelligence officials and policymakers and how to en-sure better use of intelligence on future issues is also necessary.

Intelligence affects the nation's interests through its effect on policy. No matter how much the process of intelligence gathering itself is fixed, the changes will do no good if the role of intelligence in the policymaking process is not also addressed. . . .

CHAPTER 2

Will Post-9/11 Reforms of the U.S. Intelligence System Be Effective?

U.S. Intelligence Reform: An Overview

Gary Thomas

Gary Thomas is a veteran news correspondent who writes for Voice of America, an international broadcasting service funded by the U.S. government that broadcasts news, educational, and cultural programming around the world.

Editor's Note: In January 2007, John Negroponte announced his resignation as director of National Intelligence (DNI) and his move to the U.S. Department of State, where he will serve as deputy secretary of state. President George W. Bush nominated former National Security Agency director Mike McConnell as the country's new DNI.

It took three years and an independent commission investigating the events leading up to the September 11th attacks on New York and Washington for Congress to pass legislation in 2004 designed to improve the U.S. intelligence structure as a frontline against terrorism. The core question is, has intelligence reform succeeded? Proponents say it has, pointing to the fact that there has been no terrorist attack on U.S. soil since 9-11. But some analysts say that the success of the reforms—particularly the creation of a director of national intelligence—has been marginal.

Asked how he would grade progress in intelligence reform, [now former] Director of National Intelligence [D.N.I.] John Negroponte, whose office was created by the 2004 legislation, gives himself passing marks, particularly in interagency cooperation on counter-terrorism efforts. "On a pass-fail basis, I would certainly pass us. That would be my first point. I'd say

Gary Thomas, "Terror Spurs U.S. Intelligence Reform," Voice of America, October 11, 2006. www.voanews.com. Reproduced by permission.

it's also a work in progress. But I'm encouraged, I really am. I think we've made progress in the counter-terrorism area by strengthening the National Counter-Terrorism Center, where we have a fusion of databases from 28 different agencies," says Negroponte.

Are U.S. Intelligence Capabilities Improving?

But Paul Pillar, former deputy director of the C.I.A's [Central Intelligence Agency's] counter-terrorism center, questions whether there has been overall improvement in U.S. intelligence.

The 9-11 Commission recommended creating a new chief intelligence officer to coordinate all 16 [intelligence] agencies.

"I don't think that the [intelligence] reorganization legislation of December 2004 was a net improvement. In some respects, with particular reference to counter-terrorism, I think it was a step backwards. In the creation of N.C.T.C [the National Counter-Terrorism Center], what you did was create a new 'stovepipe,' a new set of bureaucratic lines, over which information has to pass," says Pillar. "And a well-intentioned effort to try to improve cross-agency coordination and common use of information, I think, has had in some ways impeded the flow of information mainly because it is, for most intents and purposes, a new, separate agency."

The job of heading the U.S. intelligence community used to fall to the Director of Central Intelligence, who also was head of the C.I.A. and the president's chief intelligence officer. However, that post lacked any real authority among other governmental intelligence organs. The 9-11 Commission recommended creating a new chief intelligence officer to coordinate all 16 agencies.

John Negroponte, who is the first person to hold the newly-created post of Director of National Intelligence, says his job is to focus on "big picture" issues that affect all intelligence agencies. "So I think of myself, if you will, as the coach of this team of 16 agencies. And if we do our job well dealing with cross-cutting issues that affect the community as a whole, we're actually going to relieve some of these agencies of the need to worry about those things themselves, and enable them to focus on their core challenges and the core tasks. So if we do it right, and I certainly think that we're moving in the right direction, I think that it's going to be a win-win situation," says Negroponte.

Growing Bureaucracy

Negroponte's office was envisioned only as a small coordinating body of perhaps 80 people, but has grown into a staff of around 1,500. Tim Roemer, who was a member of the 9-11 Commission that drew up the recommendations on intelligence reform, says the idea of recommending the creation of the post was to streamline the bureaucracy, not enlarge it. "Many of us in the 9-11 Commission worry that the current structure of the D.N.I. is getting to be too big, too many bureaucratic layers, and too many staff people, especially some of those people picked off from already existing organizations," says Roemer.

The D.N.I. lacks authority over Defense Department intelligence activities, setting the stage for clashes between the D.N.I. and the secretary of defense.

Former C.I.A. officer Paul Pillar questions the need for a D.N.I. at all, saying that the office was created to show that something was being done to "fix" the intelligence structure. "Basically the exercise . . . , using the scheme that came out of the 9-11 Commission, was for the most part a response to strong public pressure to do something after 9-11," says Pillar. "And so the commission came up with its plan, which falls under the category of the favorite Washington technique of doing something when we don't have any other really good ideas, and that's reorganize. So we move boxes around on the [organizational] chart, and I don't see how it's really improved anything."

The D.N.I. and the Pentagon

But Greg Treverton, senior analyst on intelligence policy at the RAND Corporation [a public policy research group], says a D.N.I. was needed. The real flaw, he says, is that the D.N.I. lacks authority over Defense Department intelligence activities, setting the stage for clashes between the D.N.I. and the secretary of defense. "If it turns out over time that the Pentagon and the D.N.I. end up going separate directions, that will be a shame, and I think that will be a real failure. And that might be a time when the nation might want to consider again, do we want to take the next step, do we want to do what almost happened in December 2004 and give the D.N.I. more substantial authority over those big [intelligence] collectors in the Defense Department," says Treverton.

The Defense Department, which has the largest share of the intelligence budget, has operational control over what analysts say is the United States' biggest intelligence bureaucracy— the electronic eavesdroppers and code breakers of the super-secret National Security Agency.

Improved Organization of U.S. Intelligence Agencies Will Ensure Good Intelligence in the War on Terror

George W. Bush

George W. Bush is the forty-third president of the United States.

My most solemn duty is to protect our country. . . . Since our country was attacked [on September 11, 2001,] we've taken steps to overcome new threats. We will continue to do everything in our power to defeat the terrorist enemy and to protect the American people.

Early Action to Fight Terrorism

Recently, the commission on the terrorist attacks upon the United States came to a conclusion that I share: that our country is safer than it was on September the 11th, 2001, yet we're still not safe. The commission members have worked hard and served our country well. I speak for all Americans in thanking them for their fine work.

Their recommendations are thoughtful and valuable. My administration has already taken numerous actions consistent with the commission's recommendations. Today, we're taking additional steps. Our government's actions against the terrorist threat accelerated dramatically after the attacks on the country. Across the world, we've aggressively pursued al Qaeda terrorists, destroyed their training camps and ended their sanctuaries.

We're working closely with other countries to gather intelligence and to make arrests and to cut off terrorist finances.

George W. Bush, "President's Remarks on Intelligence Reform," August 2, 2004. www .whitehouse.gov.

We've created a new unified Department of Homeland Security and gave it resources and the authority to defend America. We're employing the latest equipment and know-how to secure our borders, air- and seaports and infrastructure. We're bringing the best technologies to bear against the threat of chemical and biological warfare. Project Bioshield will fund cutting-edge drugs and other defenses against a biological, chemical, or radiological attack.

To track terrorists and disrupt their cells and seize their assets, we're using the tools of the Patriot Act [a law that expanded domestic police surveillance powers]. . . . Congress needs to make sure law enforcement have the tools necessary to defend the country. We've transformed the FBI to focus on the prevention of terrorist attacks. We're continuing to expand and strengthen the capabilities of the Central Intelligence Agency [CIA]. We established the Terrorist Threat Integration Center to merge and analyze in a single place foreign and domestic intelligence on global terror.

[Our intelligence] reforms have a single goal: We will ensure that the people . . . countering terrorism have the best possible information to make the best decisions.

Yet, the work of securing this vast nation is not done. . . . All the institutions of our government must be fully prepared for a struggle against terror that will last into the future. Our goal is an integrated, unified national intelligence effort. Therefore, my administration will continue moving forward with additional changes to the structure and organization of our intelligence agencies.

Many of these changes are specific recommendations of the 9/11 Commission. Others will go further than the proposal of the commission's report. All these reforms have a single goal: We will ensure that the people in government responsible for defending America and countering terrorism have the best possible information to make the best decisions.

A National Intelligence Director

Today I'm asking Congress to create the position of a National Intelligence Director. That person—the person in that office—will be appointed by the President with the advice and consent of the Senate, and will serve at the pleasure of the President. The National Intelligence Director will serve as the President's principal intelligence advisor and will oversee and coordinate the foreign and domestic activities of the intelligence committee. Under this reorganization, the CIA will be managed by a separate Director. The National Intelligence Director will assume the broader responsibility of leading the intelligence community across our government.

I want, and every President must have, the best, unbiased, unvarnished assessment of America's intelligence professionals. Creating the position of the National Intelligence Director will require a substantial revision of the 1947 National Security Act. I look forward to working with the members of Congress to move ahead on this important reform.

The 9/11 Commission also made several recommendations about Congress, itself. I strongly agree with the commission's recommendation that oversight and intelligence—oversight of intelligence—and of the homeland security must be restructured and made more effective. There are too many committees with overlapping jurisdiction[s], which wastes time and makes it difficult for meaningful oversight and reform.

A National Counter-Terrorism Center

Today, I also announce that we will establish a National Counter-Terrorism Center. This new center will build on the analytical work, the really good analytical work, of the Terrorist Threat Integration Center, and will become our government's knowledge bank for information about known and suspected terrorists. The new center will coordinate and monitor counter-terrorism plans and activities of all government agencies and departments to ensure effective joint action, and that our efforts are unified in priority and purpose. The center will also be responsible for preparing the daily terrorism threat report for the President and senior officials.

The Director of the National Counter-Terrorism Center will report to the National Intelligence Director, once that position is created. Until then, the center will report to the Director of the CIA. Given the growing threat of weapons and missile proliferation in our world, it may also be necessary to create a similar center in our government to bring together our intelligence analysis planning and operations to track and prevent the spread of weapons of mass destruction. I asked the commission headed by Judge Laurence Silberman and Senator Chuck Robb to determine the merits of creating such a center. This nation must do everything we can to keep the world's most destructive weapons out of the world's most dangerous hands.

We are a nation in danger. . . . [But] we're making good progress in protecting our people and bringing our enemies to account.

Other Steps to Protect the Country

Finally, we will act on other recommendations made by the commission. In coming days, I'll issue a series of directives to various departments to underscore and further outline essential steps for the U.S. government on the war on terror. All relevant agencies must complete the task of adopting common databases and procedures so that intelligence and homeland security information can be shared and searched effectively, consistent with privacy and civil liberties.

At the same time, the FBI Director will continue his restructuring of the bureau to create a specialized workforce for collecting and analyzing domestic intelligence on terrorism. The acting CIA Director will continue to increase efforts already underway to strengthen human intelligence and analytical capabilities.

The dedicated, hardworking men and women of our intelligence community are laboring every day to keep our country safe. I'm proud of their work, and so should our American citizens [be]. We're in their debt, we're grateful for them. And the changes we're making are designed to help the professionals carry out their essential missions, as best as they possibly can. I'll work closely with the Congress to ensure that reform does not disrupt their daily work. We've got good people working hard to protect America. We don't want these efforts to . . . get in the way of their efforts to protect our fellow citizens.

We are a nation in danger. We're doing everything we can in our power to confront the danger. We're making good progress in protecting our people and bringing our enemies to account. But one thing is for certain: We'll keep our focus, and we'll keep our resolve, and we will do our duty to best secure our country.

The 2004 Intelligence Reform Bill Is an Important First Step in Improving U.S. Intelligence

Gregory F. Treverton and Peter A. Wilson

Gregory F. Treverton is director of the Intelligence Policy Center at the Rand Corporation, a nonprofit research group. Peter Wilson is a senior analyst at Rand.

The intelligence reform bill signed by President [George W.] Bush will hardly solve all the problems confronting the American intelligence community, but it is a beginning. Someone is at last in charge. The new Director of National Intelligence (DNI) will not, though, have a free hand to reshape American intelligence. The bill gives the DNI authority to move only small amounts of money. So big changes—like collapsing all the intelligence collectors into a single agency—are ruled out.

A First Step

Creating a DNI always was going to be just a first step. In pushing that measure, the 9/11 commission did an impressive job of selling a good idea that had almost nothing to do with 9/11. The failures that the commission documented are operational—too little sharing of information and insufficient attention to the counterterrorism mission, especially by the FBI. An intelligence director is only indirectly related to those failings.

In the short run, the simple fact of 9/11 has impelled better cooperation among the different elements of the intelligence community. Sure, in the long run, having someone in charge should make for better cooperation between the FBI and the CIA. But as two generations of secretaries of defense have found in pressing for more "jointness" among the military services, the task is long and arduous. Real reforms are much more matters of organizational culture than of organizational charts.

The Need for Creative Thinking

Improving analysis is one of the most important initiatives for the next phase. The 9/11 commission was eloquent about the need for more creativity, but its recommendations do not really touch that topic. Indeed, its main recommendation in the final bill—to organize the analytic part of the intelligence community around issues, as with the National Counterterrorism Center—has merit but also carries risks. The centers will be consumed by the need to provide the very hottest current intelligence.

The real challenge is to develop a cadre of intelligence analysts who are encouraged to "think creatively" and to acquire intellectual capital in the form of substantive expertise on a broad range of topics. Threats to the US, like terrorism, are global and adaptive, blurring distinctions between crime, terrorism, and war. Analysts of the future need to think more like homicide detectives who focus on solving puzzles with incomplete information.

This next phase [of intelligence reforms] will require leaders in the intelligence, national security, and law enforcement communities willing to take risks.

The need for creative thinking runs directly into the need to reform secrecy and compartmentalization. Current rhetoric about the "transformation" of the intelligence community celebrates exploiting information from the full spectrum of secret and open courses. Such terms as "multi-intelligence" and "fusion analysis" are the catchphrases. The favorite is "connecting the dots." Unfortunately, the current system is biased toward compartmentalizing information, not sharing it. To protect the US, every agency controls its own information, with access granted on a "need to know" basis. Yet creativity in analysis will come precisely from having people with no "need to know" look at data, because they may see patterns that current experts do not.

Other Needed Reforms

Workforce reforms are another important challenge. All the intelligence agencies have grown substantially since 9/11. The growth is a wonderful opportunity. The new young intelligence analysts are fearless and computer savvy. They will not stand for the information environments—compartmentalized, slow, and source-driven—that current intelligence provides. Yet they are also untrained, and given the aging of the intelligence agencies, will lack for mentors. All the agencies will have to dramatically rethink how they deal with the lives and careers of their premier asset—their people. At present, training of analysts, in particular, is mostly on the job. And almost all training is stovepiped by agency, so analysts have little idea how counterparts in other agencies work.

Yet another challenge is finding a way to keep the intelligence community from drowning in information. For one thing, while terrorists are secretive, data that is not secret— phone numbers, drivers' licenses, and the like—is also relevant. For another, America's technical capabilities to produce secret information, such as imagery from spy satellites, have mushroomed. In particular, the big collectors of imagery and signals intelligence—the National Geospatial Intelligence Agency and the National Security Agency—will be tempted to turn a firehose of data on intelligence analysts. After all, that is the way to make sure that they are not the culprits for the next intelligence failure.

A better balance is needed between investments in the emerging collection systems and enhanced forms of analytical capability. The latter means a greatly expanded investment in quality personnel and new technologies that assist analysts, instead of overwhelming them. Put simply, huge amounts of data collected but unprocessed and unanalyzed are useless to the policymaker.

Finally, there is a need for new forms of intelligence collection. Every blue-ribbon panel calls for improving America's espionage, or human intelligence capabilities. The call is worthy, but expectations have to be reasonable. However one judges the past half century of US espionage, doing better against tomorrow's much harder targets, like terrorists, will not be easy. The required actions—making much more use of America's ethnic diversity, or moving spying out of official US government buildings, for instance—take time and money.

The intelligence reform bill should be viewed as the necessary first step, but hardly as sufficient. This next phase will require leaders in the intelligence, national security, and law enforcement communities willing to take risks. Most important, Congress needs to be convinced that what it has done so far is just the beginning. The people of the US intelligence community are up to the task of real reform. The question is whether their current and prospective leaders are also up to that task.

The 2004 Intelligence Reform and Terrorism Prevention Act Has Improved U.S. Intelligence

John D. Negroponte

John D. Negroponte is a former U.S. Director of National Intelligence (DNI).

The Intelligence Reform and Terrorism Prevention Act of 2004 ... created the Office of the Director of National Intelligence [ODNI] and has served as the master plan for the ODNI's actions. In addition, the law was supplemented by those recommendations of the Robb-Silberman Commission on Weapons of Mass Destruction [charged with investigating intelligence failures in assessing Iraq's weapons of mass destruction]—of which 70 out of 74 recommendations—were endorsed by the President in the summer of 2005.

Good Results

Intelligence reform, as the President and Congress ultimately defined it, encompassed an ambitious scheme of rethinking our previous intelligence practices, rebuilding our intelligence programs in an integrated fashion, creating new entities to confront new threats, and developing fresh approaches to our fundamental way of doing business within the Intelligence Community [IC] and with the Intelligence Community's natural partners—both domestic and foreign.

The bar for intelligence reform was set high, but for our Intelligence Community, it was not set too high. ... The IC has achieved good results through a concerted effort to integrate itself more tightly, share information more freely, coor-

Remarks by the Director of National Intelligence Ambassador John D. Negroponte and Director, Central Intelligence Agency General Michael V. Hayden, "Intelligence Reform Progress Report," DNI Headquarters—Defense Intelligence Agency, Washington, D.C., January 9, 2007. www.dni.gov.

dinate its actions more efficiently, define its priorities more clearly, and align its resource expenditures against those priorities more strategically. The IC has built closer relations with the other agencies of the United States Government and our allies around the world. And the IC has improved partnerships with federal, state, and local law enforcement, homeland security officials, tribal leaders, and the private sector here in the United States. The Office of the Director of National Intelligence has assumed responsibility for strategic leadership of the Intelligence Community, but the office has attempted to do this in concert with its Intelligence Community colleagues, relying on the individual agencies to execute their missions fully and completely. There's no other way to succeed.

I do think that we have succeeded, and I think we will keep succeeding. That's because strategic leadership—and the leadership demonstrated by establishing priorities, standards, policies, and budget—is not the whole of leadership. In a true community, leadership in its fullness is a shared mandate; it extends across bureaucratic divisions and up and down the chain of command. Everyone has to feel responsible and be accountable for the effectiveness of his or her agency, programs, office, and personal actions.

A great deal of structural change has occurred within the Intelligence Community . . . in direct response both to our most important past failures and our most important pressing threats.

Indeed, I have the sense that this kind of Community-wide leadership is characteristic of our Intelligence Community. The effort to reform the IC was already under way when I took office. The professionals of the IC were doing everything in their power to improve United States intelligence and guard against another 9/11 or failure to assess correctly the capabilities and intentions of America's adversaries.

Structural Changes

To frame my assessment of intelligence reform, I'd like to focus on structural change, collection and analysis, information access, science and technology, and human capital. There are several other significant components of intelligence reform, to be sure, but I will do my best to fit them under one or more of these headings.

A great deal of structural change has occurred within the Intelligence Community ... in direct response both to our most important past failures and our most important pressing threats.

We have taken the reform legislation's call for a strong National Counterterrorism Center, established by Executive Order initially, and made it a reality. The National Counterterrorism Center stands at the center of the intelligence contribution to the War on Terror. . . .

The law also focused on the FBI's contribution to national intelligence. In my view, the FBI's senior leadership embraced this mandate and has shown a great commitment to integration within the Intelligence Community. As a result, on September 12, 2005, the FBI established the National Security Branch [NSB] to bring together under a single umbrella its counterterrorism, counterintelligence, and intelligence programs. The National Security Branch has since established a dedicated counter–Weapons of Mass Destruction [WMDs] effort within the NSB itself. And all this has greatly facilitated the FBI's participation in, among other things, community-wide intelligence training and education programs.

The Robb-Silberman Commission emphasized the critical contribution human intelligence plays in preserving national security. The WMD commission called for increased interagency HUMINT [human intelligence] coordination, better and more uniform tradecraft standards, and increased joint training for operators. This led to another important structural change in U.S. intelligence: the establishment of the National Clandestine Service in 2005.

These two changes—the establishment of the National Clandestine Service and the National Security Branch—strengthened our intelligence effort at home and abroad.

If we are going to solve the most difficult intelligence challenges, our analysts and collectors must work together hand-in-glove.

Additional innovations quickly followed: the creation of DNI's [director of national intelligence's] Open Source Center at the CIA [Central Intelligence Agency], the establishment of a National Counterproliferation Center, and the appointment of a MASINT [Measurement and Signature Intelligence] Community Executive, for example. Meanwhile, institutions of long-standing assumed important new responsibilities. NSA [National Security Agency] has been vital in helping support the Global War on Terror. . . . DIA [Defense Intelligence Agency] is on the front lines in Iraq and Afghanistan; and has taken the lead in developing the Defense Joint Intelligence Operations Center. The Department of Homeland Security has advanced the efforts to integrate homeland security intelligence and analysis. In so doing, it has assumed enormous responsibility for gathering and analyzing intelligence that is crucial to securing our land and maritime borders with Mexico and Canada. And the National Geospatial Agency [NGA] stepped "out of the box" to help our nation assess and mitigate the terrible impact of Hurricane Katrina. The innovative response to domestic challenges perfectly reflects NGA's vital role on the warfront where it is totally integrated in successful real-time operations.

Information Collection and Analysis

Virtually all observers of the Intelligence Community have focused attention on the interdependence of collection and analysis, as well as the need to continuously improve finished intelligence products through better methodology, more outreach, more alternative analysis, and more transparent sourcing. If we are going to solve the most difficult intelligence challenges, our analysts and collectors must work together hand-in-glove. While greater integration is still needed, progress is being made in terms of attacking hard targets.

The National Intelligence Council, the National Counterproliferation Center, and the North Korea, Iran, Cuba and Venezuela Mission Managers are helping close collection and analytic gaps vis-à-vis our most crucial intelligence priorities. And by the same token, we have taken many steps to bring analysts closer together. . . . The fastest way to increase the value of intelligence is to share it for collaborative critiques and make it accessible for authorized action. Two senior officials—our Chief Information Officer and the Program Manager for the Information Sharing Environment—have accomplished a great deal toward both of these ends. Under their leadership:

- We have implemented a major classified information sharing initiative with key United States allies. And this was a project that was "stuck" for quite a long time and we managed to get it "unstuck."

- We developed—they developed rather—and rolled out the Electronic Directory Services, a "virtual phone book" for terrorism information and those that have counterterrorism responsibilities in the United States Government; and

- They shaped and disseminated the *Information Sharing Environment Implementation Plan and the Presidential*

Guidelines on Information Sharing. These two documents provide the vision and road map for better information sharing within the Intelligence Community and with our Federal, State, local, and tribal counterparts, as well as with the private sector.

Neutralizing insider threats, especially technically astute spies, will take on added urgency in such an environment of more freely flowing information. Guided by our Mission Manager for Counterintelligence, our counterintelligence community is evolving to better support this and other critical national priorities.

These are just a few examples of our "problem solving" approach to information sharing and access that enhances intra-IC collaboration and cooperation with those outside the Community who share our goals and objectives.

Science and Technology

In an age of globalization that closely reflects developments in science and technology [S&T], intelligence reform would have dim prospects of success if it did not ensure our competitive advantage in the realm of S&T. As in all of our reforms, Science & Technology change cannot be effected overnight, but that is precisely why our Associate Director for S&T has chosen "Speed" as the first of his cardinal values, the other two being "Synergy" and "Surprise."

Nothing is more important to the [Intelligence Community's] future than developing its personnel.

With respect to speed, we have launched the Rapid Technology Transition Initiative to accelerate the transition of innovative technology to operations by funding 13 programs in F[iscal] Y[ear] 2007. In support of the warfighter our IC S&T team has made important contributions to General Meigs' Joint IED [improvised explosive device] Defeat Organization—and I know that has been one of [NSA director of research] Eric Haseltine's very highest priorities.

With respect to synergy, we have developed a unified Intelligence Community S&T Strategy and Plan that identifies and addresses IC-wide technology gaps, establishes new joint Science & Technology programs against high value hard targets, and institutes new joint duty programs such as the ODNI's Science & Technology Ambassadors initiative. We have also, through our Science & Technology Fellows Program, rewarded our top S&T talent with significant grants to pursue their innovative research projects and help foster greater collaboration among our most creative minds.

And with respect to surprise, we have laid the groundwork for an Intelligence Community version of DARPA [Defense Advanced Research Projects Agency], which we are calling IARPA—the Intelligence Advanced Research Projects Agency.

Human Capital

Now nothing is more important to the IC's future than developing its personnel, which includes replenishing its ranks of analysts and collectors, attracting specialists in Science & Technology and counterproliferation, and making the most of America's natural diversity.

We need to have a workforce that is fully equipped to meet every threat, and . . . that in the end looks like America.

By working closely with agencies and departments across the Community, our Chief Human Capital Officer has helped:

- Establish the framework that will make joint duty a prerequisite for promotion to senior levels of the Intelligence Community;

- He has helped complete the first Strategic Human Capital Plan for the Intelligence Community; and

- He has initiated development of a modern, performance-based compensation system for civilian employees that will be completed over the next few years.

We need to have a workforce that is fully equipped to meet every new threat, and we need to have a workforce that in the end looks like America. Building that diverse IC workforce is an area where we have made modest, but steady progress. But we still need to do significantly more as a Community to effectively recruit, hire, retain, reward, and promote women, minorities, and persons with disabilities. I strongly encourage each Intelligence Community agency director to make his commitment visible, specific, personal, and persistent, so that executives and managers will understand the importance of this mission imperative. . . .

The intelligence reform process the United States has initiated is complex and demanding. The successful implementation of these reforms is a work in progress. We need to continue to evaluate our performance concerning the work that is underway to ensure that our goal of making our nation safer is being met. Several challenges remain:

- We need to ensure that the Community does more to tap into the great diversity of ethnicities and talents our nation possesses;

- We must increase training and education in foreign languages and the human and natural sciences to deepen our understanding of an increasingly complex world; and,

- We must continue to facilitate the seamless flow and collaboration of data between analysts and collectors; and,

- We must continue to emphasize the intangible but inestimable value of a well-integrated community. . . .

Day by day we must do our utmost to thwart attacks by determined fanatics who wish to create the illusion that acts of indiscriminate murder are the emblems of political power and legitimacy. If we succeed in defeating these perpetrators of crimes against humanity—and we have succeeded in thwarting many attacks and decommissioning terrorist leaders and cells—we will have made an important contribution to national security.

And day by day we must ensure that our estimates of a hostile actor's capabilities and intentions are realistic, transparent, and immune to intellectual error and adversarial deception. In the process of initiating the reform of United States intelligence, I think that we have done this and more. We have questioned the basic premises of our collective enterprise—how we are organized, resourced, deployed, and focused. And we have rededicated ourselves to an ambitious goal: the highest quality global intelligence coverage and, within that coverage, an effective integration of the foreign, domestic, and military dimensions of our efforts. We all recognize that achieving this ambitious goal will take time, but so far, so good. We are making progress. We are heading in the right direction.

Post-9/11 Reforms of U.S. Intelligence Will Not Prevent Another Terrorist Attack

Glenn Hastedt

Glenn Hastedt is a professor and chair of the Justice Studies program at Indiana University. He is the author of American Foreign Policy, Past, Present, Future *(6th ed., Prentice-Hall). His most recent articles on intelligence have appeared in* Intelligence and National Security *and* Defense Intelligence Journal.

We have now passed the five-year anniversary of September 11, 2001. For many younger Americans the terrorist attacks of that day promise to become a generational event of the magnitude of Pearl Harbor. It may in time define how they think about America's role in the world and the steps necessary to ensure its safety. Already 9/11 has helped elevate a seldom used concept, homeland security, to a place of prominence in the rhetoric of American foreign policy much as Pearl Harbor did, over one half century ago, for the concept of national security.

From the point of view of both homeland and national security, Pearl Harbor and 9/11 raise the classic questions about surprise: How did the Japanese catch the U.S. government unaware by such an attack and what should be done to prevent another in the future? Both events offer similar answers: Surprise happened because analysts failed to connect the dots, lacked needed intelligence resources, and fell short of communicating effectively with one another. Reorganization can help avoid surprise. In response to Pearl Harbor, Congress created the Central Intelligence Agency as part of the 1947 National Security Act. Following 9/11 the government created

Glenn Hastedt, "9/11 Intelligence Reform: An Opportunity Lost," AmericanDiplomacy .org, October 27, 2006. Reproduced by permission.

the position of Director of National Intelligence (DNI). The two are linked in the minds of many. In signing the Intelligence Reform and Terrorism Prevention Act of 2004, President George W. Bush called it "the most dramatic reform of our Nation's intelligence capabilities since Harry S. Truman signed the National Security Act of 1947. Under this new law, our vast intelligence enterprise will become more unified, coordinated, and effective."

Does this presidential rhetoric accord with reality? The argument laid out below demonstrates that it does not. The overall rhetoric accompanying the creation of the DNI marks, instead, the triumph of domestic over international politics. Given the logic of administrative reorganizations, the nature of presidential commissions, and the dynamics of the rhetorical presidency this is not an unexpected outcome. That outcome, moreover, raises serious questions about the extent to which the American government fully understands the potential for future surprise attacks and their consequences for future homeland security policy debates.

Creating the Position of Director of National Intelligence

The DNI represents the signature intelligence reform proposed by the presidential commission chaired by Thomas Kean and Lee Hamilton. Officially known as the National Commission on Terrorist Attacks on the United States, the Commission . . . issued its report on July 22, 2004, [and] identified four kinds of failures that contributed to the 9/11 terrorist attacks and made forty-one recommendations. Its centerpiece reform proposal became creating the position of DNI with an office in the White House. This individual would oversee all-source national intelligence centers, serve as the president's primary intelligence advisor, manage the national intelligence program, and oversee the component agencies of the intelligence community. Included in the DNI's powers should be submitting a unified intelligence budget, appropriating funds to intelligence agencies, and setting personnel policies for the intelligence community. Although congressional leaders promised to move quickly to overhaul the intelligence community, the White House urged caution, and acting CIA Director John McLaughlin, Secretary of Defense Donald Rumsfeld, and Homeland Security Secretary Tom Ridge all spoke against creating a DNI. With Democratic presidential candidate John Kerry endorsing creation of a DNI, the Bush administration found it necessary to follow suit but wanted to limit the DNI's authority to coordination of intelligence.

Intelligence failures are inevitable.

In October 2004 the House and Senate passed different pieces of legislation creating a DNI. The Senate bill most closely followed the recommendations of the Commission by granting broad powers to the DNI. The House bill reflected the White House's position. Although the Senate bill gave the DNI the power to "determine" the intelligence budget, for example, the House bill only gave the DNI the power to develop the budget and give guidance to the intelligence community. Similarly, the Senate version placed the CIA under the authority, direction and control of the DNI while the House version only stated that the CIA director would report to the DNI. Representative Duncan Hunter (R-Calif.), chair of the House Armed Services Committee, was particularly adamant that the Pentagon not lose control over its intelligence budget and that the overall intelligence budget remain secret. In the end, behind the scenes negotiations produced a compromise bill acceptable to House Republicans and the White House. President Bush signed it into law on December 17, 2004.

Preventing Intelligence Failures

Much of the debate surrounding the ability of the DNI to prevent future intelligence failures focuses on the powers given and denied to this official. Viewed from the perspective of world politics and the literature on intelligence, this debate misses the mark for a very important reason: Intelligence failures are inevitable. Events in world politics do not move forward in neat readily identifiable bundles. They travel in odd-shaped sizes, in bits and pieces, and at different speeds. Responding to this incoherent environment, policymakers and analysts try to distinguish signals of impending events from noise—the background clutter of meaningless information that is always present. It is only with the aid of hindsight that a clear pattern becomes evident. Until then the data may support several different interpretations of the future. Two other factors compound the problem of detecting signals in world politics: First, policymakers may change their minds. Second, they may try to deceive observers.

Confronted with this operating environment, Richard Betts in "Analysis, War, and Decision" observed that "the most crucial mistakes have seldom been made by collectors of raw information, occasionally by professionals who produce finished analysis, and most often by decision makers who consume the products of intelligence services." Surprise succeeds despite warning because intelligence failures are political and psychological more often than organizational. Psychological failures occur because analysts, coping with the inherent uncertainty of evidence, impose their own logic upon it. For some that logic reflects a theoretical model, for others the notion that history repeats itself, and for still others little more than a gut feeling. The political failures occur because the assumptions underlying a country's foreign and defense policy, organizational vested interests, the rapid pace of crisis decision making, and the desire to protect personal reputations all conspire to downgrade the impact of inconvenient or unwanted information. . . .

9/11 II?

Does the creation of a DNI prevent or at least significantly reduce the possibility of another surprise terrorist attack? The differing positions taken by both the Bush administration and its critics on the Commission miss the mark and bring unrecognized risks. In the judgment of the Bush administration, its policies have significantly reduced the danger of another terrorist attack on United States soil. To bolster this claim, it periodically reveals instances of foiled terrorist plots. In July 2006, for example, the FBI announced that it had broken up, in its early stages, a plan to attack New York City transit tunnels under the Hudson River, and the month before the FBI announced it had thwarted a Miami-based terrorist plan to attack the Sears Tower in Chicago. Other highly publicized terrorist threats were directed at the New York City subway systems and a tunnel near Baltimore.

Intelligence is being viewed almost exclusively in a law enforcement context rather than a warning context.

The twin dangers here are complacency followed by recrimination and reprisals against the intelligence community. Complacency results from a false sense of accomplishment undiminished by later revelations questioning the integrity of the supporting data used. Complacency has its roots in the manner in which intelligence is defined. Three problems stand out: First, intelligence is being viewed almost exclusively in a law enforcement context rather than a warning context. The purpose of intelligence in law enforcement is to stop an illegal act. The purpose of warning intelligence is to alert policymakers to a dangerous situation so that it can be followed more closely and countering action taken. A spy is arrested and charged with espionage from a law enforcement perspective. From a warning perspective, a spy is followed and observed in hopes that he or she will lead authorities to other spies or their handlers so that the total scope of the problem becomes clear.

Second, to the extent that intelligence is viewed in a warning context there has yet to be a systematic development of a terrorist warning system. During the Cold War, the United States developed a warning system to alert policymakers to an impending military action. The system included evidence of troop build-ups, domestic political maneuvering, civil unrest, and diplomatic actions such as the recall of ambassadors. The more of these indicators observed the greater the perceived danger. The situation today appears quite different. According to [veteran intelligence expert] Arthur Hulnick ("Indications and Warning for Homeland Security") no equivalent warning system appears to exist for judging the threat posed by terrorist groups. As more evidence emerged, the Sears Tower and New York City transit tunnel attacks sounded like fantasy and loud talk. Business disputes that produced false reporting account for the phony Baltimore harbor tunnel and New York City subway attacks. This is not to say that these threats did not merit investigation, but the examples do raise questions about how their discovery made the United States any safer. At the same time, the London Subway bombings and the thwarted attempt to bring liquid explosive devices on board transatlantic flights out of London to the United States make clear that real terrorist threats do exist.

Third, complacency also has roots in a view of intelligence that equates it with fortunetelling. In "Estimates and Fortunetelling in Intelligence Work," Shlomo Gazit described as fortunetelling predicting the occurrence of a specific event on a specific day in the distant future. Given the inherent potential for surprise in world politics, governments cannot expect intelligence agencies to do this, and doing so is not an appropriate standard against which to judge their work. What intelligence can and should do is "lay out alternative outcomes and indicate the possible milestones or turning points which would help in deciding the outcome." The nearer in time to the occurrence of an event the more can be expected of intelligence, but then the key to success increasingly becomes the state of preparations to deal with an event. As Hurricane Katrina revealed, warning without preparation provides little security.

Organizational reforms can improve performance but not totally prevent surprise.

The danger of complacency is not a risk for critics of the Bush administration who argue its organizational reforms have not gone far enough. The risk inherent in their criticism is subtle. They have a misplaced faith in the ability of organizational changes to prevent intelligence failures, which leads them to pursue reforms that cannot deliver on their promise. There is no doubt that organizational factors contributed to the 9/11 intelligence failures. Prominently numbered among them are communication problems inside and between intelligence organizations, a reliance on inadequate and outmoded conceptual frameworks for analyzing information, and limited human intelligence resources directed at gathering information on terrorism.

The Value of Organizational Reform

As already noted, at their root intelligence failures result from the incoherent environment in which analysts must try to distinguish signals from noise, take account of the fact that policymakers change their minds or are uncertain what they will do, and cut through attempts at deception. Organizational reforms can improve performance but not totally prevent surprise. No universal formula exists for organizing intelligence, making learning from the past or the experiences of other countries difficult. Stung by Israel's failure to anticipate the onset of the 1973 Yom Kippur War, the Agranat Commission proposed a series of changes that in many respects copied the American intelligence system. In addition to creating a DNI, the Commission also called for the creation of a National Counterterrorism Center that would bring all relevant information and analysis of intelligence together in one place. William Casey, as Director of Central Intelligence, established America's first such joint center in 1986. As charges of politicizing intelligence became frequent during his tenure, simply creating analytic centers provides no guarantee of improved intelligence analysis.

Organizational reforms may also make a situation worse, precisely what some feared might result from creating the DNI in its initial form. [9/11 Commission member John] Lehman, for one, expressed concern that the DNI would simply add another layer of bureaucracy on the intelligence community and thereby make effective management even more difficult. Rather than a powerful and lean staff with agency heads reporting to one of three deputy directors, the Office of the DNI contained one principal deputy, four deputies, three associate deputies and more than nineteen assistant deputies. Evidence that this reorganization represented no panacea for improving control over intelligence came with Porter Goss's surprise resignation as head of the CIA on May 5, 2005. Contributing to his decision were differences with [former] DNI John Negroponte over plans to move intelligence analysts from the CIA's counterterrorism staff to other intelligence agencies. On becoming head of the CIA on September 24, 2004, Goss's principal charge had been to bring it under control after the Bush administration had come to view it as the source of a constant stream of hostile intelligence leaks.

None of this is to cast doubt on the worth of undertaking organizational reforms in pursuit of better intelligence. The chances of achieving that goal become much greater, however, if those who work in the organizations embrace the reforms rather than having them imposed externally with little or no buy-in. Such reforms alone will not, moreover, prevent surprise. Just as important as organizational reforms is altering the attitudes of policymakers. In *Improving CIA Analytic Performance*, Jack Davis, a retired intelligence official, suggests the special importance of making senior policymakers partly responsible for the quality of warning intelligence instead of simply its passive recipients. They need to become more involved in the selection of topics, allocation of resources, standard setting, and assessment of threats. They must also become more interested in the reasoning behind intelligence estimates and less inclined to reward most whatever intelligence reaches them first.

[Intelligence reforms have] failed to acknowledge the deeper sources of strategic surprise and the limitations of organizational reforms for preventing intelligence failures.

The need for attitudinal change also applies among congressional overseers of intelligence. Virtually from the creation of the intelligence community, Congress has been reluctant to receive information on the activities of the intelligence community. Matters have improved little over time. Lock Johnson's study, "Governing in the Absence of Angels," concluded that the story of congressional oversight since 1975 has been one of "discontinuous motivation, ad hoc responses to scandals, and reliance on the initiatives of just a few members of Congress—mainly the occasional dedicated chair—to carry the burden." Reporting for the *Washington Post*, Dana Milbank and Walter Pincus found that no more than six senators and a handful of representatives read more than the five-page executive summary of the ninety-two-page National Intelligence Estimate requested by the Senate Intelligence Committee prior to the Iraq War. Finally, while never totally absent from the workings of the intelligence committees, partisanship has become more pronounced recently. Not only have competing political agendas grown increasingly evident in investigations and hearings on intelligence matters, Gregory McCarthy's "GOP Oversight of Intelligence in the Clinton Era" reported charges about congressional attempts to use the intelligence budget to fund their pet projects. . . .

The intelligence reform dialogue that has taken place since 9/11 holds great peril for the U.S. intelligence community and U.S. security in general. The dialogue constituted a lost opportunity to inform and educate the American public about why surprise happens in world politics and the potential for and limitations of attempts to deal with it. Both the solution endorsed, principally creating a DNI, and critiques of that solution failed to acknowledge the deeper sources of strategic surprise and the limitations of organizational reforms for preventing intelligence failures. When a failure does occur the danger exists that the public and policymakers will turn on the intelligence community with calls either for dissolving it or for its radical reconstruction. Blame will be placed squarely on the failure of the 9/11 reorganization efforts. Perhaps such proposals will have merit but the solutions will likely fall far short of perfecting the silver bullet that prevents surprise. Instead it will set in motion a repetition of the dynamics outlined here.

The Intelligence Reforms of 2004 Will Not Fix Problems Identified in the Iraq Intelligence Failure

Charles N. Davis

Charles N. Davis is a former intelligence analyst for the Defense Intelligence Agency and the National Intelligence Council.

The Intelligence Reform Bill that Congress passed [in 2004] makes significant improvements in intelligence sharing among federal agencies and it cements into law the already created National Counterterrorism Center. It charters a new office of Director of National Intelligence. . . . But such coordination and centralized authority may come at significant costs in other areas of intelligence gathering.

Question About the Director of National Intelligence

While the restructuring answers one of the major concerns of the Sept. 11 Commission—that no one is in charge of American intelligence—the readjustment is certain to provide a jolt to the intelligence gathering community. As Douglas Jehl wrote in the Dec. 8 [2004] *New York Times*: "In some ways, the new intelligence overseer will exercise more authority than predecessors did, particularly in controlling how a $40 billion budget is divided among 15 rivalrous agencies and 200,000 employees."

Exactly what kind of authority that director would have is still uncertain. As Dana Priest and Walter Pincus pointed out in *The Washington Post,* "The new chief would not be directly in charge of any operations—not covert actions, the CIA [Central Intelligence Agency] station chiefs around the world, the army of analysts whose job is to connect the dots, or the operators of high-tech collection systems that contribute so much these days to finding and disrupting terrorist plans." They also note that the new director would not have total control over some military intelligence operations and, finally, that the new director of national intelligence would have competition for the president's ear from the director of a new national counterterrorism center, also provided for in the new bill, who will report directly to the president. . . .

Will Reforms Fix Intelligence Problems?

While I believe the bill will improve coordination among agencies, there is nothing to protect against "groupthink"—the belief that one view is the only correct one—that led, for example, to the unquestioned conviction that Iraq possessed weapons of mass destruction. Some of the improvements may actually weaken our capability for independent intelligence analysis. Even if all the intelligence forwarded to the White House from here on in were 100 percent correct, this administration's ideological biases could easily skew that intelligence.

Under the appointments of [the George W. Bush] administration, the ability of Congress and the public to gain access to intelligence judgments will be considerably restricted.

The decentralized intelligence gathering of old had an upside as far as independent analysis is concerned. The intelligence analyses that receive the greatest respect in the government are National Intelligence Estimates, which bring together representatives mainly from the State Department, CIA, the

Defense Intelligence Agency and the military services to analyze a problem and come to judgments. Any agency could dissent from the judgments and these were recorded in either "alternative views" or footnotes. In the future, because the new national intelligence director will have control over the budget of most agencies, I believe the courage of any agency to dissent by taking an intelligence view that runs contrary to administration policy will be considerably weakened. Thus, the risk of "groupthink" within the intelligence community will be considerably higher under this reorganization.

Political Control over Intelligence Information

Reorganization aside, under the appointments of this administration, the ability of the Congress and the public to gain access to intelligence judgments will be considerably restricted. [The] secretary of defense, . . . secretary of state . . . , director of the CIA . . . and . . . director of national intelligence will almost certainly severely curtail within the government the distribution of intelligence that does not back up administration policy. The administration has already shown itself prone to such actions in its handling of two bleak intelligence assessments on Iraq. One, a National Intelligence Estimate sent to the White House in August [2004] "presented a dark forecast of Iraq's future through the end of 2005." The intelligence estimate projected that "the best case was for tenuous stability and the worst case included a chain of events leading to civil war." The other assessment was a November cable from a CIA station chief that was widely disseminated within the government. The cable "warned that the situation in Iraq is deteriorating and may not rebound soon." The National Intelligence Estimate was not released during the election campaign and it is almost certain the distribution of such future CIA cables within the government will be curtailed to prevent leaks.

Finally, this administration continues to ignore intelligence from the region as it attempts to rewrite history. There is growing evidence that we are not winning the hearts and minds of ordinary Arabs in the Middle East; they believe U.S. policies give unqualified backing to Israel and support authoritarian and corrupt regimes in Egypt, Saudi Arabia and other countries in the Gulf region. Consequently, many Arabs reject "democracy" and go to Iraq to join the rebellion. Nonetheless, the administration continues to try to place an unrealistically positive spin on developments in Iraq and to deflect blame for policy failures. No amount of good intelligence will help if it is trumped by political spin.

Numerous Problems Remain in the U.S. Intelligence System Despite Reforms

Michael A. Gips

Michael A. Gips is a senior editor at Security Management *magazine, a publication for security professionals.*

Since 9-11, there have been numerous attempts to "fix" the U.S. intelligence apparatus. First, President [George W.] Bush established the Terrorism Threat Integration Center (TTIC), which was supposed to help coordinate analysis among the intelligence community's multiple players. Before that had time to coalesce, however, it was superseded by the National Counterterrorism Center, among other changes contained in the Intelligence Reform and Terrorism Prevention Act of 2004, which also established the Director of National Intelligence (DNI).

Amidst these legislative and presidential attempts to redraw reporting authority, many highly regarded Central Intelligence Agency (CIA) personnel have departed en masse, some in protest over the appointment of Porter Goss (as CIA Director), who himself was eased out in May [2006]. Meanwhile, the National Security Agency (NSA) has come under fire for harvesting records of Americans' phone calls from telephone companies.

Nearly two years after passage of the reform act, it is unclear whether the changes have helped. Among the most frequently mentioned problems dogging the reform is the persistence of contrasting cultures among intelligence entities,

Michael A. Gips, "Spying Trouble: Culture Clashes Among the FBI, CIA, and the Military Intelligence Agencies Are Some of the Problems Cited in the Intelligence Community," *Security Management*, vol. 50, August 2006, pp. 68–79. © 2006 ASIS International, 1625 Prince Street, Alexandria, VA 22314. Reprinted by permission of *Security Management* magazine.

especially between military and civilian intelligence agencies, and between members of the intelligence community and law enforcement in agencies that combine both missions. Other roadblocks to reform are a lack of access to policymakers, insufficient integration of intelligence, and difficulties in obtaining quality intelligence.

Sinking or Swimming

It's never a good sign when someone compares you to the *Titanic*. Yet that "unsinkable" ocean liner was the metaphor of choice at the Intelcon conference, a recent gathering of the intelligence community. Several speakers and attendees likened the reform effort to rearranging deck chairs on the much-maligned ship. One highly placed ex-intelligence official at the Department of Defense (DoD), who requested that his comments not be for attribution, said that the reform act "rearranged the chairs, added a couple of chairs . . . and looked at who's funding the chairs." But it neglected to consider whether the floor beneath the chairs was solid.

The [Office of the Director of National Intelligence] is actually sapping the strength of the [intelligence] community by . . . its demand for personnel, resources, and credibility.

To carry that metaphor further, one could contend that a large and ornate chair has been placed overlooking the others, next to the captain. That chair is the Office of the Director of National Intelligence (ODNI), which trumps the CIA as the conduit between the intelligence community and the White House. Critics say that the ODNI merely creates another layer of bureaucracy. "They [ODNI] have integrated almost nothing because they're too busy staffing themselves," says Dick Coffman, who served in major managerial and coordinator positions during 31 years with the CIA. The ODNI is "sucking the juice" out of the CIA and the rest of the intelligence community, he adds.

Instead of freeing intelligence officers to collect and analyze data, the ODNI is actually sapping the strength of the community by virtue of its demand for personnel, resources, and credibility. Plus, by superimposing the ODNI over the CIA, he says, the reform act is lowering the CIA on the intelligence hierarchy. As a result, what has long been considered the premiere all-source analytical arm of the intelligence community now may not be able to attract the same quality personnel.

Jason Klitenic, former deputy general counsel of the Department of Homeland Security (DHS), counters that it's far too early to assess the reform effort, likening such an exercise to judging the performance of a baseball pitcher after the first pitch of the game. While not commenting on the ODNI's performance, Klitenic says that creating the ODNI made sense because the director of the CIA had a dual role as the director of central intelligence, so there was the temptation to favor CIA intelligence over other sources when speaking to the President. The DNI "is supposed to be more objective and a little removed from the 16 intelligence agencies," he says.

The attempt to coordinate intelligence through the ODNI is being hampered by the fact that the DoD has been building up its own intelligence structure.

Among the various cultures existing in the intelligence community, two have been cited frequently as creating the most significant tension and rifts: the struggle between military and civilian agencies, and the dichotomy between the FBI's role as an intelligence agency and its role as a law enforcement agency.

Spy vs. Spy

The Defense Department's intelligence role has troubled many observers. Even though the reform act endows the ODNI with authority over DoD agencies, the Pentagon remains a powerful player because the statute does not strip the Secretary of Defense of his authority over his intelligence agencies. Many experts have expressed concern that the attempt to coordinate intelligence through the ODNI is being hampered by the fact that the DoD has been building up its own intelligence structure.

To address that concern, one expert, federal circuit court judge Richard Posner, recommends spinning off the national intelligence agencies that operate as arms of the DoD and letting them become stand-alone agencies under the control of the ODNI. That would swing the balance of power back to the civilian sector. But it's not likely to happen. . . .

[Intelligence] collection, analysis, and dissemination are the bases of successful intelligence operations.

Two Sides of a Coin

Much has been made of the wall between the FBI's investigative and intelligence functions, which some say hindered the Bureau from sniffing out the 9-11 plot. Members of the intelligence community say that intelligence continues to be subservient to investigation and law enforcement. In testimony before the Senate Judiciary Committee, John Gannon, who worked with the FBI frequently during his 24-year stint at the CIA, asserted that "the FBI is unacceptably behind . . . in developing a national intelligence collection and analytic capability."

The problem, many say, is that FBI officers are rewarded for making arrests, not for gathering data for some amorphous, distant purpose. Its officers collect evidence of possible crimes, not possible future crimes. Thus, intelligence staff are treated like "second-class citizens," according to Michael Collier, professor of national security and intelligence studies with American Military University.

The reform act directed the FBI to improve its intelligence capabilities through the development of a "national intelligence workforce." In addition, the statutory language noted the importance of rotating intelligence officers through various agencies in the community, "in order to facilitate the widest possible understanding by such personnel of the variety of intelligence requirements, methods, users, and capabilities." The law further stated that service in more than one intelligence agency should be a condition for promotion to certain positions. With that mandate in mind, [now former] DNI John D. Negroponte, speaking . . . at the National Press Club, said that his plans for 2007 included getting all the agencies to require that individuals in intelligence have joint tours of duty before they get promoted to the senior intelligence service.

Quality of Intelligence Collection

Collection, analysis, and dissemination are the bases of successful intelligence operations. The law reforming intelligence attempted to address each of these. For example, it created a National Counterterrorism Center (NCTC) for centralized analysis and distribution; it set up a framework for the alternative analysis of intelligence; and it required President [George W.] Bush to establish an Information Sharing Environment to foster sharing across all branches and levels of government. . . .

Collection continues to be a problem, especially at the national level, Gannon told the Senate Judiciary Committee. In an effort to improve the situation, the National Clandestine Service (NCS) was created . . . within the ODNI and the CIA, reporting to the director of the CIA. The NCS was "established to set standards for human intelligence collection throughout the intelligence community," said Negroponte. The NCS replaced the CIA's Directorate of Operations (formerly responsible for covert operations). The service is also charged with coordinating human intelligence operations, including with the FBI.

Within the FBI, another new organizational unit, the National Security Branch (NSB), has been established to bring together the FBI's counterintelligence and counterterrorism divisions with its Directorate of Intelligence. The NSB, explained Negroponte, "has launched pilot programs in field offices across the country focused on national security training [and it is developing] asset-validation procedures to align with the intelligence community standards." . . .

If the dots of . . . [collected] data are not analyzed to see whether they create a noteworthy pattern, the effort [to improve collection] will have been a waste of time.

When asked directly at the National Press Club whether progress has been made on intelligence collection, Negroponte's answer was an unequivocal "yes." Not all reports are as sanguine as Negroponte's. "Looking at where we are, we should be asking why it is so hard for the FBI to develop a national intelligence capability," Gannon told the Senate Judiciary Committee. Perhaps, he suggested, "We have asked too much of an otherwise-capable criminal-investigation agency."

Foreign collection has its own troubles, says one agent who has worked closely with U.S. embassy personnel who screen foreign nationals walking in with tips. These informants, who may have an agenda, such as the need for a visa, tend to be in contact only with post security officers, who may not be able to discern what constitutes good intelligence. The bluster and misinformation could easily be flushed out by trained agents, he says. . . .

The problem is not just with the lack of hard-to-procure intelligence, however. Just as with industrial espionage, a trained eye may be able to assemble disparate pieces of public information to spot patterns and intuit future intentions. The reform act encourages collectors of intelligence to use more of this type of open-source information. Steps are being taken toward this goal. For example, Negroponte announced the creation of an open-source intelligence center at Langley [CIA headquarters] late last year [2005].

At the Intelcon conference, one highly placed member of the intelligence community affirmed that information available to the general public was a hugely important element of intelligence, and not just "frosting." But, he said, the community still isn't sufficiently availing itself of that valuable information. . . .

Problems with Intelligence Analysis

Collection is, of course, not an end in itself. If the dots of that data are not analyzed to see whether they create a noteworthy pattern, the effort will have been a waste of time. Congress and the President attempted to address this issue through the establishment of TTIC and now the NCTC. Is that working as intended? Again, it depends who you ask.

At the National Press Club, Negroponte cited "many efforts underway to improve our analytic prowess, our analytic skills, as well as verifying our sources of information." He then elaborated on some of the changes he has implemented to ensure that analysis mistakes of the past would not be repeated. For example, the ODNI has created the position of an analytic ombudsman "whose job is going to be basically to look at reports that we've done on very critical issues and to then really test them very severely with respect to the analytic tradecraft . . . and also to receive complaints from anywhere in the intelligence community," said Negroponte. Gregory Treverton, a senior policy analyst with the RAND Corporation who previously worked for the first Senate Select Committee on Intelligence, says that the appointment of an ombudsman was "the right thing to do." That person can be "a focal point for spurring innovations," he says, adding, however, that it's too early to assess how well that person, or the function, is working.

The most important new force in terms of analysis of intelligence is the NCTC. In his progress report, Negroponte lauded some of the NCTC's advances. In particular, Negroponte pointed out that he had directed the transfer of 72 analyst positions to the NCTC from other intelligence agencies, and that the NCTC has created a secure Web site that reaches more than 5,000 federal users. But some observers see problems with the NCTC. For one, the center was intended to supersede the analytic function at the CIA, but the CIA's center still exists and is instead competing with the NCTC. The DHS in its own reorganization [in 2005] also established an analytic center (the Office of Intelligence and Analysis), perhaps further undermining the NCTC's goal of centralization.

One solution is turning more frequently to private-sector expertise.

[Bruce] McIndoe [CEO of the intelligence firm Jet] sees another problem: the isolation of analysts, who toil alone in cubicles and have no access to sources and agents in the field. "We should let them learn the language and the culture," he suggests, as well as talk to collectors and sources, which he says will lead to more informed and better-textured analysis. Cycling intelligence agents between collection and analysis assignments isn't feasible, however. "They're too different," says McIndoe. Analysts are typically introverted, he says, and would get frustrated with recruiting and developing sources over long periods of time.

Private Sector Role

One solution is turning more frequently to private-sector expertise. "The government has to be more agile in recruiting and coordinating external analysis with subject matter experts," says McIndoe, whose company gathers intelligence to help clients monitor and mitigate risks. Right now, McIndoe says, the government reaches out for professional or academic expertise only sporadically, and only in fields where it believes it lacks depth.

In his recent summary on implementation of intelligence reform, Negroponte said that the National Intelligence Council, which provides the government with estimates of current situations and developing trends, has been reaching out to the private sector more "to secure the full range of alternative views and analytic insights needed by our customers."

Cross-agency dissemination of intelligence has been another major focus of intelligence reform efforts, with some success.

Some intelligence experts worry that the government is ceding too much responsibility to the private sector. A compromise might be the creation of a permanent public-private partnership, rather than handing off functions piecemeal to contractors. As one intelligence professional explained it at the Intelcon conference, such a partnership would combine the best of what each brings to the table: hiring, training, and mission setting by the government, and innovating and employing new technology by the private sector.

Information Sharing

In the sinking of the *Titanic*, the warnings about icebergs that lay in the ship's path never made it from the radio room to the bridge. Similarly, the 9/11 Commission found that the CIA's failure to pass along information about terrorists to the

FBI was a factor in the government's inability to uncover the plot. As a result, cross-agency dissemination of intelligence has been another major focus of intelligence reform efforts, with some success. "Contrary to the common perception, we have already achieved several successes in key areas such as information sharing," asserted Negroponte at the National Press Club. To support that claim, Negroponte pointed out that "information from 28 different systems flows into the NCTC." He added that information sharing between intelligence groups was already taking place daily. "To keep counterterrorism officials throughout the government in constant contact, NCTC holds communitywide secure video teleconferences three times a day," Negroponte said.

The reform act called for creation of an Intelligence Sharing Environment (ISE) to facilitate the give-and-take of terrorism-related information among federal, state, local, and tribal governments, the private sector, and foreign allies. But there seems to be little real substance to the ISE. An ODNI backgrounder describes the ISE as "not a new technology, database, or system; it will be created through further defining, changing, or establishing policies, procedures, cultures, and technologies." "More than four years after September 11, the nation still lacks the government-wide policies and processes that Congress called for," investigators from the Government Accountability Office (GAO) reported [in 2006]. . . .

The bottom line, says one ex-DEA [Drug Enforcement Administration] official, is to believe that . . . [reform is] achievable. "When the United States really wants to do something, the power is awesome." A can-do attitude is healthy. But it's no substitute for real progress. "The salient fact is that, approaching five years after 9-11, we still do not have a domestic intelligence service that can collect effectively against the terrorist threat to the homeland or provide authoritative analysis of that threat," testified Gannon.

CHAPTER 3

Do Intelligence-Gathering Activities Threaten Civil or Human Rights?

Chapter Preface

The United States responded to the September 11, 2001, terrorist attacks not only by restructuring and reforming the U.S. intelligence system for detecting foreign threats, but also by expanding the federal government's surveillance powers within the United States. Indeed, just days after the 9/11 attack, on September 19, 2001, President George W. Bush proposed the Uniting and Strengthening America by Providing Appropriate Tools Required to Intercept and Obstruct Terrorism Act of 2001 (aka USA PATRIOT Act), and Congress quickly passed the law with virtually no debate or opposition. The 9/11 crisis united the country in the desire to try to prevent future terrorist attacks, and the Patriot Act's supporters claimed that its provisions were necessary to give the nation's police and intelligence officials the powers to collect information about potential terrorists living in the country.

The Patriot Act, however, soon became very controversial because it provided for greatly expanded government surveillance not only of terrorists, but of all U.S. residents, including ordinary citizens. The government's new surveillance powers, for example, authorized the Federal Bureau of Investigation (FBI), one of the nation's main intelligence agencies, to search people's homes and other properties without advance notice to the owner, to monitor their e-mails and Internet communications, and to access a wide variety of their intimate business, health, financial, and consumer records, as well as other items.

Unlike traditional police searches, searches conducted under the new Patriot Act did not require the government to show evidence that the person being targeted had committed a crime, or even that he or she was involved in terrorism. Instead, the government was authorized to conduct searches and surveillance based only on a claim that the information sought is relevant to a government terrorism investigation. In addition, the act permitted much of this surveillance to be carried out in secret and did not provide for judicial challenges or oversight to check unscrupulous or excessive government intrusions. For certain types of surveillance, the act even prohibited persons or businesses from ever revealing the fact that they had been asked to provide information to the government. Noncitizens fared even worse than citizens under the Patriot Act because the law provided that noncitizens could be detained solely on a claim that the government has reasonable grounds to believe that the person's actions threaten national security.

Critics said these loose and ambiguous provisions granted the U.S. government unprecedented domestic surveillance powers and threatened Americans' civil rights, including the constitutional rights considered central to American democracy—free speech, free association, privacy, and due process of law. Civil liberties groups such as the American Civil Liberties Union (ACLU) filed numerous lawsuits challenging the Patriot Act, and several federal courts ruled against the administration, finding parts of the law unconstitutional. President Bush and supporters of the Patriot Act, meanwhile, argued that it helped to keep the country safe from further terrorist attacks in the years following 9/11. The administration steadfastly maintained that ordinary Americans were not being targeted for government surveillance, and that the new intelligence powers in the Patriot Act were vital for fighting the war on terror and ensuring America's security.

Although widespread opposition developed against the Patriot Act, Congress ultimately reauthorized the law in 2006, with a few safeguards that supporters promised would protect citizens' civil liberties. The law's opponents, however, thought that the safeguards did not go far enough and vowed to continue their fight to expose the act's civil rights abuses. In 2006, for example, the ACLU released information indicating that the FBI was conducting surveillance of antiwar groups exercising their First Amendment rights of protest, solely because of the content of their speech—their opposition to the war in Iraq and President Bush's foreign-policy decisions. Some critics say the Patriot Act and the war on terror are being used by the Bush administration to expand the powers of the president and executive branch far beyond the separation-of-powers limits set in the U.S. Constitution.

Indeed, the Patriot Act is not the only post-9/11 intelligence-gathering activity that has been criticized for violating civil and human rights. A number of other government decisions taken in the war against terror have also stirred up controversy, both in the United States and around the world. One of these is a decision by President Bush shortly after 9/11 to authorize the National Security Agency, a super-secret U.S. intelligence arm, to monitor Americans' phone calls and e-mails without first getting court-approved search warrants—an action that critics said violated the Fourth Amendment to the U.S. Constitution. Other Bush administration actions challenged on civil and human rights grounds included the torture and imprisonment without trial of hundreds of suspected terrorists, classified as "enemy combatants," at a U.S. military base in Guantánamo Bay, Cuba. Critics claim this treatment violates both due process guarantees in the U.S. Constitution (such as the right to bail and to a speedy trial) as well as international laws against torture. Yet another concern of critics is the administration's expansion of the intelligence-gathering activities of the U.S. military, which unlike other intelligence actions, do not require an explicit presidential authorization and are not subject to Congressional oversight. The authors in this chapter describe and debate these decisions and their effects on civil and human rights.

The National Security Agency Domestic Spying Program Does Not Violate Americans' Civil Rights

Mortimer B. Zuckerman

Mortimer B. Zuckerman is the editor in chief of U.S. News & World Report, *and the publisher of the* New York Daily News.

Here is a scenario that could be right out of a spy movie or the TV hit *24*: A foreign intelligence service tells the CIA it has discovered that one of its nationals who is an active terrorist has made calls home from within the United States. The foreign spy service gives the CIA the man's aliases and the number he called from. Our counterterrorist agents leap into action. They ask the National Security Agency [NSA] to check all the phone numbers the terrorist called in the United States or elsewhere to unmask a possible sleeper cell of other terrorists.

The NSA, using its vast computer power to scan millions of "call detail" records, begins urgently examining the pattern of calls when a garbled story appears in the press that the agency is eavesdropping on the conversations of innocent Americans. A U.S. president, recently elected and unsure of himself, orders the NSA to stand down. Four weeks later, the sleeper cell explodes a bomb in a tunnel of a major American city.

Far-fetched? Not really, when you consider the media storm about NSA's "listening in" on calls placed to the United States from suspected al Qaeda members or affiliates. Except that that's not what the NSA does. It doesn't listen in on all these millions of conversations. The agency's analysts look for patterns in the timing and frequency of numbers called. This is what it was charged with doing by President Bush after 9/11. It was and is a sensible use of our comparative advantage in technology. It enables us to collect information that human intelligence has been unable to provide, given our difficulty of penetrating cells of radical Islamists, at home or abroad. The program was an essential response to the pre-9/11 failure to "connect the dots." Why? Because before you can connect the dots, you've got to be able to see them.

Uproar

Much of the rhetoric of the press now essentially charges the White House with illegally trampling on our constitutional rights and creating an ominous surveillance state. The fact is that the NSA has not been "snooping" on the conversations of Americans. Moreover, what it has been doing is presumptively legal, given the Communications Assistance to Law Enforcement Act, or CALEA, of 1994. That law made it clear that a telecommunications carrier had a duty to cooperate in the interception of communications for law enforcement purposes. The law reads, "Interception of communications or access to call-identifying information . . . can be activated only in accordance with a court order or other lawful authorization." In other words, a court order is not the only form of lawful authorization. A subpoena or "national security" letter from the FBI may also compel a telephone company to hand over these records without court approval. This action is consistent with telephone and Internet business contracts, which include provisions authorizing the company to disclose records, if necessary, to protect public safety and national security or to comply with a lawful government request.

The case for the NSA's data mining is even stronger than it was in 1994, before the 9/11 attacks. It was hardly controversial when it was passed and signed into law by a Congress and

White House controlled by Democrats. Given that the leaders in both chambers and members of the newly created intelligence subcommittees were briefed on the matter, and given that the U.S. Supreme Court had already distinguished between collecting routing information and phone numbers as acceptable and separate from obtaining the actual content of phone calls, why the uproar? Is it because the Republicans now control the White House and Congress?

The freedom we enjoy has to be protected from enemies who would destroy every vestige of it if they could.

The answer, in part, is yes. There has been such political mismanagement by this administration that the public is no longer inclined to give the president the benefit of the doubt on national security issues. Quite simply, the administration could have done a much better job of explaining both the potential and the limits of data mining. It should have made it clear that in the right context, no one's privacy would be violated.

Intelligence Is Essential

The American public is going to have to come to terms with the fact that it is better to allow such activities, as long as they are disclosed—but only to the appropriate government agencies and committees of Congress. Publicity undermines the effectiveness of these kinds of measures by alerting terrorists to change their behavior. Besides, why should we forsake our one big advantage, technology, in the war on terrorism?

Americans have a long and proud history of low tolerance for government snooping. But the freedom we enjoy has to be protected from enemies who would destroy every vestige of it if they could. The government would be lax indeed if, out of fear of criticism, it stopped collecting information. In the past, such intelligence has helped convict thousands of felons and solved or helped solve countless numbers of terrible crimes. We should not preclude its use now to help detect the enemies in our midst.

Torture Must Be Permitted in Certain Terrorism Cases to Save Innocent Lives

Charles Krauthammer

Charles Krauthammer is a Pulitzer Prize–winning columnist and commentator whose work often appears in the Washington Post, Time *and the* Weekly Standard.

The pieties about torture have lain so thick in the air that it has been impossible to have a reasoned discussion. The [John] McCain amendment that would ban "cruel, inhuman, or degrading" treatment of any prisoner by any agent of the United States sailed through the Senate by a vote of 90-9. The Washington establishment remains stunned that nine such retrograde, morally inert persons—let alone senators—could be found in this noble capital.

Now, John McCain has great moral authority on this issue, having heroically borne torture at the hands of the North Vietnamese. McCain has made fine arguments in defense of his position. And McCain is acting out of the deep and honorable conviction that what he is proposing is not only right but is in the best interest of the United States. His position deserves respect. But that does not mean, as seems to be the assumption in Washington today, that a critical analysis of his "no torture, ever" policy is beyond the pale.

Three Kinds of Prisoners

Let's begin with a few analytic distinctions. For the purpose of torture and prisoner maltreatment, there are three kinds of war prisoners:

First, there is the ordinary soldier caught on the field of battle. There is no question that he is entitled to humane treatment. Indeed, we have no right to disturb a hair on his head. His detention has but a single purpose: to keep him *hors de combat* [a French term for "out of the fight"]. The proof of that proposition is that if there were a better way to keep him off the battlefield that did not require his detention, we would let him go. Indeed, during one year of the Civil War, the two sides did try an alternative. They mutually "paroled" captured enemy soldiers, i.e., released them to return home on the pledge that they would not take up arms again.

Because the only purpose of detention in these circumstances is to prevent the prisoner from becoming a combatant again, he is entitled to all the protections and dignity of an ordinary domestic prisoner—indeed, more privileges, because, unlike the domestic prisoner, he has committed no crime. He merely had the misfortune to enlist on the other side of a legitimate war. He is therefore entitled to many of the privileges enjoyed by an ordinary citizen—the right to send correspondence, to engage in athletic activity and intellectual pursuits, to receive allowances from relatives—except, of course, for the freedom to leave the prison.

Anyone who blows up a car bomb in a market deserves to spend the rest of his life roasting on a spit over an open fire.

Second, there is the captured terrorist. A terrorist is by profession, indeed by definition, an unlawful combatant. He lives outside the laws of war because he does not wear a uniform, he hides among civilians, and he deliberately targets innocents. He is entitled to no protections whatsoever. People seem to think that the postwar Geneva Conventions were written only to protect detainees. In fact, their deeper purpose was to provide a deterrent to the kind of barbaric treatment of civilians that had become so horribly apparent during the first half of the 20th century, and in particular, during the Second World War. The idea was to deter the abuse of civilians by promising combatants who treated noncombatants well that they themselves would be treated according to a code of dignity if captured—and, crucially, that they would be denied the protections of that code if they broke the laws of war and abused civilians themselves.

Breaking the laws of war and abusing civilians are what, to understate the matter vastly, terrorists do for a living. They are entitled, therefore, to nothing. Anyone who blows up a car bomb in a market deserves to spend the rest of his life roasting on a spit over an open fire. But we don't do that because we do not descend to the level of our enemy. We don't do that because, unlike him, we are civilized. Even though terrorists are entitled to no humane treatment, we give it to them because it is in our nature as a moral and humane people. And when on rare occasions we fail to do that, as has occurred in several of the fronts of the war on terror, we are duly disgraced.

Torture is not always impermissible . . . there are circumstances in which, by any rational moral calculus, torture not only would be permissible but would be required.

The norm, however, is how the majority of prisoners at Guantanamo [a U.S. base in Cuba used to detain suspects of terrorism] have been treated. We give them three meals a day, superior medical care, and provision to pray five times a day. Our scrupulousness extends even to providing them with their own Korans, which is the only reason alleged abuses of the Koran at Guantanamo ever became an issue. That we should have provided those who kill innocents in the name of Islam with precisely the document that inspires their barbarism is a sign of the absurd lengths to which we often go in extending undeserved humanity to terrorist prisoners.

Third, there is the terrorist with information. Here the issue of torture gets complicated and the easy pieties don't so easily apply. Let's take the textbook case. Ethics 101: A terrorist has planted a nuclear bomb in New York City. It will go off in one hour. A million people will die. You capture the terrorist. He knows where it is. He's not talking. Question: If you have the slightest belief that hanging this man by his thumbs will get you the information to save a million people, are you permitted to do it? Now, on most issues regarding torture, I confess tentativeness and uncertainty. But on this issue, there can be no uncertainty: Not only is it permissible to hang this miscreant by his thumbs. It is a moral duty.

Torture Is Sometimes Necessary

Yes, you say, but that's an extreme and very hypothetical case. Well, not as hypothetical as you think. Sure, the (nuclear) scale is hypothetical, but in the age of the car and suicide bomber, terrorists are often captured who have just set a car bomb to go off or sent a suicide bomber out to a coffee shop, and you only have minutes to find out where the attack is to take place. This "hypothetical" is common enough that the Israelis have a term for precisely that situation: the ticking time bomb problem.

And even if the example I gave were entirely hypothetical, the conclusion—yes, in this case even torture is permissible—is telling because it establishes the principle: Torture is not always impermissble. However rare the cases, there are circumstances in which, by any rational moral calculus, torture not only would be permissible but would be required (to acquire life-saving information). And once you've established the principle, to paraphrase George Bernard Shaw, all that's left to haggle about is the price. In the case of torture, that means that the argument is not *whether* torture is ever permissible, but *when*—i.e., under what obviously stringent circumstances: how big, how imminent, how preventable the ticking time bomb.

Since 9/11 the United States has maintained a series of ... secret detention centers where presumably high-level terrorists ... have been imprisoned.

That is why the McCain amendment, which by mandating "torture never" refuses even to recognize the legitimacy of any moral calculus, cannot be right. There must be exceptions. The real argument should be over what constitutes a legitimate exception.

A Real-Life Example

Let's take an example that is far from hypothetical. You capture Khalid Sheikh Mohammed [an al Qaeda leader] in Pakistan. He not only has already killed innocents, he is deeply involved in the planning for the present and future killing of innocents. He not only was the architect of the 9/11 attack that killed nearly three thousand people in one day, most of them dying a terrible, agonizing, indeed tortured death. But as the top al Qaeda planner and logistical expert he also knows a lot about terror attacks to come. He knows plans, identities, contacts, materials, cell locations, safe houses, cased targets, etc. What do you do with him?

We have recently learned that since 9/11 the United States has maintained a series of "black sites" around the world, secret detention centers where presumably high-level terrorists like Khalid Sheikh Mohammed have been imprisoned. The world is scandalized. Black sites? Secret detention? Jimmy Carter calls this "a profound and radical change in the ... moral values of our country." The Council of Europe demands an investigation, calling the claims "extremely worrying." Its human rights commissioner declares "such practices" to constitute "a serious human rights violation, and further proof of the crisis of values" that has engulfed the war on terror. The gnashing of teeth and rending of garments has been considerable.

I myself have not gnashed a single tooth. My garments remain entirely unrent. Indeed, I feel reassured. It would be a gross dereliction of duty for any government *not* to keep Khalid Sheikh Mohammed isolated, disoriented, alone, despairing, cold and sleepless, in some godforsaken hidden location in order to find out what he knew about plans for future mass murder. What are we supposed to do? Give him a nice cell in a warm Manhattan prison, complete with Miranda rights, a mellifluent lawyer, and his own website? Are not those the kinds of courtesies we extended to the 1993 World Trade Center bombers, then congratulated ourselves on how we "brought to justice" those responsible for an attack that barely failed to kill tens of thousands of Americans, only to discover a decade later that we had accomplished nothing—indeed, that some of the disclosures at the trial had helped Osama bin Laden avoid U.S. surveillance?

Once you have gone public with a blanket ban on all forms of coercion, it is going to be very difficult to publicly carve out exceptions.

Have we learned nothing from 9/11? Are we prepared to go back with complete amnesia to the domestic-crime model of dealing with terrorists, which allowed us to sleepwalk through the nineties while al Qaeda incubated and grew and metastasized unmolested until on 9/11 it finished what the first World Trade Center bombers had begun? ...

The Need for Torture Rules

Given the gravity of the decision, if we indeed cross the Rubicon [i.e., take a decisive step with no return]—as we must—we need rules. The problem with the McCain amendment is that once you have gone public with a blanket ban on all forms of coercion, it is going to be very difficult to publicly carve out exceptions. The [George W.] Bush administration is to be faulted for having attempted such a codification with the kind of secrecy, lack of coherence, and lack of strict enforcement that led us to the McCain reaction.

What to do at this late date? Begin, as McCain does by banning all forms of coercion or inhuman treatment by anyone serving in the military—an absolute ban on torture by all military personnel everywhere. We do not want a private somewhere making these fine distinctions about ticking and slow-fuse time bombs. We don't even want colonels or generals making them. It would be best for the morale, discipline, and honor of the Armed Forces for the United States to maintain an absolute prohibition, both to simplify their task in making decisions and to offer them whatever reciprocal treatment they might receive from those who capture them— although I have no illusion that any anti-torture provision will soften the heart of a single jihadist holding a knife to the throat of a captured American soldier. We would impose this restriction on ourselves for our own reasons of military discipline and military honor.

Outside the military, however, I would propose, contra McCain, a ban against all forms of torture, coercive interrogation, and inhuman treatment, except in two contingencies: (1) the ticking time bomb and (2) the slower-fuse high-level terrorist. Each contingency would have its own set of rules. In the case of the ticking time bomb, the rules would be relatively simple: Nothing rationally related to getting accurate information would be ruled out. The case of the high-value suspect with slow-fuse information is more complicated. The principle would be that the level of inhumanity of the measures used would be proportional to the need and value of the information. Interrogators would be constrained to use the least inhumane treatment necessary relative to the magnitude and imminence of the evil being prevented and the importance of the knowledge being obtained.

In this real world of astonishingly murderous enemies, in two very circumscribed circumstances, we must all be prepared to torture.

These exceptions to the no-torture rule would not be granted to just any nonmilitary interrogators, or anyone with CIA credentials. They would be reserved for highly specialized agents who are experts and experienced in interrogation and who are known not to abuse it for the satisfaction of a kind of sick sadomasochism . . . indulged in at Abu Ghraib [an American prison in Iraq where Iraqi prisoners were tortured]. Nor would they be acting on their own. They would be required to obtain written permission for such interrogations from the highest political authorities in the country or from a quasi-judicial body modeled on the Foreign Intelligence Surveillance Court [special courts charged with issuing warrants for surveillance of foreign agents and terrorists]. Or, if the bomb was truly ticking and there was no time, the interrogators would be allowed to act on their own, but would require post facto authorization within, say, 24 hours of their interrogation, so that they knew that whatever they did would be subject to review by others and be justified only under the most stringent terms. . . .

In this real world of astonishingly murderous enemies, in two very circumscribed circumstances, we must all be prepared to torture. Having established that, we can then begin to work together to codify rules of interrogation for the two very unpleasant but very real cases in which we are morally permitted—indeed morally compelled—to do terrible things.

The Terrorist Threat Requires the United States to Relax Constraints on Covert Operations

Matthew S. Pape

Matthew S. Pape is an attorney in private practice in Dallas, Texas. He is a graduate of Georgetown University (BA, history, 1994) and the University of Houston Law Center (JD, 1998).

The United States is the most powerful nation on earth— the most powerful nation in the history of nations. From ancient Greece through Roman times to the age of Pax Britannica [when Britain was the dominant world power], no nation-state has influenced the world as greatly as the United States has. Much of the power America possesses directly results from its military capabilities and its willingness to use them to protect its national interests. The United States won World Wars I and II, used the first atomic weapons, and stared down the Soviet Union's numerical superiority in conventional and nuclear weapons with high technology. America continues to possess the largest and most technologically superior fighting force in history. At the tip of this powerful spear is a galaxy of satellites and sophisticated intelligence and information systems poised to deliver the latest in military, economic, and political intelligence.

A New Breed of Enemy

The events of 11 September 2001 demonstrate that a new breed of enemy exists—sinister conspirators who use asymmetric warfare to bring death, destruction, and terror to

Matthew S. Pape, "Constitutional Covert Operations: A Force Multiplier for Preemption," *Military Review*, vol. 84, March-April 2004, pp. 52-59. Copyright 2004 U.S. Army CGSC.

Americans at home and abroad. To defeat this new generation of foes, the United States must alter its geostrategy and relax its self-imposed constraints on the use of U.S. military, political, and social power. The United States can no longer rely on strategic nuclear deterrence, standing conventional armies, and fleets of carrier battle groups arrayed around the globe to ensure its citizens' safety and liberty. The international terrorist threat demands a proactive approach—preemptive action against terrorist groups and all nations that sustain and shelter them.

The U.S. Constitution contains an interesting dichotomy. Congress is responsible for raising an army, maintaining a navy, and declaring war, but the President, the Chief Executive of the United States, is the Commander-in-Chief who controls the actual deployment and use of military force. While Congress declares war's legal status and controls the funding of U.S. military forces, the President directs their conduct.

Congress and the President, in theory, share authority over the exercise of military power. In practice, war has not been "declared" by a U.S. Congress in more than 60 years. The President, as Commander-in-Chief, can send U.S. troops anywhere in the world with only a perfunctory requirement to notify Congress. This presidential power is vital if the United States is to win the Global War on Terrorism. American forces must act swiftly and decisively, at a moment's notice, to preempt attacks by the international terrorists who have brought or who want to bring devastation and mass murder to our shores.

As Chief Executive and Commander-in-Chief, the President possesses the constitutional power to engage in "little wars," "secret wars," and actions short of war to protect the Nation. The President's constitutional power permits him to train, fund, and arm pro-U.S. indigenous forces in other nations or to deploy special operations forces anywhere in the world to fight the Global War on Terrorism. Although the

United States is the most powerful nation on Earth, time, force structures, geography, and even alliances sometimes prevent direct military assaults that might quickly end a hostile threat. . . .

The debate over the power to wage war has not checked the President's dominance in controlling covert operations, but Congress's use of appropriations provisions has.

The Dispute over Covert Operations

The control of covert operations is at times a source of conflict between the President and Congress. Each proclaims power over the other to authorize and execute such operations, and each cites provisions in the Constitution to support its claim. . . .

Under the Constitution, Congress has the power "to provide for the common defense and general welfare of the United States." Specifically, Congress has the power to "declare war, grant letters of Marque and Reprisal, and make Rules concerning Captures on land and water." Congress is also charged, as part of its legislative and appropriations functions, "to raise and support Armies" and "to provide and maintain a Navy." Another provision that influences how America conducts its covert operations is the Constitution's "necessary and proper" clause, which states that Congress shall "make all laws which shall be necessary and proper for carrying into execution the foregoing powers, and all other powers vested by this Constitution in the Government of the United States, or in any Department or Officer thereof." The Constitution provides for the Senate to approve all treaties and the appointment of ambassadors and executive officers. Of its enumerated powers, Congress's two strongest arguments for requiring congressional authorization for covert operations are its power to declare war and the appropriations power, or "power of the purse."

The Constitution gives sole power to "declare war" to Congress, yet in 200 years, U.S. presidents have ordered hundreds of overt and covert military deployments, seeking formal declarations of war from Congress on only 5 occasions. Considerable debate surrounds the framers of the Constitution's intent concerning the control of U.S. covert operations. Proponents of congressional dominance cite earlier drafts of the Constitution that specified a congressional power to "make war" rather than "declare" it as proof that the framers' intent was that Congress exercise control over all forms of warfare. Clearly, the framers wanted some congressional control over the power of war rather than vesting it solely in one person.

Congressional Control over Covert Operations

The debate over the power to wage war has not checked the President's dominance in controlling covert operations, but Congress's use of appropriations provisions has. In the past 20 years, the most effective method Congress has employed to rein in Presidential power over covert operations has been tailoring appropriations bills to prohibit certain acts by the President. Two clear examples are the Hughes-Ryan Amendment and the Boland Amendment.

The Hughes-Ryan Amendment to the Foreign Assistance Act of 1974 states that a President must issue a finding that an authorized activity is "important to the national security interests of the United States" before appropriated funds may be used. The Boland Amendment and its subsequent editions proscribe the President's actions in Nicaragua.

In its first edition, the Boland Amendment to the Department of Defense Appropriation Act of 1983 prohibited the use of any funds to support any military or paramilitary group whose aim was to overthrow the Nicaraguan government. Subsequent Boland amendments placed a cap of $24 million in aid to the Contras [a rebel group] in Nicaragua and prohibited any aid at all after February 1985. The Boland Amendment led to the Iran-Contra scandal because operatives within President Ronald Reagan's administration sought alternative sources of funds outside congressional appropriations to continue funding covert resupply operations.

The President enjoys broad powers to conduct covert operations . . . subject only to notification requirements imposed by Congress.

Invoking the "war declaration" clause has been ineffective in checking executive dominance over covert operations; invoking the appropriations clauses has been an indirect check on presidential power. Congress can demand prior notification and has the power to stop all aid—overt and covert—to a region. Under this clause, congressional power is not really dominant; it is obstructionist. . . .

Thus, in an environment in which Congress rarely exercise its enumerated war-making powers (preferring to use only its appropriations power), the President enjoys broad powers to conduct covert operations. Under current law, the President can authorize covert operations subject only to notification requirements imposed by Congress. . . .

Notification Requirements

The Hughes-Ryan Amendment of 1974 requires the CIA [Central Intelligence Agency] to conduct covert operations only after a president has expressly authorized them. For a president to authorize such actions, and to receive funds from Congress for them, a president must find that such operations are necessary to U.S. national security. The Hughes-Ryan Amendment makes a president accountable for all covert operations the CIA or other agencies or forces under his control conduct. The amendment also imposes a duty on the director of the

CIA to report these actions to congressional intelligence committees before they are implemented. There are, however, exceptions.

A president can limit notification to just the intelligence committees' senior members and the majority and minority leaders of Congress if he feels it necessary to limit disclosure for national security reasons. If the President prefers not to provide prior notice to the intelligence committees, he must inform congressional oversight committees of the action in a timely fashion and provide a statement of his reasons for not giving prior notice. As the law now reads, the President must notify the intelligence committees in advance of all covert operations, save for these exceptions.

Covert operations, conducted directly by U.S. forces to intercept or capture terrorists abroad, are constitutional exercises of the President's war powers.

The laws that regulate the conduct of those covert operations that do not directly involve deployments of U.S. forces give considerable discretion and authority to the President. If the President so chooses, he could covertly supply weapons and aid to forces fighting terrorist regimes while only notifying select members of Congress. He would not need prior congressional approval. Covert operations supported by full written presidential findings are constitutionally acceptable. . . .

Covert Operations in the War on Terror

Covert operations, conducted directly by U.S. forces to intercept or capture terrorists abroad, are constitutional exercises of the President's war powers to protect the Nation, and of his Chief Executive powers.

If the President employs active-duty U.S. military personnel, even Special Forces, he must report the employment under the War Powers Resolution; that is, if he chooses to abide by the resolution. The President might try another tactic—calling his action an "interdiction," as when pursuing international terrorists or drug smugglers. If the President chooses to employ CIA paramilitary elements to perform the task, he could probably do so under the Hughes-Ryan Act's far simpler notification requirements and simply tell Congress about the action afterward.

In the Global War on Terrorism, some nations allied with the United States might prove to be allies in name only. For all practical purposes, the United States cannot rely on allies who are unwilling to root out terrorist cells within their own borders. Nor can the United States rely on allies in countries where the will to fight terror is strong, but the capability is not. The United States should consider using direct-action covert raids as an option to put its preemption doctrine into effect. Where traditional military action is not possible or feasible, direct-action covert operations might be the only definitive way to preempt or prevent asymmetric attacks on the United States.

The National Security Agency Domestic Spying Program Violates Americans' Civil Rights

American Civil Liberties Union

The American Civil Liberties Union (ACLU) is a nonprofit and nonpartisan organization dedicated to protecting the constitutional civil rights of Americans.

Editor's Note: In August 2006, a federal district court struck down the National Security Agency (NSA) surveillance program authorized by President George W. Bush as a violation of Americans' rights to free speech and privacy under the First and Fourth Amendments to the U.S. Constitution and the Foreign Intelligence Surveillance Act (FISA). The Bush administration appealed the ruling, but in January 2007 the administration abruptly disbanded the controversial NSA spy program and replaced it with one that would be subject to the FISA court, a decision that Bush officials claim should end the lawsuit.

What if it emerged that the President of the United States was flagrantly violating the Constitution and a law passed by the Congress to protect Americans against abuses by a super-secret spy agency? What if, instead of apologizing, he said, in essence, "I have the power to do that, because I say I can." That frightening scenario is exactly what we are now witnessing in the case of the warrantless NSA spying ordered by President Bush that was reported December 16, 2005 by the *New York Times*.

American Civil Liberties Union (ACLU), "NSA Spying on Americans Is Illegal," www.aclu.org, December 29, 2005. Reproduced by permission.

According to the *Times*, Bush signed a presidential order in 2002 allowing the National Security Agency to monitor without a warrant the international (and sometimes domestic) telephone calls and e-mail messages of hundreds of thousands of citizens and legal residents inside the United States. The program eventually came to include some purely internal controls—but no requirement that warrants be obtained from the Foreign Intelligence Surveillance Court as the 4th Amendment to the Constitution and the foreign intelligence surveillance laws require. In other words, no independent review or judicial oversight. . . .

NSA Surveillance Is Illegal

The day after this shocking abuse of power became public, President Bush admitted that he had authorized it, but argued that he had the authority to do so. But the law governing government eavesdropping on American citizens is well-established and crystal clear. President Bush's claim that he is not bound by that law is simply astounding. It is a Presidential power grab that poses a challenge in the deepest sense to the integrity of the American system of government—the separation of powers between the legislative and executive branches, the concept of checks and balances on executive power, the notion that the president is subject to the law like everyone else, and the general respect for the "rule of law" on which our democratic system depends. . . .

The tensions between the need for intelligence agencies to protect the nation and the danger that they would become a domestic spy agency have been explicitly and repeatedly fought out in American history. The National Security Act of 1947 contained a specific ban on intelligence operatives from operating domestically. In the 1970s, America learned about the extensive domestic political spying carried out by the FBI, the military, the CIA, and the NSA, and Congress passed new laws to prevent a repeat of those abuses. Surveillance laws were debated and modified under presidents [Gerald] Ford, [Jimmy] Carter, [Ronald] Reagan, [George] Bush Sr. and [Bill] Clinton.

But, President Bush would sweep aside this entire body of democratically debated and painstakingly crafted restrictions on domestic surveillance by the executive branch with his extraordinary assertion that he can simply ignore this law because he is the Commander-in-Chief. In a December 17 [2005] radio address, for example, Bush asserted that the spying was "fully consistent with my constitutional responsibilities and authorities." But his constitutional duty is to "take care that the laws be faithfully executed" (Article II, Section 3); the law here clearly establishes well-defined procedures for eavesdropping on U.S. persons, and the fact is, Bush ordered that those procedures not be followed.

The law on surveillance begins with the Fourth Amendment to the Constitution, which states clearly that Americans' privacy may not be invaded without a warrant.

Government eavesdropping on Americans is an extremely serious matter; the ability to intrude on the private realm is a tremendous power that can be used to monitor, embarass, control, disgrace, or ruin an individual. Because it is so invasive, the technology of wiretapping has been subject to carefully crafted statutory controls almost since it was invented. Ignoring those controls and wiretapping without a court order is a crime that carries a significant prison sentence (in fact, criminal violations of the wiretap statute were among the articles of impeachment that were drafted against President [Richard] Nixon shortly before his resignation). . . .

Unfortunately, although the law in this matter is crystal clear, many Americans, faced with President Bush's bold assertions of "inherent" authority for these actions, will not know what to believe. . . .

Electronic Surveillance by the Government Strictly Limited

The law on surveillance begins with the Fourth Amendment to the Constitution, which states clearly that Americans' privacy may not be invaded without a warrant based on probable cause. The US Supreme Court (*US v. Katz 389 US 347*) has made it clear that this core privacy protection does cover government eavesdropping. As a result, all electronic surveillance by the government in the United States is illegal, unless it falls under one of a small number of precise exceptions specifically carved out in the law. In other words, the NSA can only spy where it is explicitly granted permission to do so by statute. Citizens concerned about surveillance do not have to answer the question, "what law restricts the NSA's spying?" Rather, the government is required to supply an answer to the question "what law permits the NSA to spy?" . . .

FISA does not authorize the president to conduct warrantless eavesdropping on U.S. citizens or permanent legal residents . . . without an order from the FISA Court.

There are only three laws that authorize any exceptions to the ban on electronic eavesdropping by the government. Congress has explicitly stated that these three laws are the exclusive means by which domestic electronic surveillance can be carried out. They are:

Title III and ECPA. Title III and the Electronic Communications Privacy Act make up the statutes that govern criminal wiretaps in the United States.

FISA. The Foreign Intelligence Surveillance Act is the law that governs eavesdropping on agents of "foreign powers" within the United States, including suspected foreign terrorists. . . .

The Bush-NSA Spying Not Authorized

Title III and ECPA govern domestic criminal wiretaps and are not relevant to the NSA's spying. FISA is the law under which the NSA should have operated. It authorizes the government to conduct surveillance in certain situations without meeting all of the requirements of the Fourth Amendment that apply under criminal law, but requires that an independent Foreign Intelligence Surveillance Court oversee that surveillance to make sure that Americans who have no ties to foreign terrorist organizations or other "foreign powers" are not spied upon.

FISA was significantly loosened by the Patriot Act (which, for example, allowed it to be used for some criminal investigations), and parts of it now stand in clear violation of the Constitution's Fourth Amendment in the view of the ACLU and many others. However, even the post–Patriot Act version of FISA does not authorize the president to conduct warrantless eavesdropping on U.S. citizens or permanent legal residents in the U.S. without an order from the FISA Court. Yet it is that very court order requirement—imposed to protect innocent Americans—that the President has ignored.

In fact, one member of the FISA Court, Judge James Robertson, has apparently resigned from the court in protest of President Bush's secret authorization of this program. And the *New York Times* reported that the court's chief judge complained about the program when she was (belatedly) notified of it, and refused to allow information gathered under the program to be used as the basis for FISA wiretap orders. . . .

Use-of-Force Resolution Does Not Legitimize Spying

Congress after 9/11 approved an Authorization to Use Military Force against those responsible for the attacks in order to authorize the president to conduct foreign military operations such as the invasion of Afghanistan.

But that resolution contains no language changing, overriding or repealing any laws passed by Congress. Congress does not repeal legislation through hints and innuendos, and the Authorization to Use Military Force does not authorize the president to violate the law against surveillance without a warrant any more than it authorizes him to carry out an armed robbery or seize control of Citibank in order to pay for operations against terrorists. In fact, when President [Harry] Truman tried to seize control of steel mills that were gripped by strikes in 1952, the Supreme Court decisively rejected his authority to make such a seizure, even in the face of arguments that the strike would interfere with the supply of weapons and ammunition to American troops then under fire on the battlefields of the Korean War. . . . The Supreme Court also rejected similar assertions of inherent executive power by Richard Nixon. . . .

President Bush's claim that he has "inherent authority" as Commander-in-Chief to use our spy agencies to eavesdrop on Americans is astonishing.

FISA contains explicit language describing the president's powers "during time of war" and provides that "the President, through the Attorney General, may authorize electronic surveillance without a court order under this title to acquire foreign intelligence information *for a period not to exceed fifteen days following a declaration of war by the Congress."* . . . So even if we accept the argument that the use-of-force resolution places us on a war footing, warrantless surveillance would have been legal for only 15 days after the resolution was passed on September 18, 2001. . . .

The FISA law takes account of the need for emergency surveillance, and the need for quick action cannot be used as a rationale for going outside the law. FISA allows wiretapping without a court order in an emergency; the court must simply be notified within 72 hours. The government is aware of this emergency power and has used it repeatedly. In addition, the Foreign Intelligence court is physically located in the Justice Department building, and the FISA law requires that at least two of the FISA judges reside in the Washington, DC area, for precisely the reason that rapid action is sometimes needed.

If President Bush still for some reason finds these provisions to be inadequate, he must take his case to Congress and ask for the law to be changed, not simply ignore it.

President Bound by the Rule of Law

President Bush's claim that he has "inherent authority" as Commander-in-Chief to use our spy agencies to eavesdrop on Americans is astonishing, and such spying is clearly illegal. It must be halted immediately, and its origins must be thoroughly investigated by Congress and by a special counsel.

The Bush Administration has developed "a whole new surveillance paradigm" . . . to run communications en masse through computers.

Given the extensive (indeed, excessive) surveillance powers that the government already possesses, the Administration's blatantly illegal use of warrantless surveillance raises an important question: why? One possibility, raised by the *New York Times* in a Dec. 24, 2005 story ("Spy Agency Mined Vast Data Trove, Officials Report"), is that the NSA is relying on assistance from several unnamed telecommunications companies to "trace and analyze large volumes of communications" and is "much larger than the White House has acknowledged."

This, as security expert Bruce Schneier has noted, suggests the Bush Administration has developed a "a whole new surveillance paradigm"—exploiting the NSA's well-known capabilities to spy on individuals not one at a time, as FISA permits, but to run communications en masse through computers in the search for suspicious individuals or patterns. This "new paradigm" may well be connected to the NSA program sometimes known as "Echelon," which carries out just that kind of mass collection of communications This "wholesale" surveillance, as Schneier calls it, would constitute an illegal invasion of Americans' privacy on a scale that has never before been seen. According to the *Times*, several telecommunications companies provided the NSA with direct access to streams of communications over their networks. In other words, the NSA appears to have direct access to a large volume of Americans' communications—with not simply the assent, but the cooperation of the companies handling those communications. . . .

Regardless of the scale of this spying, we are facing a historic moment: the President of the United States has claimed a sweeping wartime power to brush aside the clear limits on his power set by our Constitution and laws—a chilling assertion of presidential power that has not been seen since Richard Nixon.

The Bush Administration's Use of Torture and Imprisonment Without Trial Is Unconstitutional

Thomas R. Eddlem

Thomas R. Eddlem is the editor of the Hanson Express *newspaper in Hanson, Massachusetts, and is a regular contributor to the* New American *and* Point South *magazines.*

CIA [Central Intelligence Agency] prisoner Benyam Mohammed al Habashi, an Ethiopian refugee who obtained residence in Britain in 1994, hung by his hands from electrical cords in a secret Moroccan jail in August 2002. After the Muslim convert had been picked up by Pakistani immigration officials and given to the American CIA Pakistani jailers had beaten him regularly with a leather strap as he hung by his hands.

But the Moroccan interrogators acting on behalf of the CIA found a new way to torture al Habashi. According to al Habashi, interrogators brandished a surgical scalpel, cut his chest, and urged him to confess to being a terrorist. The interrogators did not stop at cutting his chest: "One of [the guards] took my penis in his hand and began to make cuts. He did it once and they stood still for maybe a minute, watching my reaction. I was in agony, crying. . . . They must have done this 20 to 30 times. There was blood all over." The helpless prisoner described his two-hour ordeal: "They cut all over my private parts. One of them said it would be better just to cut it off, as I would only breed terrorists." The interrogators next poured pain-inducing chemicals over the open wounds.

Thomas R. Eddlem, "Emerging Police State: Imprisonment without Trial and the Torture of Prisoners Are Hallmarks of an Oppressive Police State, Yet George Bush and His Administration Openly Promote These Practices," *The New American*, vol. 22, July 24, 2006, pp. 19-22. Copyright © 2006 American Opinion Publishing Incorporated. Reproduced by permission.

Habashi has testified that throughout his 18-month incarceration in Morocco his interrogators cut his chest and genitals with a scalpel monthly, and subjected him to psychological torture in-between. This was al Habashi's introduction to the Bush administration policy of "extraordinary rendition," where the CIA farms out torture to the most barbaric governments on Earth. Al Habashi also spent nine months in two U.S. prisons inside Afghanistan where—he alleges—he was forced to sign confessions and swear false testimony against other prisoners before being transferred to Guantanamo Bay [a U.S. military base in Cuba].

Inhumane and Unreliable

Why should law-abiding American citizens care about the troubles of this Guantanamo Bay prisoner? Because much of his "confession" against his supposed "terrorist" confederates was made after his torture in Morocco, and this "evidence" is being used to keep at least one American citizen in jail today. Americans need to ask themselves: "Do I really want my freedom to hinge upon whether or not some suspect whimpers out my name as a surgical scalpel is applied to his genitals?"

A detainee under such a situation would understandably be willing to "confess" whatever the interrogator wanted. This explains in part why evidence obtained under torture is so notoriously unreliable. In fact, the Bush administration's case for the war against Iraq was based largely upon the false testimony of Ibn al-Shaykh al-Libi, an al-Qaeda training camp official captured in Afghanistan who concocted tales of "ties" between al-Qaeda and Saddam Hussein's Iraqi regime in order to stop his torture sessions. Hussein's ties to al-Qaeda turned out to be false.

Torturing Innocents

[Then-]Secretary of Defense Donald Rumsfeld told a radio interviewer on June 27, 2005 of the Guantanamo Bay prisoners: "These are people all of whom were captured on a battlefield.

They're terrorists, trainers, bomb makers, recruiters, financiers, [Osama bin Laden's] body guards, would-be suicide bombers, probably the 20th hijacker, 9/11 hijacker." However, they weren't all captured on the battlefield. Al Habashi had been arrested—unarmed—at the Karachi, Pakistan airport by Pakistani immigration officials before being transferred to CIA custody. Yet the CIA considers him an "enemy combatant." Al Habashi is not the only case that proves Rumsfeld wrong. A study of Guantanamo detainees on behalf of the counsel for some released defendants suing the U.S. government found that only seven percent of the detainees whose method of apprehension had been revealed had been captured on the battlefield. The rest had been "captured" by governments cooperating with the Bush administration or by bounty hunters seeking cash rewards for turning in suspected terrorists.

In December 2005, Congress passed a law banning torture by a veto-proof majority.

It should hardly be surprising that many of those captured turned out to be innocent. Coalition forces distributed leaflets promising huge bounties for Afghans and Pakistanis who informed on their neighbors. One leaflet distributed in Afghanistan promised: "Get wealth and power beyond your dreams. . . . You can receive millions of dollars helping the anti-Taliban forces catch al-Qaida and Taliban murderers. There is enough money to take care of your family, your village, your tribe for the rest of your life."

Boston-based Attorney P. Sabin Willett represents one such innocent client, Adel al Hakim, one of five innocent ethnic Uighurs (Chinese Muslims), detained at Guantanamo. Willett explains:

> Adel is innocent. I don't mean he claims to be. I mean the military says so. It held a secret tribunal and ruled that he is not al Qaeda, not Taliban, not a terrorist. The whole thing

was a mistake. The Pentagon paid $5,000 to a bounty hunter, and it got taken. The military people reached this conclusion, and they wrote it down on a memo, and then they classified the memo and Adel went from the hearing room back to his prison cell.

Adel and his four Uighur compatriots never received a trial during their more than four years of incarceration at Guantanamo. Only after a legal battle during a habeas corpus petition was Willett even informed that the military had already determined his client was innocent. But the determination did not affect his incarceration. Officials have stated that they cannot repatriate Adel to China because he may face torture from the Chinese government for being a Muslim, and don't know where to send him and his fellow Uighurs. So back to Guantanamo they went.

The Bush administration . . . has openly defied the . . . U.S. Constitution, which prohibits 'cruel and unusual punishments,' and the . . . right to a 'speedy and public trial.'

Official Torture

In December 2005, Congress passed a law banning torture by a veto-proof majority. After signing the bill, President [George W.] Bush issued a so-called signing statement: an official document in which a president lays out his interpretation of a new law. In it Bush said:

> The executive branch shall construe Title X in Division A of the Act, relating to detainees, in a manner consistent with the constitutional authority of the President to supervise the unitary executive branch and as Commander in Chief and consistent with the constitutional limitations on the judicial power, which will assist in achieving the shared objective of

the Congress and the President, evidenced in Title X, of protecting the American people from further terrorist attacks.

The *Boston Globe* reported the administration's position, in the words of an anonymous official: "Of course the president has the obligation to follow this law, [but] he also has the obligation to defend and protect the country as the commander in chief, and he will have to square those two responsibilities in each case. We are not expecting that those two responsibilities will come into conflict, but it's possible that they will." By issuing the "signing statement," Bush essentially signed the law with his fingers crossed behind his back.

How have such gross violations of justice and basic human decency occurred?

The Bush administration—from President Bush on down—has openly defied the plain meaning of the Eighth Amendment to the U.S. Constitution, which prohibits "cruel and unusual punishments," and the Seventh Amendment right to a "speedy and public trial, by an impartial jury."

The Bush administration promulgated a new torture policy shortly after 9/11 which gave the green light to any kind of torture by American interrogators short of organ failure or death. Justice Department Assistant Attorneys General Jay S. Bybee and John C. Yoo explained in a 2002 memo that for an action to be deemed torture, physical pain "must be equivalent in intensity to the pain accompanying serious physical injury, such as organ failure, impairment of bodily function, or even death." While the Bush administration officially pioneered such torture techniques such as "waterboarding," where detainees are strapped to a plank and have wet towels or cellophane wrapped around their heads to simulate drowning, other more forceful torture techniques received only tacit approval and were therefore "outsourced" to foreign governments such as Egypt, Uzbekistan, Saudi Arabia, Morocco, and Syria.

Just how far Bush administration officials are willing to carry this was revealed in a December 1, 2005 Chicago debate between Yoo, now a professor at the University of California at Berkeley, and Notre Dame professor and international human rights scholar Doug Cassel:

> Doug Cassel: If the president deems that he's got to torture somebody, including by crushing the testicles of the person's child, there is no law that can stop him?
>
> Yoo: No treaty.
>
> Cassel: Also no law by Congress—that is what you wrote in the August 2002 memo. . . .
>
> Yoo: I think it depends on why the president thinks he needs to do that.

Yoo's testimony does far more than make al Habashi's description of his torture credible; it also puts to lie the administration claim that the abusive excesses of Abu Ghraib and other detainees throughout the CIA rendition program were cases of "renegade" agents. Abu Ghraib was not a case of a few jailers who had gone wild, but rather part of the program approved by the Bush Administration, which openly claimed the power to torture—regardless of what the law as passed by Congress says.

A March 2003 Defense Department memorandum stated that laws passed by Congress are irrelevant: "In order to represent the President's inherent constitutional authority to manage a military campaign, 18 USC 2340A (the prohibition against torture) must be construed as inapplicable to interrogations undertaken pursuant to his Commander-in-Chief authority. . . . Congress may no more regulate the President's ability to detain and interrogate enemy combatants than it may regulate his ability to direct troop movements on the battlefield."

Other Innocents

The ethnic Uighurs are not the only cases of innocent persons being sent away to prisons to be tortured. The U.S. government apprehended Canadian computer programmer Maher Arar at [John F. Kennedy] airport in New York while he was on his way home from a family vacation in Tunisia, and renditioned him without trial to Syria for nine months of torture. Arar endured beatings and was forced to live in a tiny underground cell he likened to a tomb. Syrian officials eventually realized his innocence, and set him free after Canadian diplomatic pressure was brought to bear on his behalf.

Mamdouh Habib, an Australian citizen born in Egypt and father of four, was released from Guantanamo on January 11, 2005 without charges after enduring beatings, electrocution, and injection of drugs in an Egyptian CIA rendition prison. He never received a hearing or trial during his three-and-a-half years of imprisonment.

The Bush administration has openly stated that U.S. citizenship is no guarantee against indefinite detention without trial.

Khaled el-Masri, a Lebanese-born German citizen, was apprehended in Macedonia in September 2002 and renditioned to Afghanistan, where U.S. officials beat, stripped, and sodomized el-Masri. He was released without charges in May 2004.

Americans As the Enemy

Many Americans may remain unconcerned—or perhaps comforted—by the fact that most of the names of those who have been tortured at the hands of the Bush administration are Arabic names. They shouldn't be. Denial of the right to trial by jury and torture of American citizens is already underway.

The Bush administration has openly stated that U.S. citizenship is no guarantee against indefinite detention without trial. In fact, the administration took all the way to the Supreme Court the cases of two U.S. citizens—Jose Padilla and Yaser Esam Hamdi—detained without trial. The administration settled the Hamdi case out of court in order to avoid an embarrassing precedent in favor of the Seventh Amendment right to trial by jury. In a similar fashion, the administration finally decided to charge Padilla with a crime [in 2005], when it appeared likely the Supreme Court would rule that Padilla was entitled to a trial. But the charges came more than three years after Padilla had been incarcerated after being apprehended unarmed at Chicago's O'Hare Airport and personally designated as an "enemy combatant" by President Bush.

The primary proof against Padilla for alleged crimes of plotting terrorist acts in the United States are al Habashi's statements while under CIA torture in Afghanistan and statements by Khalid Sheikh Mohammed and Abu Zubaydah, senior al-Qaeda members who fingered Padilla only under torture.

That ordinary innocent Americans could be imprisoned without trial based upon "evidence" obtained through torture is hardly far-fetched. After the recent crackdown on alleged terrorist cells in Florida, Attorney General Alberto Gonzales noted on June 23 [2006] that American citizens may soon be on the "enemy combatant" block: "The terrorists and suspected terrorists in Madrid and London and Toronto were not sleeper operatives sent on suicide missions. They were students and businesspeople and members of the community. They were persons who, for whatever reason, came to view their home country as the enemy. And it's a problem that we face here in the United States as well." Also, it wasn't that long ago when some 325,000 Americans, including several congressmen, were put on the "terrorism watch list."

If Americans do not demand a restoration of the universal right to trial by jury and strict adherence to the prohibition against cruel and unusual punishment—along with prosecution of those officials who have violated and sanctioned those constitutional violations—they may find themselves the next ones on the cutting end of the surgical scalpel.

America's Use of Torture in Interrogations of Suspected Terrorists Violates Human Rights

Lisa Hajjar

Lisa Hajjar teaches in the Law and Society Program at the University of California–Santa Barbara and serves on the editorial committee of Middle East Report. *She is also the author of the 2004 book* Courting Conflict: The Israeli Military Court System in the West Bank and Gaza.

There is a popular belief that Western history constitutes a progressive move from more to less torture. Iron maidens and racks are now museum exhibits, crucifixions are sectarian iconography and scientific experimentation on twins is History Channel infotainment. This narrative of progress deftly blends ideas about "time," "place" and "culture." In the popular imagination, "civilized societies" (a.k.a. "us") do not rely on torture, whereas those societies where torture is still common remain "uncivilized," torture being both a proof and a problem of their enduring "backwardness."

George W. Bush epitomizes and mines the American popular imagination with his mantra of "spreading freedom," which carries a strong implication of stopping torture. Saddam Hussein's horrific legacy of mass torture was one of the arguments deployed to justify preemptive war against Iraq, and torture has become retroactively more important since weapons of mass destruction have failed to materialize. On April 30, 2004, Bush said, "A year ago I [gave a] speech ... saying we had achieved an important objective, accomplished a mis-

Lisa Hajjar, "Torture and the Future," Middle East Report Online, May 2004. www
.merip.org. Reproduced by permission.

sion, which was the removal of Saddam Hussein. As a result, there are no longer torture chambers or mass graves or rape rooms in Iraq."

Even as Bush spoke those words, he and millions of newspaper readers and television viewers across the world were aware that torture chambers, rape and sexual abuse of detainees in Iraq are not a thing of the past. The public exposure of torture of Iraqi detainees by US soldiers, working in interrogation wings run by military intelligence and American "security contractors," at Abu Ghraib prison outside of Baghdad—as well as allegations of torture of other Iraqis by British soldiers—are headline news. The shocking revelations and photographs provide stark proof that torture is not a relic of "our past." Nor does torture provide a meaningful geographical or cultural demarcation between "civilized" and "uncivilized" societies.

The fact is that, today, people are being tortured in two thirds of the world's countries. Yet if one were to accept the rhetoric of the world's states at face value, there is no torture in the world. No torturing regime defends or even acknowledges its own torture as torture. . . .

No one—ever, anywhere—has a "right" to torture, and . . . everyone—always, everywhere—has a right not to be tortured.

Denial of torture is articulated in many ways, but all states deny it for the same reason. Torture must be practiced in secret and denied in public because, in the mid-twentieth century, torture became an international crime. Irrespective of what penalties the arrested soldiers may face under the Uniform Code of Military Justice, the pictures from Abu Ghraib—whose authenticity no one has denied—document offenses of an especially heinous kind. . . .

A Human Right

The international criminalization of torture is inextricable from the history of human rights. The unprecedented horrors and violence of World War II provided the negative inspiration for a revolution in international law to forge the principle that people should have rights as humans, and not merely as protected classes of subjects, such as citizens, civilians or prisoners of war. However, the creation of international human rights did not undermine or substantially alter the power of states. Rather, it entailed the elaboration of new internationalized norms of government to which all states would be expected to adhere, while preserving states' sovereign fights. Human rights obtained their "universalizing" character from the fact that people are subjects of states and states are subjects of international law.

The right not to be tortured became a human right when international law prohibited the practice, and established legal liabilities and penalties. The right not to be tortured is one of many human rights, but it is stronger than almost any other human right because the prohibition of torture is absolutely non-derogable and because law recognizes no exceptions. What this means is that no one—ever, anywhere—has a "right" to torture, and that everyone—always, everywhere—has a right not to be tortured. It also means that anyone who engages in or abets torture is committing a crime.

The international prohibition of torture illuminates something very important about the rights of human beings. The right not to be tortured represents an ideal type of human rights norm because it invests people, regardless of their social status, their political identity or affiliations, with a kind of sovereign right over their bodies and minds, albeit limited to situations that fall within the legal definition of torture. In contrast, the right of persons not to be exterminated through genocide hinges on a collective identity as members of a national, religious or ethnic group. The right not to be deliberately targeted in war hinges not on one's humanity but rather on one's status as a civilian or non-combatant, or a surrendered or captured soldier.

One common reason invoked by many states [for using torture] is that they claim to be engaged in conflicts with 'terrorists.'

The prohibition of torture is customary international law and therefore attaches universal jurisdiction. Universal jurisdiction means that if a perpetrator is not prosecuted in his or her own country, he or she can be prosecuted in any competent legal system anywhere in the world. Therefore, the right not to be tortured is accorded greater weight in law than the sovereign rights of states because torture is prohibited under all circumstances, including the "ticking bomb" scenario. In the words of the UN [United Nations] Convention Against Torture and Other Cruel, Inhuman or Degrading Treatment or Punishment (1984), "No exceptional circumstances whatsoever, whether a state of war or a threat of war, internal political instability or any other public emergency, may be invoked as a justification for torture." The US ratified this convention in 1994. . . .

Torture and Terror

If torture is so strongly prohibited, and denied by all states because it is fundamentally illegitimate, then why is it so common in today's world? While states torture people for numerous reasons, one common reason invoked by many states is that they claim to be engaged in conflicts with "terrorists."

Terrorism is a broad and flexible concept, and there is no clear, internationally accepted definition. It is used, variously, to describe certain kinds of actions, including attacks on civilians, hijackings, organized resistance or repression, and to identify certain types of actors. In US national security discourse, the term terrorism typically is used to refer to non-state actors or organizations engaged in attacks or struggles against the state, emphasizing but not necessarily limited to violence, to which the state responds with "counter-terrorism." . . .

Defenders of . . . [torture as the lesser of two evils] argue that . . . [prohibiting torture] ties the hands of security agents from finding that 'ticking bomb' and saving innocent lives.

Around the world, some of the most egregious human rights violations have been perpetrated by states in the name of counter-terrorism. . . . Since September 11, [2001, for example,] the Bush administration has articulated positions and pursued policies that blatantly contravene the Geneva Conventions [international human rights laws], on the grounds that terrorists do not deserve legal rights and protections. These policies include the invention of a category, "unlawful combatants," that does not exist in international law. These unlawful combatants are being held incommunicado, at Guantánamo Bay [in Cuba] and other locations, and subjected to years of interrogation with no judicial oversight, no public accountability and virtually no visitation by representatives of the International Committee of the Red Cross. Although the US government claims that no torture is used in the interrogation of these detainees, these clandestine and extralegal conditions are an invitation for abuse. The Abu Ghraib images are a piece of hard evidence indicating that the US has joined the list of countries—Egypt, Israel, Uzbekistan—that are fighting wars on terrorism partly through the use of torture. . . .

The Torture Debate

[The] debate [about torture by the United States] circles around two clichés: the slippery slope and the lesser evil.

Jeremiads against the slippery slope argue that no cause or crisis justifies the erosion of the absolute prohibition against torture. Variations on this theme include: there is no such thing as just a "little torture," once you start torturing "terrorists" you open the door to torturing anyone in the future and using torture makes you no better than your enemy. Defenders of the lesser evil argue that the absolute prohibition on torture is immoral if it ties the hands of security agents from finding that "ticking bomb" and saving innocent lives. On *CNN's* "Crossfire," conservative commentator Tucker Carlson said, "Torture is bad. [But] some things are worse. And under some circumstances, it may be the lesser of two evils. Because some evils are pretty evil." . . .

If American law enforcement officers were ever to confront the law school hypothetical case of the captured terrorist who knew about an imminent attack but refused to provide the information necessary to prevent it, I have absolutely no doubt that they would try to torture the terrorists into providing the information. Moreover, the vast majority of Americans would expect the officers to engage in that time-tested technique for loosening tongues, notwithstanding our unequivocal treaty obligations never to employ torture, no matter how exigent the circumstances. The real question is not whether torture would be used—it would—but whether it would be used outside of the law or within the law.

[Constitutional lawyer Alan] Dershowitz offers a suggestion as to how torture can be brought "into the law": "torture warrants" issued by judges. He also offers a helpful suggestion for tactics: sterilized needles under the fingernails. He told an interviewer for *Salon.com*: "I wanted to come up with a tactic that can't possibly cause permanent physical harm but is excruciatingly painful. . . . [T]he point I wanted to make is that torture is not being used as a way of producing death. It's been used as a way of simply causing excruciating pain. . . . I want maximal pain, minimum lethality."

Lesser evilers like Dershowitz criticize the slippery slopers as human rights fundamentalists who would sacrifice innocent civilians to preserve a legal principle. They are not suggesting that we forsake the principle that torture is illegal, but rather that we suspend that principle in the handling of some people on the grounds that they are necessarily and legitimately "torturable." The implicit rationale is that terrorists are not human, and therefore are undeserving of inclusion in the universe of human beings covered by international and constitutional law that categorically prohibits torture. But the most glaring problem with this argument, as many critics have pointed out, is the implausibility of knowing with absolute certainty that the torture candidate possesses information about an imminent threat. The speculation would translate into a license to use violence on a person assumed to be guilty. Following Dershowitz's suggestion to involve judges in the dispensing of torture warrants would, at best, narrow the pool of candidates. . . .

No Room for Mistakes

The slippery slopers present a valuable and worthy defense of taking the moral and legal high road. Those who invoke the slippery slope tend to focus on the tortured and worry—with good cause, as the Abu Ghraib photos have shown—that they are defenseless and susceptible to abuse in custody. But making slippery slope arguments against torture to a public gripped by fear of "evildoers" and willing to sacrifice the rights of "enemies" is not an effective rebuttal to advocates of torture as a lesser evil.

If torture is legitimized and legalized in the future, it is not 'the terrorists' who will lose but 'the humans.'

Those who invoke the lesser evil tend to focus on the public that is vulnerable to terrorism and violence. Their arguments have appeal because many people are willing to accept the legitimacy of torturing terrorists as necessary and effective. Much of the public is willing to trust that government agents empowered to decide whom to torture are capable of discerning real from imagined threats, and restricting torture to the former. But at least 22 Guantánamo Bay detainees—people described as "the worst of the worst" by [former secretary of defense] Rumsfeld—have been released, an implicit acknowledgment that their very detention in a place where torture is likely being used had been a mistake. On May 5, [2004,] the *New York Times* published an interview with an Iraqi advancing a credible claim to be the man infamously pictured naked and hooded in Abu Ghraib prison, a female soldier pointing jokingly at his genitalia—was the torture that he is now compelled to relive also a "mistake"? Without effective oversight by a judicial body, the public cannot know or trust that other such "mistakes" will not be made. When it comes to torture, there is no room for a mistake.

Naturally, it is important to focus both on the tortured and on the vulnerable public, but the case of Abu Ghraib shows that it is most important to focus on the torturers. They are representatives of the public they serve. If torture is practiced by agents of a state that claims to be a democracy, then "we the people" are responsible for torture. Citizens of a democracy cannot or at least should not be comforted by blaming a few "aberrant agents" if torture is systemic and routine. Those citizens cannot or should not be quiescent as democratic values and laws are being trampled in a panic. "We the people" are responsible for stopping, protesting and preventing torture.

Keeping torture illegal and struggling to enforce the prohibition are the front lines, quite literally, of a global battle to defend the one core right that all human beings can claim. If torture is legitimized and legalized in the future, it is not "the terrorists" who will lose but "the humans." Should proponents of torture as a lesser evil succeed in regaining legitimacy for the execrable practice, there would be no better words than George Orwell's from *1984*: "If you want a picture of the future, imagine a boot stamping on a human face—forever."

Expanding Unsupervised Covert Operations by the Pentagon Could Be Dangerous

Jennifer D. Kibbe

Jennifer D. Kibbe is a fellow at the Brookings Institution, a non-profit, public policy research organization.

The 9-11 Commission is to be commended for many aspects of the weighty report it . . . issued [in 2004]. The report provides a wealth of detail about the tragic events of that day and of what led up to them. It also provides some thoughtful recommendations on how to fix the very serious problems with the nation's ability to confront the threat of terrorism, including expanding congressional oversight of intelligence.

Which is all the more reason to be shocked and disappointed that in one very important way, the commissioners dropped the ball. Not only did they not tighten up oversight of the crucial area of covert paramilitary operations, but they effectively loosened it, creating the potential for serious problems involving covert actions over which Congress has no say or control.

Covert Operations Without Congressional Oversight

In its recommendations regarding reorganization of the intelligence community, the commission states: "Lead responsibility for directing and executing paramilitary operations, whether clandestine or covert, should shift to the Defense Department," from the CIA [Central Intelligence Agency] where it has traditionally been housed. The commissioners' reason-

Jennifer D. Kibbe, "A Loophole for Covert Operations," Brookings Institution, August 8, 2004. www.brookings.edu. Reproduced by permission.

ing is sound. They begin from the underlying assumption that against the current enemy, more decentralized and fluid than the Soviet opponent of the Cold War, there will be more call for smaller, paramilitary-type operations. They point out, though, that before 9-11 the CIA did not invest much in developing a paramilitary capability and that it would be redundant and expensive to build one up now when the military already has the Special Forces for exactly that purpose.

[There are] two requirements for covert operations: that they be justified, before the fact, . . . and that the administration notify the congressional intelligence committees.

The problem lies in the fact that in all their recommendations about strengthening congressional oversight, the commissioners neglected to say anything about oversight of these covert paramilitary operations.

The Definition of Covert Operations

Some context may help highlight the problem. As defined by statute, a covert operation is activity meant "to influence political, economic, or military conditions abroad, where it is intended that the role of the United States government will not be apparent or acknowledged publicly." Thus, where "clandestine" refers to the secrecy of the operation itself, "covert" refers to the secrecy of its sponsor, the action itself may or may not be secret.

Ever since post–Iran/contra reforms adopted in 1991, all agencies of the U.S. government have had to meet two requirements for covert operations: that they be justified, before the fact, in a written presidential finding, and that the administration notify the congressional intelligence committees. Although the CIA has apparently met these requirements, there is considerable confusion over whether the military has or should.

For one thing, the law expressly exempts "traditional military activities." In true legislative form, the law itself does not define the phrase, but the conference committee report explained that it was meant to include actions preceding and related to anticipated hostilities that will involve U.S. military forces. That still leaves open, however, the interpretation of the word *anticipated*, since if future military hostilities are anticipated, no presidential finding or congressional notification are required. Although the conference report defines anticipated hostilities as those for which operational planning has already been approved, a knowledgeable Pentagon official maintains that some in the Defense Department believe that the act gives them the power to undertake activities "years in advance" of any overt U.S. military involvement.

The Pentagon reasons that it can send Special Forces on a covert operation to wherever it wants, with Congress having no knowledge, input, or recourse.

The second aspect of the problem is broader and more direct. Administration officials have been nothing if not consistent in portraying the events since 9-11 as part of a "war on terrorism." The phrase has been repeated so often that it has become second nature to most sentient Americans. But administration and Pentagon officials mean it quite literally: We are in an active war, they say, and therefore anything the military does, including Special Forces, is a "traditional military activity." The upshot? Under either one of the above interpretations, the Pentagon reasons that it can send Special Forces on a covert operation to wherever it wants, with Congress having no knowledge, input or recourse.

A Recipe for Disaster

Although many Special Forces operations are necessary and well-thought out, combining that kind of blank-check authority with a civilian administration that has a taste for pre-emption and whose judgment is already in question is a recipe for potential disaster.

There is, of course, the additional question of who would or should conduct the oversight, since the intelligence committees have traditionally had the responsibility of determining if an operation is covert yet the Special Forces fall within the purview of the more powerful Armed Services committees.

The 9-11 Commission's efforts to strengthen congressional oversight of intelligence are welcome and should be applauded. Nonetheless, by calling for paramilitary operations to be handled solely by the military without providing for the oversight of covert paramilitary actions, the commissioners have, whether knowingly or not, created a dangerous loophole in congressional control of intelligence operations. . . . It is up to the congressional committees holding hearings to identify and close this loophole.

The requirements regarding covert operations evolved over time in response to several dangerous and embarrassing chapters in U.S. history, including the CIA's efforts to assassinate Fidel Castro, Richard Nixon's efforts to overthrow Chile's Salvador Allende, and the Iran-contra affair. Just because the military may be better suited than the CIA to conduct today's covert paramilitary operations does not mean that military leaders are somehow immune from the pressures and poor judgment that led to previous mistakes.

Moreover, with the enemy as decentralized as it is, the potential for covert operations has spread to many more countries, meaning that the risk of collateral damage, diplomatic disputes and retaliation is much greater than it ever was in the past.

CHAPTER 4

What Can Be Done to Improve U.S. Intelligence-Gathering Abilities?

Chapter Preface

The reforms of the U.S. intelligence system begun in the wake of the September 11, 2001, terrorist attacks and the Iraq War, according to many analysts, will likely take many years. In the meantime, the intelligence community is expected to face a number of challenges, some of which could be as serious and significant for U.S. security as the 9/11 attack or the Iraq invasion. In early 2007, many commentators were predicting that the next important intelligence challenge would be Iran, a country bordering Iraq with an authoritarian Islamic government that may be seeking to expand its power in the Middle East.

Relations between the United States and Iran have been bitter since the Iranian revolution in early 1979, when Islamic clerics took control of the country and ousted its former ruler, the Shah of Iran, who had long been supported by the United States. The relationship between the two countries deteriorated even further in the fall of 1979, when radical Iranian students aligned with the new Iranian government captured and held hostage sixty-three American diplomats and three other U.S. citizens for 444 days, finally releasing them in January 1981. American-Iranian tensions continued thereafter, and in President George W. Bush's State of the Union address on January 29, 2002, the president even claimed that Iran was part of an "axis of evil," along with Iraq and North Korea, and charged that it sponsors terrorism and seeks to develop weapons of mass destruction—that is, chemical, biological, and nuclear weapons.

In recent years, the Bush administration has viewed Iran as a growing national security threat, for several reasons. First, the United States, along with other countries, suspected that Iran was developing a nuclear weapons program in violation of the Nuclear Non-Proliferation Treaty, an international agreement designed to limit the spread of nuclear weapons. The Bush administration publicly supported diplomatic efforts led by European countries to stop Iran from building nuclear weapons, but some evidence suggested that, privately, the United States was preparing for a military strike against Iran. As early as 2005, for example, the *New Yorker* magazine published an article by investigative reporter Seymour Hersh reporting that the United States had been conducting secret reconnaissance missions inside Iran since the summer of 2004 to identify possible bombing sites and suggesting that "the next strategic target was Iran." Later newspaper reports said that the U.S. military was actively making plans for a military attack. In December 2006, U.S. diplomats were successful in getting the United Nations Security Council to approve a resolution demanding that Iran stop all efforts to produce weapons-grade nuclear fuel and imposing sanctions to ban the supply of nuclear-related technology and materials to Iran.

In 2007, as Iraq descended deeper into civil strife, the United States also began implicating Iran in the Iraqi violence. In a speech to the nation on January 10, 2007, President Bush accused Iran of supporting insurgents in Iraq and "providing material support for attacks on American troops." The president vowed to stop this flow of support to Iraq and to prevent Iran from "gaining nuclear weapons and dominating the region." Shortly after the speech, the administration ordered two U.S. aircraft carriers to the Persian Gulf and positioned a Patriot missile battalion in the region—actions that military experts said could be used to carry out air strikes against Iran and defend U.S. bases in the region from Iranian retaliation. U.S. troops also raided an Iranian consulate in northern Iraq and detained several Iranian diplomats. Some commentators interpreted President Bush's speech and actions toward Iran as tough measures designed to encourage Iran to give up its nuclear ambitions and back away from Iraq, but others saw the comments and actions as confirmation that the Bush administration was preparing to launch a military attack against Iran.

Some critics, however, said the Bush administration lacked strong intelligence information to support its saber-rattling against Iran. A National Intelligence Estimate (NIE) produced by U.S. intelligence agencies in 2005, for example, concluded that Iran was about a decade away from manufacturing the key ingredient necessary for building a nuclear weapon. In addition, a January 2007 NIE on Iraq downplayed the threat from Iran's activities in Iraq, stating that they were "not likely to be a major driver of violence or the prospects for stability" in Iraq. The Bush administration's harsh posture toward Iran despite these intelligence findings that the country was not an imminent security threat to the United States, many critics charged, looked like a replay of the scenario that preceded the U.S. invasion of Iraq in 2003. As was the case with Iraq, U.S. intelligence on Iran is at best questionable, because the United States has had no diplomatic presence in the country since 1979 and U.S. sanctions against the country have made it difficult for American spies to enter Iran or obtain information about the Iranian government and military. Many commentators worried that Bush administration officials might try to manipulate the intelligence on Iran to support their desire to take military action, as many critics say was the case regarding the alleged weapons of mass destruction in Iraq.

Whatever the final outcome regarding Iran, the importance of good U.S. intelligence is only emphasized by the Iranian controversy. Further improving U.S. intelligence capabilities to produce badly needed accurate information is the focus of this chapter. The authors present a variety of suggestions for future intelligence reforms.

Recent Reforms in U.S. Intelligence Will Keep America Secure

Peter Brookes

Peter Brookes is a columnist for the New York Post *and a senior fellow at the Heritage Foundation, a conservative Washington, D.C., think tank. He is the author of* A Devil's Triangle: Terrorism, Weapons of Mass Destruction, and Rogue States.

[On April 20, 2006], [former] Director of National Intelligence [DNI] John Negroponte, ha[d] a chance to appease his growing chorus of critics. He failed. The crowd for the speech at the National Press Club in Washington, D.C., expected the DNI to mark the end of his first year in office by regaling listeners with dazzling stories of cloak-and-dagger successes on the battlefields of Iraq, or in the shadows of the War on Terror. Instead, he lulled them to sleep with fusty tales of management and bureaucratic triumph. The best Negroponte could muster was a detail-less anecdote about how he, in his role as the new intelligence czar, had made a critical decision that broke an impasse over the future of the nation's spy satellite architecture. Some pundits seized the opportunity to wield Negroponte as the latest political-appointee truncheon with which to pummel President Bush. In fact, though, the speech shows that he's kept his eye on the fusty bureaucratic ball. That's his job.

Negroponte's Success

The problem is not that Negroponte is failing. In fact, the DNI is doing a good job in serving as the president's primary intelligence adviser, while undertaking what President [George

W.] Bush called "the most dramatic reform of our nation's intelligence capabilities" since 1947. Our expectations are wildly excessive. In fact, the DNI is not supposed to be the reincarnation of "Wild Bill" Donovan, founder of the heralded [World War] II Office of Strategic Services. Negroponte's job is, let us just say, a bit more mundane. The mission of the Office of the Director of National Intelligence (ODNI) mission is pretty unexciting: Manage the intelligence budget, ensure coordination and information-sharing among the intelligence community's (IC) agencies to provide the best intelligence available to policymakers.

It's no small task. Leading and managing an intelligence community with a $40 billion budget, and 100,000 people—both civilian and military—across 16 federal departments would be a Herculean project anytime. Doing it while implementing sorely-needed reform—and at war—is a nightmare. As Negroponte put it in his recent speech, "We are in the process of remaking a loose confederation [of intelligence agencies] into a unified enterprise. This will take time—certainly more than a year—but with the right approach, it can be done."

And despite the volley of raspberries, Negroponte is making progress. As critical as some in Congress have been, the House Intelligence Authorization bill noted: "The effort by the DNI to create an intelligence community that is greater than the sum of its parts is beginning to bear fruit."

Communications

One of the failings that led to 9/11 was the lack of communications between the intelligence and law enforcement communities, particularly the CIA and FBI. Today, information flow between agencies on intelligence matters has drastically improved. In addition, during the DNI's tenure, the FBI finally merged their counterintelligence and counterterrorism divisions with their directorate of intelligence analysis into an integrated National Security Branch. Hallelujah!

In February, Negroponte grew the IC from 15 to 16 agencies by incorporating the Drug Enforcement [Administration]. This is an important move considering the growing ties between the drug trade and terrorist financing in places like Afghanistan.

[The DNI is] leading a revolution in intelligence that, done right, will keep this country secure far beyond these difficult times.

Focus

The U.S. government (rightly) sees terrorism, the proliferation of weapons of mass destruction, Iran, Iraq, North Korea and China as the country's top-tier intelligence priorities—thus needing laser-like attention. To meet this challenge, Negroponte strengthened the counterterrorism center and established a counterproliferation center. He also set up North Korea, Iran, China and Iraq "mission managers" to improve interagency collection/analytical work against these "hard targets."

The DNI has also begun using "red teams"—outside experts who look at the same intelligence questions as government analysts to see if they reach the same conclusion—and, if not, why. He needs to extend the practice much further than he has so far.

Let's face it: The DNI's job is a tough one: Implement reform, change bureaucratic cultures and integrate foreign, domestic and military intelligence to seal the gaps in our defenses that the 9/11 Commission and others studies revealed. In fact, it's probably the second most thankless job in U.S. government after the FEMA [Federal Emergency Management Agency] director in the wake of Hurricane Katrina. You're just not going to make everyone happy, no matter what you do.

Negroponte hasn't got it all right yet. Constructive criticism and congressional oversight are great motivators for improvement. But he's leading a revolution in intelligence that, done right, will keep this country secure far beyond these difficult times.

A Clear Command Structure Is Essential for Responding to Future Terrorist Threats

Ivo H. Daalder and Anthony Lake

Ivo H. Daalder is a senior fellow at the Brookings Institution, a nonprofit public policy organization. Anthony Lake served as President Bill Clinton's national security adviser and is currently a professor at Georgetown University in Washington, D.C.

The debate about intelligence reform has rapidly turned to the issues that always dominate Washington: Who would win and who would lose control over people, money, and power? But for citizens outside Washington, the issue is seen through a far more important prism: What will actually work best? The stakes in seeing the problem this way are enormous, because intelligence constitutes the first line of defense in the war on terror and the fight against weapons proliferation. To win the war, we need to get its command structure right.

This is the first war in our nation's history in which the intelligence community is the point of the spear. The director of central intelligence, not the secretary of defense, is held primarily accountable for its management. It is also the first war in our history in which the overall commander has not had direct control over his troops. The responsibility of the director of central intelligence is far greater than his power. The Pentagon, not the director, controls over 80 percent of the intelligence community's assets and budget. This has distorted our priorities, skewed our strategy, and undermined our effectiveness.

What is required to make our first line of defense more effective? Most important, we need a war commander who has

Ivo H. Daalder and Anthony Lake, "Smart Choices About Intelligence Reform," *The Boston Globe*, August 19, 2004. Reproduced by permission of the authors.

real authority not only over personnel and budgets but also over intelligence operations. We also need to bring together all the troops—the intelligence collectors and analysts—in a single focused effort to fight the war on every front. And we will need to bring operational clarity to the defense of our homeland, especially in confronting immediate terrorist threats or dealing with the aftermath of an attack. The 9-11 Commission identified some of these requirements, while it ignored others.

We need to focus the work of the entire intelligence community—of collectors, analysts, and operators—on specific missions, starting with counterterrorism.

Director of National Intelligence

There is now widespread agreement in Washington that we need a director of national intelligence to oversee the entire intelligence community. Differences have predictably emerged over how much power this person must have. President [George W.] Bush, in endorsing the 9-11 Commission's recommendation to create this position, insisted that the person occupying the office have a coordinating rather than controlling role. The real power would remain where it has always been—with the secretary of defense, the CIA director, and other departmental heads. Unfortunately, this would constitute intelligence reform in name only. As the 9-11 Commission recognized, real change requires that the new director be vested with all the necessary attributes of Washington power—including over people, money, and operations.

Yet, even as it recommended a new director with real power, the commission sought to soften the blow by proposing that his key deputies for foreign, defense, and homeland intelligence be dual-hatted as CIA director and top officials in the defense and homeland security departments. But the officials at Defense and Homeland Security would inevitably have divided loyalties. Real reform would ensure that the director of national intelligence have complete and unvarnished control over all intelligence collection agencies.

It isn't just budgets and personnel that should concern the director of national intelligence. As the 9-11 Commission recognized, his effectiveness also requires that he control intelligence operations. This is where the most important, and largely ignored, recommendation of the commission comes in—the proposal to reorganize the intelligence community into mission specific task forces, starting with the creation of a National Counter-Terrorism Center. Today, the community consists of 15 separate bureaucratic fiefdoms. Each department has its own intelligence analysis agencies—State, Treasury, Energy, and Justice have intelligence divisions and the Pentagon has separate agencies for itself and for each of the five military services. Other agencies are divided according to the type of intelligence they collect (signal, imagery, or human intelligence).

These internal divisions no longer make any sense, if they ever did. Instead, as the 9-11 Commission rightly concluded, we need to focus the work of the entire intelligence community—of collectors, analysts, and operators—on specific missions, starting with counterterrorism. Of course, operators engaged in special operations and covert actions must remain separate from the centers, either within the Pentagon or the CIA. But to ensure effective fusion of intelligence those collecting and analyzing information in specific areas like counterterrorism and weapons proliferation must be co-located in newly created intelligence centers. To guard against the kind of groupthink that occurred in regard to the assessment of Iraqi weapons of mass destruction, all analytical work in the centers must constantly be subjected to countervailing analysis (so-called red-teaming) and all intelligence product must clearly indicate what is known, what is disputed, and what is not known.

Homeland Security Command Structure

Better command and more far-reaching integration are all necessary to ensure commanders can fight the war against terror effectively. Yet, one other change, which the 9-11 Commission did not address, is also necessary: a clear homeland security command structure.

Much of our national debate about homeland security has focused on a confusing alert system, continued vulnerabilities of critical infrastructure, and the failure to provide adequate resources to first responders. There has also been some attention to the continuing problems confronting reform efforts at the FBI, and to the organization of the new department of homeland security and the coordination among them and other agencies. But there has been no attention, in the press or by the 9-11 Commission, to what could be a tragic oversight: organizing to deal on the ground with a fast-breaking, major terrorist threat or its aftermath.

Under current procedures, the FBI will be in charge on the scene. (The Department of Homeland Security will assume a greater role over time.) Yet, as any military commander can tell you, in a crisis you need a clear command structure. What we have now is a highly imperfect coordinating system. Making it more efficient may make it better in producing policy. But in a real crisis—with terrorists poised to attack in one of our cities or after a massive strike in some location even less prepared than New York City was on 9/11—there will be no time for traditional interagency coordination. Someone must be in charge.

It is a fact of life in any bureaucracy that no agency easily takes orders from another. There is only one place that can exercise such authority, and that is the White House. A command structure must therefore be rooted there. Specifically, we should create three interagency teams as part of the White House Homeland Security Council structure which would be ready at all times to respond to an emergency. One of the teams would always be on alert, ready to fly immediately to the scene of imminent or actual disaster—to assume command for the federal government and to coordinate with local police, firefighters, emergency personnel, and other first responders. The members of the federal team would have direct access, in such a circumstance, to the highest level of their home agency. But the team leader, who would be in constant communications with the White House, would have clear authority to issue orders to the others if there were no time for Washington coordination.

This proposal will sound radical to any bureaucrat resistant to giving up advance authority to such a team. But there is precedent for the idea of Executive Office teams standing ready to go to disaster areas in the Federal Emergency Management Agency (which was once responsible for responding not only to natural disasters but also to a nuclear attack). A more compelling precedent would be the centuries of experience of militaries the world over who have learned the importance of clear command structures to help cut through the fogs of conflict and crisis.

It could well be that we will only learn the importance of clear command the hard way—through the work of some future commission investigating our response to the next major terrorist attack. It would be far better to see its importance now.

The United States Must Improve Its Ability to Collect Human Intelligence

Michael Scheuer, interviewed by Foreign Policy

Michael Scheuer served in the CIA for more than twenty years. He is the author of Through My Enemies' Eyes: Osama bin Laden, Radical Islam, and the Future of America *and* Imperial Hubris: Why the West Is Losing the War on Terror. Foreign Policy *is a bimonthly international affairs magazine published by the Carnegie Endowment for International Peace, a think tank on global issues.*

The selection of Gen. Michael Hayden to succeed Porter Goss as director of the CIA [Central Intelligence Agency] raises questions about intelligence reform once again. Michael Scheuer, former chief of the Osama bin Laden unit at the CIA, explains to *FP* [*Foreign Policy* magazine] why he thinks Hayden is the wrong choice for the job, why intelligence on Iran is so poor, and why he thinks Iraq "is finished."

Foreign Policy: *Is Michael Hayden the right choice for the CIA?*

Michael Scheuer: No. As a professional intelligence officer, the last people you want to report to are generals and diplomats. And if General Hayden comes to the CIA, we'll have . . . a general as the head of the CIA. They are not particularly good at taking bad news to the president, in the experience of most intelligence officers. So General Hayden is not the right choice. I also think that it kind of beggars the imagination in the sense that every one of the commissions that investigated 9/11 or Iraq said that we didn't have enough HUMINT [hu-

Michael Scheuer, interviewed by *Foreign Policy*, "Seven Questions: Fixing U.S. Intelligence; Interview with Michael Scheuer," May 2006, www.foreignpolicy.com. Reproduced by permission.

man intelligence] and now we're going to have 16 or 17 intelligence community components—not one of which will have anyone with HUMINT experience at its head.

The last time we had a flag-rank officer at CIA was Adm. Stansfield Turner. He gutted the human collection capability to focus on technical collection: satellites and wiretaps and that sort of thing. So one hopes that's not repeated. But General Hayden's experience is almost entirely in technical collection.

How do you view Porter Goss's tenure at the CIA?

I personally believe that Porter Goss is a good man, in the sense that I think he's smart. The people I know who worked with him on terrorist issues, for example, found him engaged, knowledgeable, and asking good questions. Yet he surrounded himself with a bunch of people that appear to have been sycophants and really civility-challenged. There was no need to be as abrasive and, frankly, as rude and crude as that bunch was. And I'm afraid that history will show that Mr. Goss may have been a good director but crippled himself by his choice of lieutenants.

[The Central Intelligence Agency] should concentrate on what we do best, which is human intelligence.

What role should the agency have in this enlarged intelligence structure, with the addition of the Director of National Intelligence (DNI)?

We should concentrate on what we do best, which is human intelligence. The agency, more than anything, needs someone to defend it. We had the information that would have enabled the [Bill] Clinton administration to kill Osama bin Laden [the leader of al Qaeda, the Islamic terrorist group responsible for 9/11] in 1998 and 1999. We provided the information that would have enabled the [George W.] Bush administration to kill Moqtada al-Sadr [the leader of an insurgent group in Iraq] two summers ago [in 2004]. We provided the information that would have allowed [al Qaeda leader Abu Musab al-] Zarqawi to be yesterday's memory. Someone needs to stand up and say, "Listen, is the agency perfect? The answer is no. Has it done its job to the best of its ability? Yes." And most of the intelligence failures we have had have been failures to act on information, not from lack of information.

[The DNI] has bloated the intelligence system as far as I can tell. It's just another layer of control, editing, review. And it's another step in preventing the truth as the intelligence community sees it from getting to the president. It's a tremendously unfortunate situation. Congress needed to help the intelligence community and instead allowed themselves to be railroaded by the families of the 9/11 victims to pass a bill that was disastrous. It was a shameful performance. It was like [President] Franklin Roosevelt and [Secretary of State] George Marshall calling in the families of the sailors that died at Pearl Harbor [in 1941] and saying, "Listen, we have a problem here with imperial Japan. What should we do?" It doesn't make sense. It's not professional, and now we're stuck with a law that's a travesty.

Does the CIA have the resources it needs to properly fulfill its role?

I don't think we're lacking in resources, at least on the terrorism issue. Among the cheapest operations to run are HUMINT operations. We were never short of money to conduct counterterrorism operations. What we were short of was leadership. The agency has had a long track record now of very mediocre people being at its head. We had two very good directors in William J. Casey and William Webster followed by a really abysmal parade of people. James Woolsey was a neocon ideologue whom the White House hated. We had John Deutsch, who at the end of the day had to be pardoned by President Clinton to avoid legal problems. George Tenet seemed more interested in being everyone's friend than in being a leader. He was really our first rock star. And Porter Goss really never gave himself a chance to prove his capabilities because he surrounded himself with people who were both untalented and obnoxious.

People have said that U.S. intelligence on Iran is poor. Why is that?

It's poor because we haven't been there since 1979. People talk about new ways of doing intelligence, and new ways of working without a presence in a country. That's all talk. You can do a certain amount of that. But without a physical presence, it's very hard to collect intelligence. If you don't have an embassy, a consulate, or a physical presence, you're dependent on people coming out to meet you or on signals intelligence. One of the big problems in Iraq was that we hadn't had a presence there since the first Gulf War, and we depended on opposition people to give us information about [Iraqi dictator] Saddam [Hussein]. And it appears that the information supplied by [Ahmad] Chalabi [an Iraqi that the United States relied upon for prewar intelligence] and others was pretty close to perfect, in the sense of being perfectly wrong.

What is your one-year outlook on Iraq?

I think Iraq is finished. We'll just find a way to get out. I frankly don't think we ever intended to win there. We certainly didn't send enough troops to close borders, to control the country. [Former defense secretary Donald] Rumsfeld was obsessed, apparently with his new, lighter, faster military. The inflow of fighters is growing. The pace of the insurgency, both there and in Afghanistan, is increasing. I don't hold much of a brief for Sen. John McCain, but he's right, in an unpalatable way: Unless we greatly increase the number of troops we have in Iraq, we're going to have to leave. I think the question is how do we leave? Do we leave with some dignity, or do we leave by flying off the top of the embassy as we did in Saigon [at the end of the Vietnam War]?

Apart from Iran and Iraq, where do you think the intelligence community needs to be focusing its attention?

It's an absolute disaster for American law enforcement and for the FBI to have no control over who comes into and out of our country. They spend tens of billions of dollars on gadgets and electronics at official checkpoints. Well, if al Qaeda is stupid enough to carry their weapons through the gate at the Windsor-Detroit Tunnel, then they might get stopped. If they roll across the Niagara River near Buffalo, then they're home free. Sadly, neither party in Congress has helped law enforcement.

The second thing we desperately need is an accelerated program to control the former Soviet nuclear arsenal. We know that bin Laden has been using hired scientists and engineers to acquire these weapons since 1992. He has now had 14 years to try and do that. And I recently read that the program to control the Soviet nuclear arsenal is well less than half complete. To me, the two touchstones of American security are controlling the borders and securing all of the Soviet nuclear weapons. If you don't do those [things], the intelligence community can help you overseas, but the domestic target is wide open.

New Technologies and an Effective Knowledge Management System Will Transform U.S. Intelligence

David Rothkopf

David Rothkopf is chairman of Intellibridge, a company that provides intelligence and analysis for the U.S. government, and author of the book Running the World: The Inside Story of the NSC and the Architects of American Power.

The recently enacted intelligence reform bill was the best Washington could do, probably. That's the bad news. The good news is that the marketplace knows that intelligence reform is much too important to be left to politicians and bureaucrats. The new legislation seeks to improve intelligence coordination through the appointment of a new layer of management. This alone can be a formula for failure. However, the chances of real reform are poor for other reasons as well.

The U.S. intelligence bureaucracy remains, unfortunately, convoluted and full of conflicting interests. The government's answer to September 11 has been to create new bureaucracies: the office of the national intelligence director is only one example. The response to management failures and communications breakdowns has been to make the system more complex, not simpler. In fact, a number of the steps taken or proposed have not even been necessary. The United States already has legislation calling for centralized control of its intelligence community. It's called the National Security Act of 1947. The [George W. Bush] administration failed to manage the system as it should have.

David Rothkopf, "Technology Can Fix U.S. Intelligence: The Intelligence Reform Bill Evaded Real Reform," *Technology Review*, vol. 108, February 2005, p. 34. © 2005 by the Association of Alumni and Alumnae of MIT. Reproduced by permission.

The Need for Effective Knowledge Management

The real problems within the intelligence community are much deeper and more ingrained. One way a technology audience might view them is as a failure to build an effective knowledge management system to support U.S. government policymakers. That perspective reveals an abundance of obvious flaws. There is a government culture that values secrecy and hoards knowledge rather than sharing with those who need it most. Secrecy is important, but while emerging technologies—like quantum encryption, which will prevent eavesdropping—make it ever easier to protect information you want to hold close, they should be used to increase, not decrease, opportunities for openness. One senior military commander told me that perhaps 95 percent of what is now deemed secret is available via open sources, thanks to the Internet. Unnecessary secrecy costs billions and impedes the flow of vital information. It is also an exercise in futility. I've seen instances where Web-harvested information was received by the government and immediately classified.

---

*It is the larger marketplace and technological innovators
... who will produce the intelligence reforms we urgently
need.*

As detrimental are the cultural biases institutionalized through a system of "stovepipes" that forces information to go up one management chain, across at the top, and down another before it can get to the people who need it the most. Furthermore, information producers within the intelligence community have too much control over who gets to see what—when every other new knowledge-based system in the world is being designed otherwise.

It is well within our power to create a flatter, more distributed knowledge management system that makes all data within the government available to users in real time regardless of agency affiliation, simply based on privileges assigned to them. But we don't have it yet.

A Few Key Steps

Nonetheless, the existing system can be enhanced via a few key steps. Unbelievably, many in the national-security community don't have full access to the Web—because counterintelligence specialists worry that that would permit spies to hack into U.S. systems. Furthermore, much of what is out there is uninterpretable even to those who see it: the United States lacks specialized analysts, and those it does have don't have the linguistic skill to translate important data. But outsourcing the analysis and translation of open-source information to the private sector would enhance U.S. capabilities. In addition, the advent of the Semantic Web (which adds definition tags to information in Web pages so that computers can interact more productively) will further empower end users of information and make the Web a much more efficient tool.

If the government stopped spending billions producing what was already available for free or at low cost on the Web, then it could devote more money to the new technologies that will truly transform intelligence. These include everything from unmanned reconnaissance vehicles to the long-envisioned ubiquitous-sensing networks that deploy vast quantities of microsensors to capture live data. Learning to better massage, intelligently search, interpret, and use the resulting information and to get good analysis to users is the ultimate challenge for U.S. intelligence—not adding new bosses to the system.

Getting intelligence to the field in real time and moving analysts closer to end users—and out of the echo chambers of intelligence institutions—are achievable ends. It is the larger marketplace and technological innovators . . . who will produce the intelligence reforms we urgently need—reforms that the recent bill, for all the fanfare around it, largely ignored.

CIA Hiring Policies Should Be Less Cautious in Order to Attract Good Agents

Robert Elliott

Robert Elliott is an assistant editor for Security Management, *a magazine for security professionals.*

R obert Baer spent 21 years working for the Central Intelligence Agency's (CIA's) Directorate of Operations, serving mostly as an on-the-ground field officer in the Middle East. His first-person recounting of that experience in *See No Evil: The True Story of a Ground Soldier in the CIA's War on Terrorism* probably should be required reading for anyone interested in how we got where we are today. These days, he is traversing the more lush terrain of the novel, but he stays in touch with the real-world intelligence community and finds many of today's trends to be troubling.

CIA's Conservative Hiring Policies

Baer admits that the youthful stunts he pulled in his early days—such as rappelling off the top of the Kennedy Center during a performance—probably would have precluded his entry into today's CIA, but he's doubtful that's a good thing. The level of security checks in place now may be turning away the very type of people that make good agents, he says. "At this point they just wouldn't even look at you—no one wants to take any risks. It's much more strict," Baer told *Security Management* in between planes on the book tour promoting his first fictional work, *Blow the House Down.* "I've talked to a

Robert Elliott, "Is the CIA Too Cautious? Former CIA Agent Robert Baer Weighs in on the State of the U.S. Intelligence Community and Offers Suggestions for Improvement," *Security Management*, vol. 50, October 2006, p. 30. © 2006 ASIS International, 1625 Prince Street, Alexandria, VA 22314. Reprinted by permission of *Security Management* magazine.

lot of people who have tried [and failed] to get into the outfit, and unless they are lying to me, they have very minor transgressions," he says. "I think that as the government comes under more criticism, the less likely [hiring managers] are going to take any chances at all."

Analysts are often isolated in offices, but they need to get out in the field to know what they are looking for while sifting through the information.

Baer says the super-conservative hiring policy is crippling the agency's effectiveness. The agency is not getting the talent where it desperately needs it—on the ground gathering information. That's because only people open to and comfortable with various cultural experiences can get the goods while remaining inconspicuous and blending into their natural environment, says Baer. "If you are a Yemeni living in Aden, you had better chew qat [a leafy narcotic], or be ready to," he says. But that's not the behavior of a cautious, timid soul. Rather, that's the behavior of a daredevil who crosses the line now and then. And that's what an agent needs to be—but those types no longer pass the security clearance, he says.

Solutions

Baer has a suggestion for getting around the problem. He calls for different classes of security clearances. The recruit from abroad, who may not be as clean cut and pure a character as the agency now seeks, would not need to be granted access to the most sensitive intelligence within the agency. "So you could hire the Pakistani, send him to Karachi, or Riyadh, or Mecca, and stick him in a mosque, and have him come out and tell his story, but you don't have him sitting down and reading this compartmented intelligence," says Baer. The current clearance needlessly gives access to all information inside, he says.

That could strengthen human intelligence (HUMINT) gathered in the field. But HUMINT is only one piece of the puzzle. Technology should not be discounted either, says Baer. He believes the best domestic information is gleaned through National Security Agency (NSA) methods, such as telephone taps. "You get people in unguarded moments and you can figure out a lot of things about them by listening to their telephone," he says.

Equally critical are data mining operations, such as the examination of databases of phone and financial records, says Baer. The recent flap about the NSA spying on American citizens was overdone, he says. "They are building a giant phonebook, which you can do privately, so why can't the government do it?"

The collection of an exorbitant amount of information that overwhelms the analytical side of spy houses has long been trumpeted as a major problem, but Baer says that is not the problem. "It's not that the analysts have too much information, it's that a lot of the stuff, they don't see," he says. "You have to get a software program that protects the source, yet lets the content go to the analysts. There are ways to do this."

Analysts are often isolated in offices, but they need to get out in the field to know what they are looking for while sifting through the information, he says. "One of the problems we had in Iraq is that the analysts didn't know who the exiles were," says Baer. "They just saw this reporting. If they were actually out dealing with exiles . . . they would have understood what they were up against."

The U.S. Intelligence Community Must Be Better Insulated from Political Influence

Shaun Waterman

Shaun Waterman is homeland and national security editor for United Press International, a leading provider of news and information to media outlets, businesses, governments, and researchers worldwide.

The man who ran the CIA's [Central Intelligence Agency's] covert activities in Europe during the run-up to the invasion of Iraq says U.S. intelligence needs to be better insulated from political influence if the nation is to avoid another disaster in Iran.

"I can see the same thing happening with (intelligence on) Iran," Tyler Drumheller told United Press International [UPI] in an interview about his [2006] book, "On the Brink."

He said there was "a core of intelligence professionals who can do the job if they're allowed to." But there was a real risk of repeating what he said was the two-pronged failure on Iraq: policy-makers brought their preconceptions to the table and senior intelligence officials failed to confront them with uncomfortable truths. Policy-makers, he said, had to learn that "when someone doesn't agree with your preconceptions, you can't interpret that as disloyalty or stupidity." But they must also be able to "rely on intelligence officials to tell them things they don't want to hear." He said that recent reforms of the structure of U.S. intelligence, including the appointment of Director of National Intelligence John Negroponte, were "an impediment, not an improvement."

Shaun Waterman, "Analyisis: U.S. Intelligence on Iran Needs Insulation from Political Interference," *United Press International*, November 3, 2006. www.upi.com. Reproduced by permission.

"On the Brink," offers a few fresh details about several episodes of the now familiar tale of how U.S. officials ended up making a case for war based on inaccurate statements about Iraq's weapons of mass destruction capabilities. "The White House took our work and twisted it for its own ends," he writes, accusing then-CIA Director George Tenet of having "set a tone whereby people knew what he and the White House wanted to hear ... The bureaucratic imperative was to prove one's worth by supporting the president's case for war." CIA spokesman Mark Mansfield declined to comment on the book beyond saying that Drumheller no longer worked for the agency and was "expressing his own opinion."

Much of the blame for the errors [must be placed] on the CIA's Weapons Intelligence, Non-Proliferation and Arms Control Center, known as WINPAC.

One former U.S. intelligence official said many who had worked the issue at the time felt Tenet "had fallen into the trap of believing he was his own best analyst." CIA management was sometimes "very dismissive of (the agency's) own products" when they did not fit what seemed to be the emerging picture. Colleagues have defended Tenet from similar charges in the past, pointing out that the published reports of two inquiries into the matter have concluded that there was no politicization of the CIA's analysis on his watch, but rather a failure of analytic creativity, and the predominance of so-called "groupthink."

Drumheller's book also echoes the conclusions of the special presidential commission that probed pre-war intelligence failures on Iraqi weapons of mass destruction, in placing much of the blame for the errors on the CIA's Weapons Intelligence, Non-Proliferation and Arms Control Center, known as WINPAC. "The truth is (Tenet) over-empowered WINPAC," he writes. The presidential commission [in 2005] recommended fundamental overhaul of the center. "We didn't quite say, 'Bulldoze it,' but we came close," a commission official told UPI at the time.

Mansfield praised the center's analysts as "smart, extraordinarily dedicated officers" and said changes had been made there. "We have improved our analytical tradecraft and our intelligence-sharing (with people working the issue at different agencies)," he said, adding that the center was doing more analysis focused on the research U.S. adversaries are doing on weapons development. He said a so-called Red Cell, or alternative analysis team, had been put in place at the center. "We are including alternative analysis in many more of our products, and are bolstering (intelligence) efforts to improve interdiction capabilities."

Many critics of the [George W. Bush] administration have discerned a similar tunnel vision . . . as was evident in the run up to war with Iraq.

He said WINPAC analysts had predicted both North Korea's missile test in July [2006] and its recent effort to detonate a nuclear bomb. "We have taken the lessons learned from the Iraq episode," he said, "and are applying them every day." One congressional staffer with access to intelligence products agreed. "I have seen no evidence that the intelligence community is being pushed or is shaping their analysis" on Iran, the staffer told UPI. "They have in fact learned fairly well the lessons of Iraq," the staffer went on. "They are much clearer about the degree of confidence they have in their judgments, much readier to acknowledge uncertainty, much better at laying out what they don't know."

But Drumheller is not alone in his concerns. Many critics of the administration have discerned a similar tunnel vision on the part of senior officials as was evident in the run up to war with Iraq. Negroponte has said it is the consensus assessment of U.S. intelligence that Iran is seeking a nuclear weapon, and is five to 10 years away from developing one. In August [2006], the GOP [Republican] Chairman of the House Permanent Select Committee on Intelligence, Peter Hoekstra of Michigan, released [a report] titled, "Recognizing Iran as a Strategic Threat: An Intelligence Challenge for the United States." "We lack critical information needed for analysts to make many of their judgments with confidence about Iran, and we don't know nearly enough about Iran's nuclear weapons program," read the report. "I would suspect we do know quite a bit about what's going on in Iran, but it's not what they want to hear, so they say, 'We're blind,'" Drumheller said.

The report was slammed by critics, including the International Atomic Energy Authority, as presenting an overblown and exaggerated picture of the threat. The authority's former head, Hans Blix, [in September 2006] gave evidence to a congressional panel, and told them that Iran was "not a threat today. It could become (one) later on." He said U.S. intelligence analysts looking before the war at Iraq's weapons programs had "chose(n) to replace question marks by exclamation marks," and urged against repeating that error on Iran.

He said it was not certain that Iran was pursuing a nuclear weapon. "I think there have been some indications pointing in that direction, but I don't think it is conclusive. And I think that after the experience we have had in Iraq, one should be a little careful to jump to conclusions."

It Will Take Decades to Rebuild the U.S. Intelligence Community

Patrick Radden Keefe

Patrick Radden Keefe is a fellow at the Century Foundation, a public policy research organization, and author of the book Chatter: Uncovering the Echelon Surveillance Network and the Secret World of Global Eavesdropping.

The lessons of 9/11 and of Iraq for intelligence reform are anything but consonant. The failure of American Intelligence to prevent the attacks on the Pentagon and World Trade Center was a false negative, in which analysts neglected to connect obliquely related dots and identify a threat where there was one. The rush to war in Iraq, on the other hand, represented a false positive, in which analysts too readily connected dots and saw a threat where there was none.

The weakness that got us into Iraq should be relatively easy to fix. The institutional pathologies that led to Sept. 11 are far more intractable, however, as testified by the Cs and Ds in the report card issued by the 9/11 Commission [in] December [2005]. Reforming intelligence institutions—and institutional cultures—to avert false negatives in the future won't take five years, or even 10. It will take a generation.

Fixing Iraq Failures

False positives are easier to guard against because when confronted with an apparent threat, analysts can focus their energies on a single target and weigh the credibility of each piece of the evidentiary puzzle. The danger is that political manipulation pollutes this process. This has long been a risk—think of the Gulf of Tonkin incident in 1964 [that led to U.S. military engagement in the Vietnam War]. But Vice President Dick Cheney's repeated visits to the CIA [Central Intelligence Agency] before the war in Iraq marked an unusually bold perversion of the long-standing analytical process of American espionage. As Paul Pillar, who oversaw Iraq Intelligence for the CIA from 2000 to 2005, wrote, "analysts . . . felt a strong wind consistently blowing in one direction. The desire to bend with such a wind is natural and strong."

That strong wind had unquestionably calamitous results. But it was not a symptom of deeply engrained dysfunction. In fact, outside the Bush White House, there is near universal agreement today that political pressure corrupts intelligence analysis. A report [in August 2006] that administration officials are angry at America's spies for failing to issue "more ominous" warnings about Iran—that rather than sexing the intel up, analysts were, in effect, sexing it down—suggests that our spies have already learned a thing or two from the Iraq debacle. That's the good news.

Fixing 9/11 Failures

But overhauling U.S. intelligence to better prevent false negatives represents a much greater challenge. A few central lessons have emerged from what CIA head Michael Hayden called the post-9/11 "archaeology" of intelligence failure. Chief among them is that the intelligence "community" is in fact a collection of warring fiefdoms, with each territorial agency disinclined to share intelligence with the rest. Traditionally, the director of the CIA was a walking conflict of interests— the titular leader of the whole community, on the one hand, and the boss of his own personal agency on the other.

The ambitious solution to this problem was a new entity, the Office of the Director of National Intelligence, which was supposed to provide a "command structure" for the nation's

16 spy agencies. Proposed by the 9/11 commission, the idea was politicized by the 2004 election and rapidly made law. It had critics from the start. But the clearest indictment of the new office was that nobody wanted the head job. It was a thankless one: The director of national intelligence would face a White House that had opposed the 9/11 commission and was lukewarm on reform, and, in [former] Defense Secretary Donald Rumsfeld, a bureaucratic heavyweight who controlled 80 percent of the intelligence budget and had prevailed against the last spy boss who encroached on his turf, former CIA Director George Tenet.

It will take decades to train linguists and analysts and case officers who are proficient enough in the languages and cultures of America's terrorist adversaries to establish more than patchwork vigilance.

In fact, when President Bush finally found someone willing to be the nation's top spy, it wasn't a spy at all. Ambassador John Negroponte took office in February 2005, and it was unclear whether he represented an inspired, counterintuitive choice—a diplomat who could persuade others to play together nicely—or just the bottom of the barrel. Still, he was a marked improvement on Porter Goss, Bush's spectacularly ineffectual choice to run the CIA. As the new chief liaison to the president, Negroponte relieved Goss of one of his key duties: delivering the president's daily intelligence brief. Given that Goss was spending six hours a day preparing the brief, rather than chasing terrorists, this simple personnel change alone may have made the country safer.

But Goss resisted Negroponte's effort to refocus the CIA and the "Gosslings," as his arrogant and combative staffers became known, alienated numerous seasoned hands at the agency's elite Directorate of Operations, prompting a devastating brain drain. So, Goss' resignation in May [2006] affirmed both Negroponte's willingness to flex his political muscle and his commitment to transformation.

The appointment of Michael Hayden to replace Goss was a promising sign. Hayden faced various detractors, most significantly because of his defense of the National Security Agency's warrantless surveillence program. But during his six years running the NSA he had ushered a hopelessly analog agency into the digital age and established his bona fides as someone capable of transforming a large organization. The surest sign that real reform was under way was the creation of the National Counterterrorism Center, a central clearinghouse for intelligence on terrorist threats. Sept. 11 happened, in part, because numerous different pieces of intelligence that in the aggregate might have sounded alarms were instead scattered across various offices and agencies. NCTC is controlled by Negroponte's office, which means it's independent of the 16 other agencies but accessible to them all. A single intelligence communitywide database is precisely the sort of innovation that can prevent false negatives like 9/11 in the future.

Still, by spring [2006] Negroponte was worrying critics and supporters alike. Even in blueprint form, his office seemed in danger of mushrooming into yet another bureaucratic layer between intelligence gatherers and the White House. As Negroponte staffed up, aiming to expand to 1,500 employees, legislators feared that the lean and mean nerve center they had envisioned was becoming less a conduit than a clog. On the critical matter of intelligence-sharing, the 9/11 commission issued America's spies a pair of Ds. A July [2006] assessment of intelligence reform by the House intelligence committee faulted Negroponte's "incremental approach."

Incremental Reform

But is it realistic to think that the ambitious overhaul of a professional community comprising 100,000 employees could be anything *but* incremental? "We established the national security structure in this country in 1947," retired Adm. William Studerman told *GovExec.com* magazine [in 2005]. "And the intel community . . . took 10 or 20 years before it started to really run on all eight cylinders." It will take decades to train linguists and analysts and case officers who are proficient enough in the languages and cultures of America's terrorist adversaries to establish more than patchwork vigilance. And it will take longer still to undo a half-century of suspicion and territoriality and get our spies to share rather than hoard their information and capabilities.

The lesson of Iraq for U.S. intelligence was that . . . spies [must] do their analysis independently and then provide it to policymakers.

It may be, as John McLaughlin, former deputy director of the CIA, recently worried, that another terrorist attack will blindside us while our spies are still "trying to figure out who works for who." It may also be, as Judge Richard Posner has suggested, that no amount of tinkering with the organizational chart of the intelligence community will do away with "the inevitability of failure," because false negatives are impossible to avoid.

But we've got to try. The lesson of Iraq for U.S. intelligence was that there is a way things have always been done—spies do their analysis independently and then provide it to policymakers—and we should not mess with it. Lesson learned. The lesson of 9/11, by contrast, is precisely that we *should* mess with the way things have always been done: that we should rebuild from the foundations. And five years after 9/11, that process—ambitious, frustrating, and utterly necessary—is still in its infancy.

Organizations to Contact

The editors have compiled the following list of organizations concerned with the issues debated in this book. The descriptions are derived from materials provided by the organizations. All have publications or information available for interested readers. The list was compiled on the date of publication of the present volume; the information provided here may change. Be aware that many organizations take several weeks or longer to respond to inquiries, so allow as much time as possible.

Brookings Institution
1775 Masachusetts Ave. NW, Washington, DC 20036
(202) 797-6000 • fax: (202) 797-6004
e-mail: brookinfo@brook.edu
Web site: www.brookings.org

The Brookings Institution is a think tank that conducts research and education in the areas of foreign policy, economics, government, and the social sciences. Numerous briefings and publications on the topic of U.S. intelligence reform can be found on its Web site. Examples include *Intelligence Reform in the Wake of the 9/11 Commission Report*, *The 9/11 Commission Report: The Limits of Hasty Reform*, and *The Bloat That Hurts Our Spies*.

The Center for National Policy
One Massachusetts Ave. NW, Suite 333
Washington, DC 20001
(202) 682-1800 • fax: (202) 682-1818
e-mail: info@cnponline.org
Web site: www.cnponline.org

The Center for National Policy is a nonprofit, nonpartisan public policy organization dedicated to providing policy solutions to American and global security issues, including U.S. engagement abroad, national security and intelligence reform, terrorism, nuclear proliferation, homeland security, and post-conflict reconstruction. The center's Web site contains links to a number of publications on U.S. intelligence matters.

Central Intelligence Agency (CIA)
Office of Public Affairs, Washington, DC   20505
(703) 482-0623 • fax: (703) 482-1739
Web site: www.cia.gov

The CIA was created in 1947 with the signing of the National Security Act by President Harry S. Truman. It is the nation's leading intelligence agency and its mission is to collect and analyze information about the plans, intentions, and capabilities of U.S. adversaries relevant to the nation's defense. The agency's Web site contains information about the history and structure of the agency and its use of intelligence data, including speeches and testimony of CIA officials.

Commission on the Intelligence Capabilities of the United States Regarding Weapons of Mass Destruction
Washington, DC
Web site: www.wmd.gov

The commission was established by President George W. Bush on February 6, 2004, and charged with assessing whether the U.S. intelligence community is capable of identifying and providing adequate intelligence information concerning the proliferation of weapons of mass destruction (WMD) and other security threats of the twenty-first century. The commission ceased operations after producing a report to the president on March 31, 2005, assessing the status of U.S. intelligence and offering seventy-four suggestions for improvement. The report is available on the commission's Web site.

Defense Intelligence Agency (DIA)
The Pentagon, Washington, DC
(703) 695-0071 • fax: (703) 614-3692
e-mail: dia-pao@dia.mil
Web site: www.dia.mil

The Defense Intelligence Agency is a Department of Defense combat support agency and an important member of the U.S. intelligence community. DIA has over eleven thousand military and civilian employees worldwide and is a major producer and manager of foreign military intelligence. The DIA Web site, under its Public Affairs category, provides information such as press releases, congressional testimony, and speeches on intelligence matters.

Federal Bureau of Investigation (FBI)
J. Edgar Hoover Bldg., Washington, DC   20535-0001
(202) 324-3000
Web site: www.fbi.gov

The Federal Bureau of Investigation is one of the many U.S. intelligence agencies and is charged with protecting the United States from terrorist and foreign intelligence threats, enforcing the criminal laws of the United States, and providing leadership and criminal justice services to federal, state, municipal, and international agencies and partners. The FBI Web site contains information about the FBI's operations, including its counterterrorism plans.

Federation of American Scientists (FAS) Intelligence Resource Program
1717 K St. NW, Suite 209, Washington, DC   20036
(202) 454-4691 • fax: (202) 675-1010
e-mail: saftergood@fas.org
Web site: www.fas.org/irp

The Federation of American Scientists was formed in 1945 by atomic scientists from the Manhattan Project, which produced the world's first atomic bomb. FAS seeks to promote humanitarian uses of science and technology through research and education projects in nuclear arms control and global security, conventional arms transfers, proliferation of weapons of mass destruction, information technology for human health, and government information policy. The federation's Intelligence

Resource Program Web site provides a wide selection of official and unofficial resources on intelligence policy, structure, function, organization, and operations.

Foreign Policy In Focus (FPIF)
1112 Sixteenth St NW, Suite 600, Washington, DC   20036
(202) 234-9382
e-mail: infocus@fpif.org
Web site: www.fpif.org

Foreign Policy In Focus is a public policy think tank for research and analysis of U.S. foreign policy and international affairs. It is jointly managed by the International Relations Center (IRC) in Silver City, New Mexico, and the Institute for Policy Studies in Washington, D.C. FPIF's Web site references a wide variety of publications relating to U.S. foreign policy matters.

The Heritage Foundation
214 Massachusetts Ave. NE, Washington, DC   20002-4999
(202) 546-4400 • fax: (202) 546-8328
e-mail: info@heritage.org
Web site: www.heritage.org

The Heritage Foundation is a research and educational institute dedicated to formulating and promoting conservative public policies based on the principles of free enterprise, limited government, individual freedoms, traditional American values, and a strong national defense. The organization's Web site contains a section titled Homeland Security and Terrorism, and offers numerous publications relating to U.S. intelligence issues.

National Commission on Terrorist Attacks upon the United States
Washington, DC
Web site: www.9-11commission.gov

The National Commission on Terrorist Attacks upon the United States (aka the 9-11 Commission) was an independent, bipartisan commission created by congressional legislation and authorized by President George W. Bush in late 2002. Its mission was to prepare a full and complete account of the circumstances surrounding the September 11, 2001, terrorist attacks and to provide recommendations for preventing future attacks. The commission disbanded after releasing its report on July 22, 2004, which made numerous recommendations for improving U.S. intelligence capabilities. The ten members of the commission, however, created the 9/11 Public Discourse Project to continue monitoring the issues studied by the commission. The commission's report is available on its Web site.

Office of the Director of National Intelligence (ODNI)
Washington, DC   20511
(703) 733-8600
Web site: www.odni.gov

The Director of National Intelligence serves as the head of the intelligence community and acts as the principal adviser to the president, the National Security Council, and the Homeland Security Council for intelligence matters related to national security. The ODNI's Web site contains reports, interviews, speeches, congressional testimony, and other documents relating to U.S. intelligence matters.

Rand Corporation
1776 Main St., Santa Monica, CA   90407-2138
(310) 393-0411 • fax: (310) 393-4818
Web site: www.rand.org

Rand is a nonprofit think tank that conducts research and analysis on national security, business, education, health, law, and science. Its Web site features a "Hot Topics" section on intelligence gathering that provides links to various publications about intelligence reform, terrorism, and other related topics.

Strategic Intelligence—Loyola College in Maryland
4501 N. Charles St., Baltimore, MD   21210-2699
(410) 617-2000
e-mail: politics@loyola.edu

Web site: www.loyola.edu/dept/politics/intel.html

Strategic Intelligence is an informational Web site run by the Political Science Department of Loyola College in Maryland. The site contains a wealth of information about U.S. intelligence, including links to the various intelligence agencies, laws, and reports.

Bibliography

Books

Peter Berkowitz, ed.
The Future of American Intelligence. Washington, DC: Hoover Institution, 2005.

Richard Betts
Surprise Attack: Lessons for Defense Planning. New York: Public Affairs, 2001.

Peter Brookes
A Devil's Triangle: Terrorism, Weapons of Mass Destruction, and Rogue States. Lanham, MD: Rowman & Littlefield, 2005.

David Cole and James X. Dempsey
Terrorism and the Constitution: Sacrificing Civil Liberties in the Name of National Security. New York: New Press, 2006.

Tyler Drumheller and Elaine Monaghan
On the Brink: An Insider's Account of How the White House Compromised American Intelligence. New York: Carroll & Graf, 2006.

Craig Eisendrath, ed.
National Insecurity: U.S. Intelligence After the Cold War. Philadelphia: Temple University Press, 1999.

Stephen Grey
Ghost Plane: The True Story of the CIA Torture Program. New York: St. Martin's, 2006.

Michael Ignatieff *The Lesser Evil: Political Ethics in an Age of Terror.* Princeton, NJ: Princeton University Press, 2005.

Chalmers Johnson *Blowback: The Costs and Consequences of American Empire. New York: Metropolitan/Owl, 2004.*

Chalmers Johnson *The Sorrows of Empire: Militarism, Secrecy and the End of the Republic.* New York: Metropolitan, 2004.

Patrick Radden Keefe *Chatter: Uncovering the Echelon Surveillance Network and the Secret World of Global Eavesdropping.* New York: Random House, 2006.

Joseph Margulies *Guantánamo and the Abuse of Presidential Power.* New York: Simon & Schuster, 2006.

Alfred McCoy *A Question of Torture: CIA Interrogation, from the Cold War to the War on Terror.* New York: Metropolitan, 2006.

Richard A. Posner *Not a Suicide Pact: The Constitution in a Time of National Emergency.* Oxford, UK: Oxford University Press, 2006.

Richard A. Posner *Preventing Surprise Attacks.* Lanham, MD: Rowman & Littlefield, 2005.

Richard A. Posner *Uncertain Shield: The U.S. Intelligence System in the Throes of Reform.* Lanham, MD: Rowman & Littlefield, 2006.

John Prados	*Safe for Democracy: The Secret Wars of the CIA.* Chicago: Ivan R. Dee, 2006.
David Pugliese	*Shadow Wars: Special Forces in the New Battle Against Terrorism.* Ottawa, ON: Esprit de Corps, 2003.
Scott Ritter	*Iraq Confidential: The Untold Story of America's Intelligence Conspiracy.* London: I. B. Tauris, 2005.
David Rothkopf	*Running the World: The Inside Story of the NSC and the Architects of American Power.* New York: Public Affairs, 2005.
Michael Scheuer	*Imperial Hubris: Why the West Is Losing the War on Terror.* Dulles, VA: Potomac, 2004.
Michael Scheuer	*Through My Enemies' Eyes: Osama bin Laden, Radical Islam, and the Future of America.* Dulles, VA: Potomac, 2006.
Jennifer E. Sims and Burton Gerber, eds.	*Transforming U.S. Intelligence.* Washington, DC: Georgetown University Press, 2005.
Gregory F. Treverton	*Reshaping National Intelligence for an Age of Information.* Cambridge, UK: Cambridge University Press, 2001.
Michael A. Turner	*Why Secret Intelligence Fails.* Dulles, VA: Potomac, 2005.

Curt Weldon — *Countdown to Terror: The Top-Secret Information That Could Prevent the Next Terrorist Attack on America . . . and How the CIA Has Ignored It.* Washington, DC: Regnery, 2005.

John Yoo — *War by Other Means: An Insider's Account of the War on Terror.* New York: Atlantic Monthly Press, 2006.

Periodicals and Newspapers

Ehsan Ahrari — "Intelligence Fallout: U.S. Spy Agency Failures May Hinder Future Action," *Defense News*, April 18, 2005. www.defensenews.com.

Paul Anderson — "U.S. Intelligence Didn't Catch 9/11 Clues?," *ERRI Daily Intelligence Report*, February 21, 2002. www.emergency.com.

Robert Baer — "How the CIA Can Be Fixed," *Time*, May 14, 2006. www.time.com.

Bryan Bender — "US Intelligence Shake-Up Meets Growing Criticism," *Boston Globe*, January 2, 2005. www.boston.com.

Julian Borger — "US Intelligence Fears Iran Duped Hawks into Iraq War," *Guardian* (Manchester, UK), May 25, 2004. www.guardian.co.uk.

Faye Bowers and Peter Grier — "Major Work Left to Fix US Intelligence," *Christian Science Monitor*, April 01, 2005. www.csmonitor.com.

CBS News   "A Spy Speaks Out," April 23, 2004.
                     www.cbsnews.com.

CNN   "NSA Eavesdropping Program Ruled
                     Unconstitutional," Thursday, August
                     17, 2006. www.cnn.com.

David D. Cole   "Reviving the Nixon Doctrine: NSA
                     Spying, the Commander-in-Chief,
                     and Executive Power in the War on
                     Terror," *Washington and Lee Journal
                     of Civil Rights and Social Justice*,
                     2006, vol. 13. http://ssrn.com.

Michael Duffy   "The Spy Master Cracks the Whip,"
                     Time, May 15, 2006.

John Fortier   "Intel Reform Takes Hold," *Hill
                     News*, May 10, 2006.
                     www.hillnews.com.

Joshua Frank   "'US Intelligence' Dead Wrong: Skep-
                     tics Were Right All Along," *Dissident
                     Voice*, April 1, 2005.
                     www.dissidentvoice.org.

Mark Hosenball   "'Foot-Dragging': Administration
                     Sources Claim that One of Porter
                     Gosss Top Deputies Stonewalled Ef-
                     forts to Reform U.S. Intelligence
                     Gathering," *Newsweek*, May 10, 2006.

Mark Hosenball   "Out from the Shadows; The Presi-
                     dent Announced He's Emptying the
                     CIA's Secret Prisons. Now What Will
                     Become of Its Former Inmates?"
                     Newsweek, September 18, 2006.

Mark Hosenball, Evan Thomas, and Michael Isikoff	"Intelligence: Goss Goes Out—But the CIA's Struggles Go On," *Newsweek*, May 15, 2006.
Arthur S. Hulnick	"U.S. Intelligence Reform: Problems and Prospects," *International Journal of Intelligence and Counterintelligence*, summer 2006.
William F. Jasper	"Intelligence Reform Charade: Republican Insiders Teamed Up with the Bush White House and Liberal-Left Democrats to Pass Dangerous 9/11 Commission Recommendations," *New American*, January 10, 2005.
Robert Jervis	"The Politics and Psychology of Intelligence and Intelligence Reform," *Forum*, 2006, vol. 4, no. 1. www.bepress.com/forum.
Thomas Joscelyn	"Spook Spin: A How-to Guide for Intelligence Cherry-Picking," *Weekly Standard*, September 11, 2006.
Rahul Mahajan	"WMD Commission: Yet Another Intelligence Failure," *Dissident Voice*, April 1, 2005. www.dissidentvoice.org.
Scott Michaelsen and Scott Cutler Shershow	"The Guantánamo 'Black Hole': The Law of War and the Sovereign Exception," *Middle East Report Online*, January 11, 2004. www.merip.org.

Ralph Nader and Kevin Zeese — "Another Whitehouse Whitewash: Iraq Commission Issues Report on Massive Intel Failure, but No One Is to Blame and Role of White House in Manipulating Intelligence Is Not Examined," *Dissident Voice*, March 30, 2005. www.dissidentvoice.org.

Walter Pincus — "Intelligence Redo Is Harshly Judged: A Judge Critiques 9/11 Overhaul, and Finds It Top-Heavy," *Washington Post*, March 31, 2006.

Richard A. Posner — "We Need Our Own MI5," *Washington Post*, August 15, 2006.

Scott Shane — "Year into Revamped Spying, Troubles and Some Progress," *New York Times*, February 28, 2006.

Mark Steyn — "The Death of Intelligence," *National Review*, December 27, 2004.

Robert D. Vickers Jr. — "The Intelligence Reform Quandary," *International Journal of Intelligence and Counterintelligence*, Summer 2006.

Matthew Wall — "The Bellicose Curve: Faulty Intelligence Has Catapulted the United States into War All Too Many Times Before," *Slate*, February 3, 2004. www.slate.com.

Weekly Standard, "The Agency Problem; Will the Next CIA Director Be Willing to Challenge CIA Careerists and Continue the Reforms of the Dysfunctional Bureaucracy?" May 15, 2006.

Index

THE LIBRARY WINDOW
A STORY OF THE SEEN AND THE UNSEEN

Margaret Oliphant

a *Broadview Anthology of British Literature* edition

Contributing Editor, *The Library Window*:
Annmarie S. Drury, Queens College

General Editors,
Broadview Anthology of British Literature:

Joseph Black, University of Massachusetts, Amherst
Leonard Conolly, Trent University
Kate Flint, University of Southern California
Isobel Grundy, University of Alberta
Don LePan, Broadview Press
Roy Liuzza, University of Tennessee
Jerome J. McGann, University of Virginia
Anne Lake Prescott, Barnard College
Barry V. Qualls, Rutgers University
Claire Waters, University of California, Davis

broadview press

Broadview Press – www.broadviewpress.com
Peterborough, Ontario, Canada

Founded in 1985, Broadview Press remains a wholly independent publishing house. Broadview's focus is on academic publishing: our titles are accessible to university and college students as well as scholars and general readers. With over 600 titles in print, Broadview has become a leading international publisher in the humanities, with world-wide distribution. Broadview is committed to environmentally responsible publishing and fair business practices.

The interior of this book is printed on 100% recycled paper.

How to cite this book: Broadview Anthology editions are stand-alone volumes presenting material that is also available within the stated anthology. Taken as a whole, each of these anthologies is typically the result of a highly collaborative editorial process. Where a contributing editor for a stand-alone volume is identified, however, that individual has taken primary responsibilitiy for editing the particular volume, and should be named in any citation of that volume. (For example, this book should be cited as "edited by Annmarie S. Drury"; in citing this volume there is no need to reference the general editors of *The Broadview Anthology of British Literature*.)

Library and Archives Canada Cataloguing in Publication

Title: The library window : a story of the seen and the unseen / Margaret Oliphant ; contributing
    editor, The library window: Annmarie S. Drury, Queens College.
Names: Oliphant, Mrs. (Margaret), 1828-1897, author. | Drury, Annmarie, editor.
Series: Broadview anthology of British literature edition.
Description: Series statement: A Broadview anthology of British literature edition
Identifiers: Canadiana 20190042842 | ISBN 9781554814183 (softcover)
Classification: LCC PR5113 .L53 2019 | DDC 823/.8—dc23

Broadview Press handles its own distribution in North America:
PO Box 1243, Peterborough, Ontario, K9J 7H5, Canada
555 Riverwalk Parkway, Tonawanda, NY 14150, USA
Tel: (705) 743-8990; Fax: (705) 743-8353
email: customerservice@broadviewpress.com

Distribution is handled by Eurospan Group in the UK, Europe, Central Asia, Middle East, Africa, India, Southeast Asia, Central America, and the Caribbean. Distribution is handled by Footprint Books in Australia and New Zealand.

Broadview Press acknowledges the financial
support of the Government of Canada
for our publishing activities.

Canada

Developmental Editor: Jennifer McCue
Cover Designer: Lisa Brawn
Typesetter: Alexandria Stuart

PRINTED IN CANADA

Contents

Introduction

Margaret Oliphant
1828–1897

A prolific author both of fiction and non-fiction, Margaret Oliphant wrote domestic narratives while training a keen critical gaze on her contemporaries—and, in her posthumously published *Autobiography* (1899), on her own life and work. Reading, writing, and domestic duty defined her life and were deeply intertwined. She belonged to an early generation of British women who succeeded in supporting themselves by writing, although the accomplishment was for her inseparable from personal sorrows, including the early death of her husband, that assigned her a heavy burden of financial responsibility. The six books that comprise her *Chronicles of Carlingford* (1861–76) remain among the most successful of her more than 90 novels; her *Autobiography* conveys an astute and feeling account of a life that spanned nearly the entire Victorian era; her stories of supernaturality, particularly "The Library Window," number among the most distinctive to emerge from the time; and her numerous works set in or relating to Scotland—where she lived for much of her childhood and to which she remained attached—place her among the era's most accomplished Scottish writers.

Oliphant was born in 1828 in Wallyford, Midlothian, where her father was a clerk. Her mother taught her at home, where Oliphant's girlhood pursuits included reading periodicals and writing. Her first published novel, *Passages in the Life of Mrs. Margaret Maitland* (1849), appeared when she was 21 and was well received. A few years later, in 1852, she married her cousin Francis (Frank) Oliphant, an aspiring painter who designed stained-glass windows. Their first daughter, Maggie, was born in 1853, and their second, Marjorie, the following year; but in 1855, Marjorie died, as did a newborn son. A second son was born the following year. Despite the deaths of her young children, Oliphant in her *Autobiography* describes oases of joy in the early years of her marriage. She writes of delight in the "curiously common and homely" daily experience of an evening routine: "I can see it now, the glimmer of the outside lights, the room dark, the faint reflection in the glasses, and my heart full of joy and peace—for what?—for nothing—that there was no harm anywhere, the children well above stairs and their father below."

Much would soon change. Frank Oliphant showed symptoms of tuberculosis in 1857—in the *Autobiography*, Margaret vividly describes his coughing up blood as an awful turning point in her life—and died of the disease in 1859 in Rome, where he had relocated his family in search of a curative climate; he seems never to have told his wife how grim his medical prognosis was. Margaret nursed him until his death and then, pregnant with their last child, inherited debt from his business. The terms of her responsibility had been set. She returned to Britain in 1860 and soon began to publish installments of *The Chronicles of Carlingford*. In ensuing years, she supported her daughter Maggie (who died in 1864, aged 9); her sons Cyril ("Tiddy") and Francis Romano ("Cecco"); her brother Willie, an alcoholic who never found steady employment; the children of her brother Frank after his bankruptcy, and then Frank himself. Despite her scrupulous planning on behalf of her children and wards, prospects for their independence and for their help in supporting the household continually receded. All her children died in her lifetime. The emotional toll of loss was considerable. In her *Autobiography*, Oliphant writes of experiencing her first occasion of a kind of supernatural consolation, "a great quiet and calm," as she walked in twilight in Scotland, worrying about the fortunes of Cecco and Tiddy.

Oliphant's writing career was closely linked to a single periodical, *Blackwood's Edinburgh Magazine*, an influential publication founded in 1817. She had started writing for *Blackwood's* before Frank's death. In the year of her marriage, the magazine serialized her novel *Katie Stewart* (1852), and in 1854, it published her first review article (about the English writer Mary Russell Mitford). In her widowhood, publication took on a new financial urgency. During the four decades from the mid-1850s to the mid-1890s, Oliphant contributed about six essays a year to the magazine, on a remarkably wide range of subjects; her topics included "The Life of Jesus," the social position of women, the poetry of Alfred Tennyson, and the modern identity of Scotland. Among her many non-fiction books were the three-volume *Literary History of England* (1882), the two-volume *Victorian Age of English Literature* (1892), and *A Child's History of Scotland* (1895). She was also a travel writer and translator. She often wrote about other women writers, and her perspectives illuminate the complexity of Victorian conversations among and about women of letters.

In her own literary practice, Oliphant merged domestic and writerly duties. In one sense, she had little choice but to proceed in this way after her husband's death. Yet the approach seems also to have been part of an ethos, one with roots in her girlhood. In the *Autobiography*, she speculates that one of the triumphs of her writing, from her mother's point of view, lay in how she pursued it amidst all the activity of the household, and Oliphant seems to have adopted something of that perspective as her own. Then again, she did not fail to interrogate her own choices and the nature of her literary career, wondering in her *Autobiography* with a "curious kind of self-compassion" whether she should have focused on creating a smaller number of great works, and what would have happened if she had lived more like George Eliot—been "kept, like her, in a mental greenhouse and taken care of," with few family responsibilities.

Oliphant had opinions and expressed them frankly. She liked the novels of Anthony Trollope. She thought Thomas Hardy underestimated the canniness of country girls, and she found his *Jude the Obscure* (1895) "indecent." She believed that John Stuart Mill, in *The Subjection of Women* (1869), advanced a distorted picture of marriage and a flawed theory of gender equality, and she regarded with skepticism the ideal of the New Woman. While not a Scottish nationalist, she objected to the myriad misrepresentations of Scotland in Victorian Britain.

If Oliphant was often frank in her criticisms of other writers' work, so too have others been frank in their criticisms of Oliphant—though, interestingly, those criticisms have focused more often on her approach to writing than on the writings themselves. That she maintained a high level of visibility in the literary community for so long seems sometimes in itself to have been held against her; Henry James remarked in an obituary that "no woman had ever, for half a century, had her personal 'say' so publicly and irresponsibly." Her prolific output and her need for the money she made through writing have made many readers uncomfortable, both in her own time and since—and many have concluded that the quality of her work suffered as a result of her having produced so much of it. Virginia Woolf, in *Three Guineas*, presents Oliphant's career as a lamentable instance of a wasted writing life. Oliphant, she says, "sold her brain, her very admirable brain, prostituted her culture and enslaved her intellectual liberty in order that she might earn her living and educate her children[.]"

Oliphant's acumen had alerted her to the likelihood of such complaints, and more. "It has been my fate in a long life of production to be credited chiefly with the equivocal virtue of industry, a quality so excellent in morals, so little satisfactory in art," she reflected. It is precisely this sort of critical insight, born in no small part from self-interrogation and evident in her fictional representations of domestic worlds, that commends Oliphant's work to us. Of few authors can it be said that writing was so perfectly coextensive with living. When Oliphant died in London in June 1897, she was still writing columns for *Blackwood's*, although none had been accepted for publication since the prior fall; she perceived, as she explained to her editor William Blackwood III, that something of the "lightness" they required had departed.

The Library Window

"The Library Window," one of Oliphant's last published works, appeared in *Blackwood's Edinburgh Magazine* for January 1896 as the opening piece, and was included among Oliphant's *Stories of the Seen and the Unseen* (1902), a collection of four short fictions dealing in supernaturality. The story is set mainly in Scotland, in the fictional town of St. Rule's, the name of which alludes to Saint Regulus (also known as Saint Rule), who in a legend with political significance for Scotland brought relics of Saint Andrew from Greece to the Scottish town of St. Andrews in the fourth century. Although Oliphant tended to take a dim view of literature in dialect, she makes considerable use of Scottish terms and expressions and of idiosyncratic spellings to represent Scottish pronunciation in this story.

The narrator of "The Library Window" communicates some familiarity with the customs of the town and the Scottish expressions of her Aunt Mary, in whose home she is staying. Though details of her illness are scarce, it is clear that she has come to her aunt's house to recuperate. The narrator's condition provides Oliphant with a rationale for the story's restricted viewpoint. Much of the story takes place in one room, the drawing room. (Called in earlier decades the "withdrawing-room," the Victorian drawing room was a private space connected to a more public one in a home.) In a nook of this room the narrator reads and undertakes her "usual occupation" of "doing nothing."

Oliphant's narrative incorporates a leap in time but is set primarily in the period near the summer solstice, also known as Midsummer's Day, when the days are the longest of the year. The narrator speaks of St. John's Day, the feast day of the Christian martyr St. John the Baptist, celebrated on 24 June, and thus roughly coinciding with the summer solstice. In Scotland, bonfires traditionally mark this holiday, and St. John's Eve has magical associations. The Scottish poet and novelist Sir Walter Scott (1771–1832), twice mentioned in "The Library Window," draws on those associations in his poem "The Eve of St. John" (1800). A reference in the story to "the great new buildings on the Earthen Mound in Edinburgh" may have encouraged Oliphant's first readers to place the story's events around 1859, when the Scottish National Gallery, a key part of new construction on the Mound, opened to the public.

While the narrator communicates hints as to her age, it is never made clear. What Oliphant does make clear is the difference between young and old that her narrator feels, and the link her narrator perceives between that distinction and differences in the experience of seeing.

A Note on the Text

The present text is that of the original publication in *Blackwood's Edinburgh Magazine* for January 1896, where the fiction ran under the subtitle "A Story of the Seen and the Unseen." Though spelling and punctuation have largely been modernized in accordance with the conventions of *The Broadview Anthology of British Literature*, there are some exceptions. Notably, Oliphant's pattern of using lower case when a new sentence starts after an exclamation or question has been retained. Oliphant, who was devoted to the dash, used at least three varieties in the original printing, and these have here been edited into one.

The Library Window

I

I was not aware at first of the many discussions which had gone on about that window. It was almost opposite one of the windows of the large old-fashioned drawing-room of the house in which I spent that summer, which was of so much importance in my life. Our house and the library were on opposite sides of the broad High Street of St. Rule's, which is a fine street, wide and ample, and very quiet, as strangers think who come from noisier places; but in a summer evening there is much coming and going, and the stillness is full of sound—the sound of footsteps and pleasant voices, softened by the summer air. There are even exceptional moments when it is noisy: the time of the fair, and on Saturday nights sometimes, and when there are excursion trains. Then even the softest sunny air of the evening will not smooth the harsh tones and the stumbling steps; but at these unlovely moments we shut the windows, and even I, who am so fond of that deep recess where I can take refuge from all that is going on inside, and make myself a spectator of all the varied story out of doors, withdraw from my watch-tower. To tell the truth, there never was very much going on inside. The house belonged to my aunt, to whom (she says, Thank God!) nothing ever happens. I believe that many things have happened to her in her time; but that was all over at the period of which I am speaking, and she was old, and very quiet. Her life went on in a routine never broken. She got up at the same hour every day, and did the same things in the same rotation, day by day the same. She said that this was the greatest support in the world, and that routine is a kind of salvation. It may be so; but it is a very dull salvation, and I used to feel that I would rather have incident, whatever kind of incident it might be. But then at that time I was not old, which makes all the difference.

At the time of which I speak the deep recess of the drawing-room window was a great comfort to me. Though she was an old lady (perhaps because she was so old) she was very tolerant, and had a kind of feeling for me. She never said a word, but often gave me a smile when she saw how I had built myself up, with my books and my basket of work.[1] I did very little work, I fear—now and then a few stitches when the spirit moved me, or when I had got well afloat in a dream, and was more tempted to follow it out than to read my book, as sometimes happened. At other times, and if the book were interesting, I used to get through volume after volume sitting there, paying no attention to anybody. And yet I did pay a kind of attention. Aunt Mary's old ladies came in to call, and I heard them talk, though I very seldom listened; but for all that, if they had anything to say that was interesting, it is curious how I found it in my mind afterwards, as if the air had blown it to me. They came and went, and I had the sensation of their old bonnets gliding out and in, and their dresses rustling; and now and then had to jump up and shake hands with some one who knew me, and asked after my papa and mamma. Then Aunt Mary would give me a little smile again, and I slipped back to my window. She never seemed to mind. My mother would not have let me do it, I know. She would have remembered dozens of things there were to do. She would have sent me up-stairs to fetch something which I was quite sure she did not want, or down-stairs to carry some quite unnecessary message to the housemaid. She liked to keep me running about. Perhaps that was one reason why I was so fond of Aunt Mary's drawing-room, and the deep recess of the window, and the curtain that fell half over it, and the broad window-seat where one could collect so many things without being found fault with for untidiness. Whenever we had anything the matter with us in these days, we were sent to St. Rule's to get up our strength. And this was my case at the time of which I am going to speak.

---

1 *work* Needlework.

Everybody had said, since ever I learned to speak, that I was fantastic and fanciful and dreamy, and all the other words with which a girl who may happen to like poetry, and to be fond of thinking, is so often made uncomfortable. People don't know what they mean when they say fantastic. It sounds like Madge Wildfire[1] or something of that sort. My mother thought I should always be busy, to keep nonsense out of my head. But really I was not at all fond of nonsense. I was rather serious than otherwise. I would have been no trouble to anybody if I had been left to myself. It was only that I had a sort of second-sight, and was conscious of things to which I paid no attention. Even when reading the most interesting book, the things that were being talked about blew in to me; and I heard what the people were saying in the streets as they passed under the window. Aunt Mary always said I could do two or indeed three things at once—both read and listen, and see. I am sure that I did not listen much, and seldom looked out, of set purpose—as some people do who notice what bonnets the ladies in the street have on; but I did hear what I couldn't help hearing, even when I was reading my book, and I did see all sorts of things, though often for a whole half-hour I might never lift my eyes.

This does not explain what I said at the beginning, that there were many discussions about that window. It was, and still is, the last window in the row, of the College Library, which is opposite my aunt's house in the High Street. Yet it is not exactly opposite, but a little to the west, so that I could see it best from the left side of my recess. I took it calmly for granted that it was a window like any other till I first heard the talk about it which was going on in the drawing-room. "Have you never made up your mind, Mrs. Balcarres," said old Mr. Pitmilly, "whether that window opposite is a window or no?" He said Mistress Balcarres—and he was always called Mr. Pitmilly, Morton: which was the name of his place.

---

1 *Madge Wildfire* Character in Sir Walter Scott's *Heart of Midlothian* (1818) who suffers from madness.

"I am never sure of it, to tell the truth," said Aunt Mary, "all these years."

"Bless me!" said one of the old ladies, "and what window may that be?"

Mr. Pitmilly had a way of laughing as he spoke, which did not please me; but it was true that he was not perhaps desirous of pleasing me. He said, "Oh, just the window opposite," with his laugh running through his words; "our friend can never make up her mind about it, though she has been living opposite it since—"

"You need never mind the date," said another; "the Leebrary[1] window! Dear me, what should it be but a window? up at that height it could not be a door."

"The question is," said my aunt, "if it is a real window with glass in it, or if it is merely painted, or if it once was a window, and has been built up. And the oftener people look at it, the less they are able to say."

"Let me see this window," said old Lady Carnbee, who was very active and strong-minded; and then they all came crowding upon me—three or four old ladies, very eager, and Mr. Pitmilly's white hair appearing over their heads, and my aunt sitting quiet and smiling behind.

"I mind the window very well," said Lady Carnbee; "ay: and so do more than me. But in its present appearance it is just like any other window; but has not been cleaned, I should say, in the memory of man."

"I see what ye mean," said one of the others. "It is just a very dead thing without any reflection in it; but I've seen as bad before."

"Ay, it's dead enough," said another, "but that's no rule; for these hizzies[2] of women-servants in this ill age—"

---

1   *Leebrary*   Library; here and elsewhere, Oliphant's spelling represents the pronunciation of her Scottish characters.

2   *hizzies*   Disreputable or ill-mannered women or girls, or uncouth rural women; Scottish form of "hussies."

"Nay, the women are well enough," said the softest voice of all, which was Aunt Mary's. "I will never let them risk their lives cleaning the outside of mine. And there are no women-servants in the Old Library: there is maybe something more in it than that."

They were all pressing into my recess, pressing upon me, a row of old faces, peering into something they could not understand. I had a sense in my mind how curious it was, the wall of old ladies in their old satin gowns all glazed with age, Lady Carnbee with her lace about her head. Nobody was looking at me or thinking of me; but I felt unconsciously the contrast of my youngness to their oldness, and stared at them as they stared over my head at the Library window. I had given it no attention up to this time. I was more taken up with the old ladies than with the thing they were looking at.

"The framework is all right at least, I can see that, and pented black—"

"And the panes are pented black too. It's no window, Mrs. Balcarres. It has been filled in, in the days of the window duties:[1] you will mind, Leddy Carnbee."

"Mind!" said that oldest lady. "I mind when your mother was marriet,[2] Jeanie: and that's neither the day nor yesterday. But as for the window, it's just a delusion: and that is my opinion of the matter, if you ask me."

"There's a great want of light in that muckle[3] room at the college," said another. "If it was a window, the Leebrary would have more light."

"One thing is clear," said one of the younger ones, "it cannot be a window to see through. It may be filled in or it may be built up, but it is not a window to give light."

---

1 *window duties* Tax on the windows in a building, abolished in Scotland in 1851.
2 *marriet* Married.
3 *muckle* Great, large; form of *mickle*, a word most common in Scotland and the north of England.

"And who ever heard of a window that was no[1] to see through?" Lady Carnbee said. I was fascinated by the look on her face, which was a curious scornful look as of one who knew more than she chose to say: and then my wandering fancy was caught by her hand as she held it up, throwing back the lace that dropped over it. Lady Carnbee's lace was the chief thing about her—heavy black Spanish lace with large flowers. Everything she wore was trimmed with it. A large veil of it hung over her old bonnet. But her hand coming out of this heavy lace was a curious thing to see. She had very long fingers, very taper, which had been much admired in her youth; and her hand was very white, or rather more than white, pale, bleached, and blood-less, with large blue veins standing up upon the back; and she wore some fine rings, among others a big diamond in an ugly old claw setting. They were too big for her, and were wound round and round with yellow silk to make them keep on: and this little cushion of silk, turned brown with long wearing, had twisted round so that it was more conspicuous than the jewels; while the big diamond blazed underneath in the hollow of her hand, like some dangerous thing hiding and sending out darts of light. The hand, which seemed to come almost to a point, with this strange ornament underneath, clutched at my half-terrified imagination. It too seemed to mean far more than was said. I felt as if it might clutch me with sharp claws, and the lurking, dazzling creature bite—with a sting that would go to the heart.

Presently, however, the circle of the old faces broke up, the old ladies returned to their seats, and Mr. Pitmilly, small but very erect, stood up in the midst of them, talking with mild authority like a little oracle among the ladies. Only Lady Carnbee always contradicted the neat, little, old gentleman. She gesticulated, when she talked, like a Frenchwoman, and darted forth that hand of hers with the lace hanging over it, so that I

---

1 *no* Not.

always caught a glimpse of the lurking diamond. I thought she looked like a witch among the comfortable little group which gave such attention to everything Mr. Pitmilly said.

"For my part, it is my opinion there is no window there at all," he said. "It's very like the thing that's called in scienteefic language an optical illusion. It arises generally, if I may use such a word in the presence of ladies, from a liver that is not just in the perfitt order and balance that organ demands—and then you will see things—a blue dog, I remember, was the thing in one case, and in another—"

"The man has gane gyte,"[1] said Lady Carnbee; "I mind the windows in the Auld Leebrary as long as I mind anything. Is the Leebrary itself an optical illusion too?"

"Na, na," and "No, no," said the old ladies; "a blue dogue would be a strange vagary: but the Library we have all kent[2] from our youth," said one. "And I mind when the Assemblies were held there one year when the Town Hall was building," another said.

"It is just a great divert[3] to me," said Aunt Mary: but what was strange was that she paused there, and said in a low tone, "now": and then went on again, "for whoever comes to my house, there are aye[4] discussions about that window. I have never just made up my mind about it myself. Sometimes I think it's a case of these wicked window duties, as you said, Miss Jeanie, when half the windows in our houses were blocked up to save the tax. And then, I think, it may be due to that blank kind of building like the great new buildings on the Earthen Mound in Edinburgh,[5] where the windows are just ornaments. And then whiles[6] I am

---

1 *gane gyte* Gone mad, lost his senses (Scottish).
2 *kent* Known.
3 *divert* Amusement, entertainment.
4 *aye* Always.
5 *the Earthen Mound in Edinburgh* A human-made hill between the Old Town and New Town of Edinburgh constructed between 1781 and 1830 that became a site for new buildings.
6 *whiles* Sometimes.

sure I can see the glass shining when the sun catches it in the afternoon."

"You could so easily satisfy yourself, Mrs. Balcarres, if you were to—"

"Give a laddie[1] a penny to cast a stone, and see what happens," said Lady Carnbee.

"But I am not sure that I have any desire to satisfy myself," Aunt Mary said. And then there was a stir in the room, and I had to come out from my recess and open the door for the old ladies and see them down-stairs, as they all went away following one another. Mr. Pitmilly gave his arm to Lady Carnbee, though she was always contradicting him; and so the tea-party dispersed. Aunt Mary came to the head of the stairs with her guests in an old-fashioned gracious way, while I went down with them to see that the maid was ready at the door. When I came back Aunt Mary was still standing in the recess looking out. Returning to my seat she said, with a kind of wistful look, "Well, honey: and what is your opinion?"

"I have no opinion. I was reading my book all the time," I said.

"And so you were, honey, and no' very civil; but all the same I ken[2] well you heard every word we said."

---

1 *laddie* Boy.
2 *ken* Know.

It was a night in June; dinner was long over, and had it been winter the maids would have been shutting up the house, and my Aunt Mary preparing to go upstairs to her room. But it was still clear daylight, that daylight out of which the sun has been long gone, and which has no longer any rose reflections, but all has sunk into a pearly neutral tint—a light which is daylight yet is not day. We had taken a turn in the garden after dinner, and now we had returned to what we called our usual occupations. My aunt was reading. The English post had come in, and she had got her *Times*, which was her great diversion. The *Scotsman* was her morning reading, but she liked her *Times* at night.

As for me, I too was at my usual occupation, which at that time was doing nothing. I had a book as usual, and was absorbed in it: but I was conscious of all that was going on all the same. The people strolled along the broad pavement, making remarks as they passed under the open window which came up into my story or my dream, and sometimes made me laugh. The tone and the faint sing-song, or rather chant, of the accent, which was "a wee Fifish,"[1] was novel to me, and associated with holiday, and pleasant; and sometimes they said to each other something that was amusing, and often something that suggested a whole story; but presently they began to drop off, the footsteps slackened, the voices died away. It was getting late, though the clear soft daylight went on and on. All through the lingering evening, which seemed to consist of interminable hours, long but not weary, drawn out as if the spell of the light and the outdoor life might never end, I had now and then, quite unawares, cast a glance at the mysterious window which my aunt and her friends had discussed, as I felt, though I dared not say it even to myself, rather foolishly. It caught my eye without any intention

---

1 *a wee Fifish* A little peculiar; the phrase draws on an idea that inhabitants of the Scottish region of Fife tended towards eccentricity.

on my part, as I paused, as it were, to take breath, in the flowing and current of undistinguishable thoughts and things from without and within which carried me along. First it occurred to me, with a little sensation of discovery, how absurd to say it was not a window, a living window, one to see through! Why, then, had they never *seen* it, these old folk? I saw as I looked up suddenly the faint greyness as of visible space within—a room behind, certainly—dim, as it was natural a room should be on the other side of the street—quite indefinite: yet so clear that if some one were to come to the window there would be nothing surprising in it. For certainly there was a feeling of space behind the panes which these old half-blind ladies had disputed about whether they were glass or only fictitious panes marked on the wall. How silly! when eyes that could see could make it out in a minute. It was only a greyness at present, but it was unmistakable, a space that went back into gloom, as every room does when you look into it across a street. There were no curtains to show whether it was inhabited or not; but a room—oh, as distinctly as ever room was! I was pleased with myself, but said nothing, while Aunt Mary rustled her paper, waiting for a favourable moment to announce a discovery which settled her problem at once. Then I was carried away upon the stream again, and forgot the window, till somebody threw unawares a word from the outer world, "I'm goin' hame; it'll soon be dark." Dark! what was the fool thinking of? it never would be dark if one waited out, wandering in the soft air for hours longer; and then my eyes, acquiring easily that new habit, looked across the way again.

Ah, now! nobody indeed had come to the window; and no light had been lighted, seeing it was still beautiful to read by—a still, clear, colourless light; but the room inside had certainly widened. I could see the grey space and air a little deeper, and a sort of vision, very dim, of a wall, and something against it; something dark, with the blackness that a solid article, however indistinctly seen, takes in the lighter darkness that is only space—a large, black, dark thing coming out into the grey. I looked more intently, and made sure it was a piece of furniture, either a writing-table or perhaps a large bookcase. No doubt it must be the last, since this was part of the old library. I never visited the old College Library, but I had seen such places before, and I could well imagine it to myself. How curious that for all the time these old people had looked at it, they had never seen this before!

It was more silent now, and my eyes, I suppose, had grown dim with gazing, doing my best to make it out, when suddenly Aunt Mary said, "Will you ring the bell, my dear? I must have my lamp."

"Your lamp?" I cried, "when it is still daylight." But then I gave another look at my window, and perceived with a start that the light had indeed changed: for now I saw nothing. It was still light, but there was so much change in the light that my room, with the grey space and the large shadowy bookcase, had gone out, and I saw them no more: for even a Scotch night in June, though it looks as if it would never end, does darken at the last. I had almost cried out, but checked myself, and rang the bell for Aunt Mary, and made up my mind I would say nothing till next morning, when to be sure naturally it would be more clear.

Next morning I rather think I forgot all about it—or was busy: or was more idle than usual: the two things meant nearly the same. At all events I thought no more of the window, though I still sat in my own, opposite to it, but occupied with some other fancy. Aunt Mary's visitors came as usual in the afternoon; but their talk was of other things, and for a day or two nothing at all happened to bring back my thoughts into this channel. It might be nearly a week before the subject came back, and once more it was old Lady Carnbee who set me thinking; not that she said anything upon that particular theme. But she was the last of my aunt's afternoon guests to go away, and when she rose to leave she threw up her hands, with those lively gesticulations which so many old Scotch ladies have. "My faith!" said she, "there is that bairn[1] there still like a dream. Is the creature bewitched, Mary Balcarres? and is she bound to sit there by night and by day for the rest of her days? You should mind that there's things about, uncanny for women of our blood."

I was too much startled at first to recognise that it was of me she was speaking. She was like a figure in a picture, with her pale face the colour of ashes, and the big pattern of the Spanish lace hanging half over it, and her hand held up, with the big diamond blazing at me from the inside of her uplifted palm. It was held up in surprise, but it looked as if it were raised in malediction; and the diamond threw out darts of light and glared and twinkled at me. If it had been in its right place it would not have mattered; but there, in the open of the hand! I started up, half in terror, half in wrath. And then the old lady laughed, and her hand dropped. "I've wakened you to life, and broke the spell," she said, nodding her old head at me, while the large black silk flowers of the lace waved and threatened. And she took my arm to go downstairs, laughing and bidding me be steady, and no' tremble and shake like a broken reed. "You should be as steady as a rock at your age. I was like a young tree," she said, leaning so heavily that my willowy girlish frame quivered—"I was a support to virtue, like Pamela,[2] in my time."

"Aunt Mary, Lady Carnbee is a witch!" I cried, when I came back.

"Is that what you think, honey? well: maybe she once was," said Aunt Mary, whom nothing surprised.

And it was that night once more after dinner, and after the post came in, and the *Times*, that I suddenly saw the Library window again. I had seen it every day—and noticed nothing; but tonight, still in a little tumult of mind over Lady Carnbee and her wicked diamond which wished me harm, and her lace which waved threats and warnings at me, I looked across the

---

1   *bairn*   Child.
2   *Pamela*   Heroine of Samuel Richardson's epistolary novel *Pamela: Or, Virtue Rewarded* (1740).

street, and there I saw quite plainly the room opposite, far more clear than before. I saw dimly that it must be a large room, and that the big piece of furniture against the wall was a writing-desk. That in a moment, when first my eyes rested upon it, was quite clear: a large old-fashioned escritoire,[1] standing out into the room: and I knew by the shape of it that it had a great many pigeon-holes and little drawers in the back, and a large table for writing. There was one just like it in my father's library at home. It was such a surprise to see it all so clearly that I closed my eyes, for the moment almost giddy, wondering how papa's desk could have come here—and then when I reminded myself that this was nonsense, and that there were many such writing-tables besides papa's, and looked again—lo! it had all become quite vague and indistinct as it was at first; and I saw nothing but the blank window, of which the old ladies could never be certain whether it was filled up to avoid the window-tax, or whether it had ever been a window at all.

This occupied my mind very much, and yet I did not say anything to Aunt Mary. For one thing, I rarely saw anything at all in the early part of the day; but then that is natural: you can never see into a place from outside, whether it is an empty room or a looking-glass, or people's eyes, or anything else that is mysterious, in the day. It has, I suppose, something to do with the light. But in the evening in June in Scotland—then is the time to see. For it is daylight, yet it is not day, and there is a quality in it which I cannot describe, it is so clear, as if every object was a reflection of itself.

I used to see more and more of the room as the days went on. The large escritoire stood out more and more into the space: with sometimes white glimmering things, which looked like papers, lying on it: and once or twice I was sure I saw a pile of books on the floor close to the writing-table, as if they had gilding upon them in broken specks, like old books. It was always about the

---

1 *escritoire* Writing desk.

time when the lads in the street began to call to each other that they were going home, and sometimes a shriller voice would come from one of the doors, bidding somebody to "cry upon the laddies" to come back to their suppers. That was always the time I saw best, though it was close upon the moment when the veil seemed to fall and the clear radiance became less living, and all the sounds died out of the street, and Aunt Mary said in her soft voice, "Honey! will you ring for the lamp?" She said honey as people say darling: and I think it is a prettier word.

Then finally, while I sat one evening with my book in my hand, looking straight across the street, not distracted by anything, I saw a little movement within. It was not any one visible—but everybody must know what it is to see the stir in the air, the little disturbance—you cannot tell what it is, but that it indicates some one there, even though you can see no one. Perhaps it is a shadow making just one flicker in the still place. You may look at an empty room and the furniture in it for hours, and then suddenly there will be the flicker, and you know that something has come into it. It might only be a dog or a cat; it might be, if that were possible, a bird flying across; but it is some one, something living, which is so different, so completely different, in a moment from the things that are not living. It seemed to strike quite through me, and I gave a little cry. Then Aunt Mary stirred a little, and put down the huge newspaper that almost covered her from sight, and said, "What is it, honey?" I cried "Nothing," with a little gasp, quickly, for I did not want to be disturbed just at this moment when somebody was coming! But I suppose she was not satisfied, for she got up and stood behind to see what it was, putting her hand on my shoulder. It was the softest touch in the world, but I could have flung it off angrily: for that moment everything was still again, and the place grew grey and I saw no more.

"Nothing," I repeated, but I was so vexed I could have cried. "I told you it was nothing, Aunt Mary. Don't you believe me, that you come to look—and spoil it all!"

I did not mean of course to say these last words; they were forced out of me. I was so much annoyed to see it all melt away like a dream: for it was no dream, but as real as—as real as—myself or anything I ever saw.

She gave my shoulder a little pat with her hand. "Honey," she said, "were you looking at something? Is't that? is't that?" "Is it what?" I wanted to say, shaking off her hand, but something in me stopped me: for I said nothing at all, and she went quietly back to her place. I suppose she must have rung the bell herself, for immediately I felt the soft flood of the light behind me, and the evening outside dimmed down, as it did every night, and I saw nothing more.

It was next day, I think, in the afternoon that I spoke. It was brought on by something she said about her fine work. "I get a mist before my eyes," she said; "you will have to learn my old lace stitches, honey—for I soon will not see to draw the threads."

"Oh, I hope you will keep your sight," I cried, without thinking what I was saying. I was then young and very matter-of-fact. I had not found out that one may mean something, yet not half or a hundredth part of what one seems to mean: and even then probably hoping to be contradicted if it is anyhow against one's self.

"My sight!" she said, looking up at me with a look that was almost angry; "there is no question of losing my sight—on the contrary, my eyes are very strong. I may not see to draw fine threads, but I see at a distance as well as ever I did—as well as you do."

"I did not mean any harm, Aunt Mary," I said. "I thought you said—But how can your sight be as good as ever when you are in doubt about that window? I can see into the room as clear as—" My voice wavered, for I had just looked up and across the street, and I could have sworn that there was no window at all, but only a false image of one painted on the wall.

"Ah!" she said, with a little tone of keenness and of surprise: and she half rose up, throwing down her work hastily, as if she meant to come to me: then, perhaps seeing the bewildered look on my face, she paused and hesitated—"Ay, honey!" she said, "have you got so far ben[1] as that?"

What did she mean? Of course I knew all the old Scotch phrases as well as I knew myself; but it is a comfort to take refuge in a little ignorance, and I know I pretended not to understand whenever I was put out. "I don't know what you mean by 'far ben,'" I cried out, very impatient. I don't know what might have followed, but some one just then came to call, and she could only give me a look before she went forward, putting out her hand to her visitor. It was a very soft look, but anxious, and as if she did not know what to do: and she shook her head a very little, and I thought, though there was a smile on her face, there was something wet about her eyes. I retired into my recess, and nothing more was said.

But it was very tantalising that it should fluctuate so; for sometimes I saw that room quite plain and clear—quite as clear as I could see papa's library, for example, when I shut my eyes. I compared it naturally to my father's study, because of the shape of the writing-table, which, as I tell you, was the same as his. At times I saw the papers on the table quite plain, just as I had seen his papers many a day. And the little pile of books on the floor at the foot—not ranged regularly in order, but put down one above the other, with all their angles going different ways, and a speck of the old gilding shining here and there. And then again at other times I saw nothing, absolutely nothing, and was no better than the old ladies who had peered over my head, drawing their eyelids together, and arguing that the window had been shut up because of the old long-abolished window tax, or else that it had never been a window at all. It annoyed me very much at those dull moments to feel that I too puckered up my eyelids and saw no better than they.

---

1   *ben*   Inside, within.

Aunt Mary's old ladies came and went day after day while June went on. I was to go back in July, and I felt that I should be very unwilling indeed to leave until I had quite cleared up—as I was indeed in the way of doing—the mystery of that window which changed so strangely and appeared quite a different thing, not only to different people, but to the same eyes at different times. Of course I said to myself it must simply be an effect of the light. And yet I did not quite like that explanation either, but would have been better pleased to make out to myself that it was some superiority in me which made it so clear to me, if it were only the great superiority of young eyes over old—though that was not quite enough to satisfy me, seeing it was a superiority which I shared with every little lass and lad in the street. I rather wanted, I believe, to think that there was some particular insight in me which gave clearness to my sight—which was a most impertinent assumption, but really did not mean half the harm it seems to mean when it is put down here in black and white. I had several times again, however, seen the room quite plain, and made out that it was a large room, with a great picture in a dim gilded frame hanging on the farther wall, and many other pieces of solid furniture making a blackness here and there, besides the great escritoire against the wall, which had evidently been placed near the window for the sake of the light. One thing became visible to me after another, till I almost thought I should end by being able to read the old lettering on one of the big volumes which projected from the others and caught the light; but this was all preliminary to the great event which happened about Midsummer Day—the day of St. John,[1] which was once so much thought of as a festival, but now means nothing at all in Scotland any more than any other of the saints' days: which I shall always think a great pity and loss to Scotland, whatever Aunt Mary may say.

---

1 *day of St. John* Feast day of the Christian martyr St. John the Baptist on 24 June.

3

It was about midsummer, I cannot say exactly to a day when, but near that time, when the great event happened. I had grown very well acquainted by this time with that large dim room. Not only the escritoire, which was very plain to me now, with the papers upon it, and the books at its foot, but the great picture that hung against the farther wall, and various other shadowy pieces of furniture, especially a chair which one evening I saw had been moved into the space before the escritoire,—a little change which made my heart beat, for it spoke so distinctly of some one who must have been there, the some one who had already made me start, two or three times before, by some vague shadow of him or thrill of him which made a sort of movement in the silent space: a movement which made me sure that next minute I must see something or hear something which would explain the whole—if it were not that something always hap- pened outside to stop it, at the very moment of its accomplish- ment. I had no warning this time of movement or shadow. I had been looking into the room very attentively a little while before, and had made out everything almost clearer than ever; and then had bent my attention again on my book, and read a chapter or two at a most exciting period of the story: and consequently had quite left St. Rule's, and the High Street, and the College Library, and was really in a South American forest, almost throttled by the flowery creepers, and treading softly lest I should put my foot on a scorpion or a dangerous snake. At this moment something suddenly calling my attention to the outside, I looked across, and then, with a start, sprang up, for I could not contain myself. I don't know what I said, but enough to startle the people in the room, one of whom was old Mr. Pitmilly. They all looked round upon me to ask what was the matter. And when I gave my usual answer of "Nothing," sitting down again shamefaced but very much excited, Mr. Pitmilly got up and came forward, and looked out, apparently to see what was the cause. He saw nothing, for he went back again, and I could hear him telling Aunt Mary not to be alarmed, for Missy had fallen into a doze with the heat, and had startled herself waking up, at which they all laughed: another time I could have killed him for his impertinence, but my mind was too much taken up now to pay any attention. My head was throbbing and my heart beating. I was in such high excitement, however, that to restrain myself completely, to be perfectly silent, was more easy to me then than at any other time of my life. I waited until the old gentleman had taken his seat again, and then I looked back. Yes, there he was! I had not been deceived. I knew then, when I looked across, that this was what I had been looking for all the time—that I had known he was there, and had been waiting for him, every time there was that flicker of movement in the room—him and no one else. And there at last, just as I had expected, he was. I don't know that in reality I ever had expected him, or any one: but this was what I felt when, suddenly looking into that curious dim room, I saw him there.

He was sitting in the chair, which he must have placed for himself, or which some one else in the dead of night when nobody was looking must have set for him, in front of the escritoire—with the back of his head towards me, writing. The light fell upon him from the left hand, and therefore upon his shoulders and the side of his head, which, however, was too much turned away to show anything of his face. Oh, how strange that there should be some one staring at him as I was doing, and he never to turn his head, to make a movement! If any one stood and looked at me, were I in the soundest sleep that ever was, I would wake, I would jump up, I would feel it through everything. But there he sat and never moved. You are not to suppose, though I said the light fell upon him from the left hand, that there was very much light. There never is in a room you are looking into like that across the street; but there was enough to see him by—the outline of his figure dark and solid, seated in the chair, and the fairness of his head visible faintly, a clear spot against the dimness. I saw this outline against the dim gilding of the frame of the large picture which hung on the farther wall.

I sat all the time the visitors were there, in a sort of rapture, gazing at this figure. I knew no reason why I should be so much moved. In an ordinary way, to see a student at an opposite window quietly doing his work might have interested me a little, but certainly it would not have moved me in any such way. It is always interesting to have a glimpse like this of an unknown life—to see so much and yet know so little, and to wonder, perhaps, what the man is doing, and why he never turns his head. One would go to the window—but not too close, lest he should see you and think you were spying upon him—and one would ask, Is he still there? is he writing, writing always? I wonder what he is writing! And it would be a great amusement: but no more. This was not my feeling at all in the present case. It was a sort of breathless watch, an absorption. I did not feel that I had eyes for anything else, or any room in my mind for another thought. I no longer heard, as I generally did, the stories and the wise remarks (or foolish) of Aunt Mary's old ladies or Mr. Pitmilly. I heard only a murmur behind me, the interchange of voices, one softer, one sharper; but it was not as in the time when I sat reading and heard every word, till the story in my book, and the stories they were telling (what they said almost always shaped into stories), were all mingled into each other, and the hero in the novel became somehow the hero (or more likely heroine) of them all. But I took no notice of what they were saying now. And it was not that there was anything very interesting to look at, except the fact that he was there. He did nothing to keep up the absorption of my thoughts. He moved just so much as a man will do when he is very busily writing, thinking of nothing else. There was a faint turn of his head as he went from one side to another of the page he was writing; but it appeared to be a long long page which never wanted turning. Just a little inclination when he was at the end of the line, outward, and then a little inclination inward when he began the next. That was little enough to keep one gazing. But I suppose it was the gradual course of events leading up to this, the finding out of one thing after another as the eyes got accustomed to the vague light: first the room itself, and then the writing-table, and then the other furniture, and last of all the human inhabitant who gave it all meaning. This was all so interesting that it was like a country which one had discovered. And then the extraordinary blindness of the other people who disputed among themselves whether it was a window at all! I did not, I am sure, wish to be disrespectful, and I was very fond of my Aunt Mary, and I liked Mr. Pitmilly well enough, and I was afraid of Lady Carnbee. But yet to think of the—I know I ought not to say stupidity—the blindness of them, the foolishness, the insensibility! discussing it as if a thing that your eyes could see was a thing to discuss! It would have been unkind to think it was because they were old and their faculties dimmed. It is so sad to think that the faculties grow dim, that such a woman as my Aunt Mary should fail in seeing, or hearing, or feeling, that I would not have dwelt on it for a moment, it would have seemed so cruel! And then such a clever old lady as Lady Carnbee, who could see through a millstone, people said—and Mr. Pitmilly, such an old man of the world. It did indeed bring tears to my eyes to think that all those clever people, solely by reason of being no longer young as I was, should have the simplest things shut out from them; and for all their wisdom and their knowledge be unable to see what a girl like me could see so easily. I was too much grieved for them to dwell upon that thought, and half ashamed, though perhaps half proud too, to be so much better off than they.

All those thoughts flitted through my mind as I sat and gazed across the street. And I felt there was so much going on in that room across the street! He was so absorbed in his writing, never looked up, never paused for a word, never turned round in his chair, or got up and walked about the room as my father did. Papa is a great writer, everybody says: but he would have come to the window and looked out, he would have drummed with his fingers on the pane, he would have watched a fly and helped it over a difficulty, and played with the fringe of the curtain, and done a dozen other nice, pleasant, foolish things, till the next sentence took shape. "My dear, I am waiting for a word," he would say to my mother when she looked at him, with a question why he was so idle, in her eyes; and then he would laugh, and go back again to his writing-table. But He over there never stopped at all. It was like a fascination. I could not take my eyes from him and that little scarcely perceptible movement he made, turning his head. I trembled with impatience to see him turn the page, or perhaps throw down his finished sheet on the floor, as somebody looking into a window like me once saw Sir Walter[1] do, sheet after sheet. I should have cried out if this Unknown had done that. I should not have been able to help myself, whoever had been present; and gradually I got into such a state of suspense waiting for it to be done that my head grew hot and my hands cold. And then, just when there was a little movement of his elbow, as if he were about to do this, to be called away by Aunt Mary to see Lady Carnbee to the door! I believe I did not hear her till she had called me three times, and then I stumbled up, all flushed and hot, and nearly crying. When I came out from the recess to give the old lady my arm (Mr. Pitmilly had gone away some time before), she put up her hand and stroked my cheek. "What ails the bairn?" she said; "she's fevered. You must not let her sit her lane in the window, Mary Balcarres. You and me know what comes of that." Her old fingers had a strange touch, cold like something not living, and I felt that dreadful diamond sting me on the cheek.

I do not say that this was not just a part of my excitement and suspense; and I know it is enough to make any one laugh when the excitement was all about an unknown man writing in a room on the other side of the way, and my impatience because

---

1   *Sir Walter*   Sir Walter Scott (1771–1832), Scottish author noted for his ballads and for developing the historical novel.

he never came to an end of the page. If you think I was not quite as well aware of this as any one could be! but the worst was that this dreadful old lady felt my heart beating against her arm that was within mine. "You are just in a dream," she said to me, with her old voice close at my ear as we went downstairs. "I don't know who it is about, but it's bound to be some man that is not worth it. If you were wise you would think of him no more."

"I am thinking of no man!" I said, half crying. "It is very unkind and dreadful of you to say so, Lady Carnbee. I never thought of—any man, in all my life!" I cried in a passion of indignation. The old lady clung tighter to my arm, and pressed it to her, not unkindly.

"Poor little bird," she said, "how it's strugglin' and flutterin'! I'm not saying but what it's more dangerous when it's all for a dream."

She was not at all unkind; but I was very angry and excited, and would scarcely shake that old pale hand which she put out to me from her carriage window when I had helped her in. I was angry with her, and I was afraid of the diamond, which looked up from under her finger as if it saw through and through me; and whether you believe me or not, I am certain that it stung me again—a sharp malignant prick, oh full of meaning! She never wore gloves, but only black lace mittens, through which that horrible diamond gleamed.

I ran upstairs—she had been the last to go—and Aunt Mary too had gone to get ready for dinner, for it was late. I hurried to my place, and looked across, with my heart beating more than ever. I made quite sure I should see the finished sheet lying white upon the floor. But what I gazed at was only the dim blank of that window which they said was no window. The light had changed in some wonderful way during that five minutes I had been gone, and there was nothing, nothing, not a reflection, not a glimmer. It looked exactly as they all said, the blank form of a window painted on the wall. It was too much: I sat down in my excitement and cried as if my heart would break. I felt that they had done something to it, that it was not natural, that I could not bear their unkindness—even Aunt Mary. They thought it not good for me! not good for me! and they had done something—even Aunt Mary herself—and that wicked diamond that hid itself in Lady Carnbee's hand. Of course I knew all this was ridiculous as well as you could tell me; but I was exasperated by the disappointment and the sudden stop to all my excited feelings, and I could not bear it. It was more strong than I.

I was late for dinner, and naturally there were some traces in my eyes that I had been crying when I came into the full light in the dining room, where Aunt Mary could look at me at her pleasure, and I could not run away. She said, "Honey, you have been shedding tears. I'm loth, loth that a bairn of your mother's should be made to shed tears in my house."

"I have not been made to shed tears," cried I; and then, to save myself another fit of crying, I burst out laughing and said, "I am afraid of that dreadful diamond on old Lady Carnbee's hand. It bites—I am sure it bites! Aunt Mary, look here."

"You foolish lassie,"[1] Aunt Mary said; but she looked at my cheek under the light of the lamp, and then she gave it a little pat with her soft hand. "Go away with you, you silly bairn. There is no bite; but a flushed cheek, my honey, and a wet eye. You must just read out my paper to me after dinner when the post is in: and we'll have no more thinking and no more dreaming for tonight."

"Yes, Aunt Mary," said I. But I knew what would happen; for when she opens up her *Times*, all full of the news of the world, and the speeches and things which she takes an interest in, though I cannot tell why—she forgets. And as I kept very quiet and made not a sound, she forgot tonight what she had said, and the curtain hung a little more over me than usual, and

---

1 *lassie* Girl.

I sat down in my recess as if I had been a hundred miles away. And my heart gave a great jump, as if it would have come out of my breast; for he was there. But not as he had been in the morning—I suppose the light, perhaps, was not good enough to go on with his work without a lamp or candles—for he had turned away from the table and was fronting the window, sitting leaning back in his chair, and turning his head to me. Not to me—he knew nothing about me. I thought he was not looking at anything; but with his face turned my way. My heart was in my mouth: it was so unexpected, so strange! though why it should have seemed strange I know not, for there was no communication between him and me that it should have moved me; and what could be more natural than that a man, wearied of his work, and feeling the want perhaps of more light, and yet that it was not dark enough to light a lamp, should turn round in his own chair, and rest a little, and think—perhaps of nothing at all? Papa always says he is thinking of nothing at all. He says things blow through his mind as if the doors were open, and he has no responsibility. What sort of things were blowing through this man's mind? or was he thinking, still thinking, of what he had been writing and going on with it still? The thing that troubled me most was that I could not make out his face. It is very difficult to do so when you see a person only through two windows, your own and his. I wanted very much to recognise him afterwards if I should chance to meet him in the street. If he had only stood up and moved about the room, I should have made out the rest of his figure, and then I should have known him again; or if he had only come to the window (as papa always did), then I should have seen his face clearly enough to have recognised him. But, to be sure, he did not see any need to do anything in order that I might recognise him, for he did not know I existed; and probably if he had known I was watching him, he would have been annoyed and gone away.

But he was as immovable there facing the window as he had been seated at the desk. Sometimes he made a little faint stir with a hand or a foot, and I held my breath, hoping he was about to rise from his chair—but he never did it. And with all the efforts I made I could not be sure of his face. I puckered my eyelids together as old Miss Jeanie did who was shortsighted, and I put my hands on each side of my face to concentrate the light on him: but it was all in vain. Either the face changed as I sat staring, or else it was the light that was not good enough, or I don't know what it was. His hair seemed to me light—certainly there was no dark line about his head, as there would have been had it been very dark—and I saw, where it came across the old gilt frame on the wall behind, that it must be fair: and I am almost sure he had no beard. Indeed I am sure that he had no beard, for the outline of his face was distinct enough; and the daylight was still quite clear out of doors, so that I recognised perfectly a baker's boy who was on the pavement opposite, and whom I should have known again whenever I had met him: as if it was of the least importance to recognise a baker's boy! There was one thing, however, rather curious about this boy. He had been throwing stones at something or somebody. In St. Rule's they have a great way of throwing stones at each other, and I suppose there had been a battle. I suppose also that he had one stone in his hand left over from the battle, and his roving eye took in all the incidents of the street to judge where he could throw it with most effect and mischief. But apparently he found nothing worthy of it in the street, for he suddenly turned round with a flick under his leg to show his cleverness, and aimed it straight at the window. I remarked without remarking that it struck with a hard sound and without any breaking of glass, and fell straight down on the pavement. But I took no notice of this even in my mind, so intently was I watching the figure within, which moved not nor took the slightest notice, and remained just as dimly clear, as perfectly seen, yet as indistinguishable, as before. And then the light began to fail a little, not diminishing the prospect within, but making it still less distinct than it had been.

Then I jumped up, feeling Aunt Mary's hand upon my shoulder. "Honey," she said, "I asked you twice to ring the bell; but you did not hear me."

"Oh, Aunt Mary!" I cried in great penitence, but turning again to the window in spite of myself.

"You must come away from there: you must come away from there," she said, almost as if she were angry: and then her soft voice grew softer, and she gave me a kiss: "never mind about the lamp, honey; I have rung myself, and it is coming; but, silly bairn, you must not aye be dreaming—your little head will turn."

All the answer I made, for I could scarcely speak, was to give a little wave with my hand to the window on the other side of the street.

She stood there patting me softly on the shoulder for a whole minute or more, murmuring something that sounded like, "She must go away, she must go away." Then she said, always with her hand soft on my shoulder, "Like a dream when one awaketh." And when I looked again, I saw the blank of an opaque surface and nothing more.

Aunt Mary asked me no more questions. She made me come into the room and sit in the light and read something to her. But I did not know what I was reading, for there suddenly came into my mind and took possession of it, the thud of the stone upon the window, and its descent straight down, as if from some hard substance that threw it off: though I had myself seen it strike upon the glass of the panes across the way.

4

I am afraid I continued in a state of great exaltation and commotion of mind for some time. I used to hurry through the day till the evening came, when I could watch my neighbour through the window opposite. I did not talk much to any one, and I never said a word about my own questions and wonderings. I wondered who he was, what he was doing, and why he never came till the evening (or very rarely); and I also wondered much to what house the room belonged in which he sat. It seemed to form a portion of the old College Library, as I have often said. The window was one of the line of windows which I understood lighted the large hall; but whether this room belonged to the library itself, or how its occupant gained access to it, I could not tell. I made up my mind that it must open out of the hall, and that the gentleman must be the Librarian or one of his assistants, perhaps kept busy all the day in his official duties, and only able to get to his desk and do his own private work in the evening. One has heard of so many things like that—a man who had to take up some other kind of work for his living, and then when his leisure-time came, gave it all up to something he really loved—some study or some book he was writing. My father himself at one time had been like that. He had been in the Treasury all day, and then in the evening wrote his books, which made him famous. His daughter, however little she might know of other things, could not but know that! But it discouraged me very much when somebody pointed out to me one day in the street an old gentleman who wore a wig and took a great deal of snuff, and said, That's the Librarian of the old College. It gave me a great shock for a moment; but then I remembered that an old gentleman has generally assistants, and that it must be one of them.

Gradually I became quite sure of this. There was another small window above, which twinkled very much when the sun shone, and looked a very kindly bright little window, above that dullness of the other which hid so much. I made up my mind this was the window of his other room, and that these two chambers at the end of the beautiful hall were really beautiful for him to live in, so near all the books, and so retired and quiet, that nobody knew of them. What a fine thing for him! and you could see what use he made of his good fortune as he sat there, so constant at his writing for hours together. Was it a book he was writing, or could it be perhaps Poems? This was a thought which made my heart beat; but I concluded with much regret that it could not be Poems, because no one could possibly write Poems like that, straight off, without pausing for a word or a rhyme. Had they been Poems he must have risen up, he must have paced about the room or come to the window as papa did—not that papa wrote Poems: he always said, "I am not worthy even to speak of such prevailing mysteries," shaking his head—which gave me a wonderful admiration and almost awe of a Poet, who was thus much greater even than papa. But I could not believe that a Poet could have kept still for hours and hours like that. What could it be then? perhaps it was history; that is a great thing to work at, but you would not perhaps need to move nor to stride up and down, or look out upon the sky and the wonderful light.

He did move now and then, however, though he never came to the window. Sometimes, as I have said, he would turn round in his chair and turn his face towards it, and sit there for a long time musing when the light had begun to fail, and the world was full of that strange day which was night, that light without colour, in which everything was so clearly visible, and there were no shadows. "It was between the night and the day, when the fairy folk have power." This was the after-light of the wonderful, long, long summer evening, the light without shadows. It had a spell in it, and sometimes it made me afraid: and all manner of strange thoughts seemed to come in, and I always felt that if only we had a little more vision in our eyes we might see beautiful folk walking about in it, who were not of our world. I thought most likely he saw them, from the way he sat there looking out: and this made my heart expand with the most curious sensation, as if of pride that, though I could not see, he did, and did not even require to come to the window, as I did, sitting close in the depth of the recess, with my eyes upon him, and almost seeing things through his eyes.

I was so much absorbed in these thoughts and in watching him every evening—for now he never missed an evening, but was always there—that people began to remark that I was look- ing pale and that I could not be well, for I paid no attention when they talked to me, and did not care to go out, nor to join the other girls for their tennis, nor to do anything that others did; and some said to Aunt Mary that I was quickly losing all the ground I had gained, and that she could never send me back to my mother with a white face like that. Aunt Mary had begun to look at me anxiously for some time before that, and, I am sure, held secret consultations over me, sometimes with the doctor, and sometimes with her old ladies, who thought they knew more about young girls than even the doctors. And I could hear them saying to her that I wanted diversion, that I must be diverted, and that she must take me out more, and give a party, and that when the summer visitors began to come there would perhaps be a ball or two, or Lady Carnbee would get up a picnic. "And there's my young lord coming home," said the old lady whom they called Miss Jeanie, "and I never knew the young lassie yet that would not cock up her bonnet at the sight of a young lord."

But Aunt Mary shook her head. "I would not lippen[1] much to[2] the young lord," she said. "His mother is sore set upon siller[3] for him; and my poor bit honey has no fortune to speak of. No, we must not fly so high as the young lord; but I will gladly take her about the country to see the old castles and towers. It will perhaps rouse her up a little."

---

1 *lippen* Trust, depend upon.
2 *lippen much to* Depend much upon; much trust.
3 *siller* Silver, money.

"And if that does not answer we must think of something else," the old lady said.

I heard them perhaps that day because they were talking of me, which is always so effective a way of making you hear—for latterly I had not been paying any attention to what they were saying; and I thought to myself how little they knew, and how little I cared about even the old castles and curious houses, having something else in my mind. But just about that time Mr. Pitmilly came in, who was always a friend to me, and, when he heard them talking, he managed to stop them and turn the conversation into another channel. And after a while, when the ladies were gone away, he came up to my recess, and gave a glance right over my head. And then he asked my Aunt Mary if ever she had settled her question about the window opposite, "that you thought was a window sometimes, and then not a window, and many curious things," the old gentleman said.

My Aunt Mary gave me another very wistful look; and then she said, "Indeed, Mr. Pitmilly, we are just where we were, and I am quite as unsettled as ever; and I think my niece she has taken up my views, for I see her many a time looking across and wondering, and I am not clear now what her opinion is."

"My opinion!" I said, "Aunt Mary." I could not help being a little scornful, as one is when one is very young. "I have no opinion. There is not only a window but there is a room, and I could show you—" I was going to say, "show you the gentleman who sits and writes in it," but I stopped, not knowing what they might say, and looked from one to another. "I could tell you— all the furniture that is in it," I said. And then I felt something like a flame that went over my face, and that all at once my cheeks were burning. I thought they gave a little glance at each other, but that may have been folly. "There is a great picture, in a big dim frame," I said, feeling a little breathless, "on the wall opposite the window—".

"Is there so?" said Mr. Pitmilly, with a little laugh. And he said, "Now I will tell you what we'll do. You know that there is a conversation party, or whatever they call it, in the big room tonight, and it will be all open and lighted up. And it is a handsome room, and two-three things well worth looking at. I will just step along after we have all got our dinner, and take you over to the pairty, madam—Missy and you—"

"Dear me!" said Aunt Mary. "I have not gone to a pairty for more years than I would like to say—and never once to the Library Hall." Then she gave a little shiver, and said quite low, "I could not go there."

"Then you will just begin again tonight, madam," said Mr. Pitmilly, taking no notice of this, "and a proud man will I be leading in Mistress Balcarres that was once the pride of the ball!"

"Ah, once!" said Aunt Mary, with a low little laugh and then a sigh. "And we'll not say how long ago;" and after that she made a pause, looking always at me: and then she said, "I accept your offer, and we'll put on our braws;[1] and I hope you will have no occasion to think shame of us. But why not take your dinner here?"

That was how it was settled, and the old gentleman went away to dress, looking quite pleased. But I came to Aunt Mary as soon as he was gone, and besought her not to make me go. "I like the long bonnie night and the light that lasts so long. And I cannot bear to dress up and go out, wasting it all in a stupid party. I hate parties, Aunt Mary!" I cried, "and I would far rather stay here."

"My honey," she said, taking both my hands, "I know it will maybe be a blow to you, but it's better so."

"How could it be a blow to me?" I cried; "but I would far rather not go."

"You'll just go with me, honey, just this once: it is not often I go out. You will go with me this one night, just this one night, my honey sweet."

I am sure there were tears in Aunt Mary's eyes, and she kissed me between the words. There was nothing more that I could

---

1   *braws*   Fancy clothes.

say; but how I grudged the evening! A mere party, a *conversazione* (when all the College was away, too, and nobody to make conversation!), instead of my enchanted hour at my window and the soft strange light, and the dim face looking out, which kept me wondering and wondering what was he thinking of, what was he looking for, who was he? all one wonder and mystery and question, through the long, long, slowly fading night!

It occurred to me, however, when I was dressing—though I was so sure that he would prefer his solitude to everything—that he might perhaps, it was just possible, be there. And when I thought of that, I took out my white frock—though Janet had laid out my blue one—and my little pearl necklace which I had thought was too good to wear. They were not very large pearls, but they were real pearls, and very even and lustrous though they were small; and though I did not think much of my appearance then, there must have been something about me—pale as I was but apt to colour in a moment, with my dress so white, and my pearls so white, and my hair all shadowy—perhaps, that was pleasant to look at: for even old Mr. Pitmilly had a strange look in his eyes, as if he was not only pleased but sorry too, perhaps thinking me a creature that would have troubles in this life, though I was so young and knew them not. And when Aunt Mary looked at me, there was a little quiver about her mouth. She herself had on her pretty lace and her white hair very nicely done, and looking her best. As for Mr. Pitmilly, he had a beautiful fine French cambric[1] frill to his shirt, plaited in the most minute plaits, and with a diamond pin in it which sparkled as much as Lady Carnbee's ring; but this was a fine frank kindly stone, that looked you straight in the face and sparkled, with the light dancing in it as if it were pleased to see you, and to be shining on that old gentleman's honest and faithful breast: for he had been one of Aunt Mary's lovers in their early days, and still thought there was nobody like her in the world.

---

1   *cambric*   Thin, plain cotton or linen of fine weave, usually white.

I had got into quite a happy commotion of mind by the time we set out across the street in the soft light of the evening to the Library Hall. Perhaps, after all, I should see him, and see the room which I was so well acquainted with, and find out why he sat there so constantly and never was seen abroad. I thought I might even hear what he was working at, which would be such a pleasant thing to tell papa when I went home. A friend of mine at St. Rule's—oh, far, far more busy than you ever were, papa!—and then my father would laugh as he always did, and say he was but an idler and never busy at all.

The room was all light and bright, flowers wherever flowers could be, and the long lines of the books that went along the walls on each side, lighting up wherever there was a line of gild-ing or an ornament, with a little response. It dazzled me at first all that light: but I was very eager, though I kept very quiet, looking round to see if perhaps in any corner, in the middle of any group, he would be there. I did not expect to see him among the ladies. He would not be with them,—he was too studious, too silent: but, perhaps among that circle of grey heads at the upper end of the room—perhaps—

No: I am not sure that it was not half a pleasure to me to make quite sure that there was not one whom I could take for him, who was at all like my vague image of him. No: it was absurd to think that he would be here, amid all that sound of voices, under the glare of that light. I felt a little proud to think that he was in his room as usual, doing his work, or thinking so deeply over it, as when he turned round in his chair with his face to the light.

I was thus getting a little composed and quiet in my mind, for now that the expectation of seeing him was over, though it was a disappointment, it was a satisfaction too—when Mr. Pitmilly came up to me, holding out his arm. "Now," he said, "I am going to take you to see the curiosities." I thought to myself that after I had seen them and spoken to everybody I knew, Aunt Mary would let me go home, so I went very willingly, though I did not care for the curiosities. Something, however, struck me strangely as we walked up the room. It was the air, rather fresh and strong, from an open window at the east end of the hall. How should there be a window there? I hardly saw what it meant for the first moment, but it blew in my face as if there was some meaning in it, and I felt very uneasy without seeing why.

Then there was another thing that startled me. On that side of the wall which was to the street there seemed no windows at all. A long line of bookcases filled it from end to end. I could not see what that meant either, but it confused me. I was altogether confused. I felt as if I was in a strange country, not knowing where I was going, not knowing what I might find out next. If there were no windows on the wall to the street, where was my window? My heart, which had been jumping up and calming down again all this time, gave a great leap at this, as if it would have come out of me—but I did not know what it could mean.

Then we stopped before a glass case, and Mr. Pitmilly showed me some things in it. I could not pay much attention to them. My head was going round and round. I heard his voice going on, and then myself speaking with a queer sound that was hollow in my ears; but I did not know what I was saying or what he was saying. Then he took me to the very end of the room, the east end, saying something that I caught—that I was pale, that the air would do me good. The air was blowing full on me, lifting the lace of my dress, lifting my hair, almost chilly. The window opened into the pale daylight, into the little lane that ran by the end of the building. Mr. Pitmilly went on talking, but I could not make out a word he said. Then I heard my own voice, speaking through it, though I did not seem to be aware that I was speaking. "Where is my window?—where, then, is my window?" I seemed to be saying, and I turned right round, dragging him with me, still holding his arm. As I did this my eye fell upon something at last which I knew. It was a large picture in a broad frame, hanging against the farther wall.

What did it mean? Oh, what did it mean? I turned round again to the open window at the east end, and to the daylight, the strange light without any shadow, that was all round about this lighted hall, holding it like a bubble that would burst, like something that was not real. The real place was the room I knew, in which that picture was hanging, where the writing-table was, and where he sat with his face to the light. But where was the light and the window through which it came? I think my senses must have left me. I went up to the picture which I knew, and then I walked straight across the room, always dragging Mr. Pitmilly, whose face was pale, but who did not struggle but allowed me to lead him, straight across to where the window was—where the window was not;—where there was no sign of it. "Where is my window?—where is my window?" I said. And all the time I was sure that I was in a dream, and these lights were all some theatrical illusion, and the people talking; and nothing real but the pale, pale, watching, lingering day standing by to wait until that foolish bubble should burst.

"My dear," said Mr. Pitmilly, "my dear! Mind that you are in public. Mind where you are. You must not make an outcry and frighten your Aunt Mary. Come away with me. Come away, my dear young lady! and you'll take a seat for a minute or two and compose yourself; and I'll get you an ice or a little wine." He kept patting my hand, which was on his arm, and looking at me very anxiously. "Bless me! bless me! I never thought it would have this effect," he said.

But I would not allow him to take me away in that direction. I went to the picture again and looked at it without seeing it: and then I went across the room again, with some kind of wild thought that if I insisted I should find it. "My window—my window!" I said.

There was one of the professors standing there, and he heard me. "The window!" said he. "Ah, you've been taken in with what appears outside. It was put there to be in uniformity with the window on the stair. But it never was a real window. It is just behind that bookcase. Many people are taken in by it," he said.

His voice seemed to sound from somewhere far away, and as if it would go on for ever; and the hall swam in a dazzle of shining and of noises round me; and the daylight through the open window grew greyer, waiting till it should be over, and the bubble burst.

5

It was Mr. Pitmilly who took me home; or rather it was I who took him, pushing him on a little in front of me, holding fast by his arm, not waiting for Aunt Mary or any one. We came out into the daylight again outside, I, without even a cloak or a shawl, with my bare arms, and uncovered head, and the pearls round my neck. There was a rush of the people about, and a baker's boy, that baker's boy, stood right in my way and cried, "Here's a braw ane!"[1] shouting to the others: the words struck me somehow, as his stone had struck the window, without any reason. But I did not mind the people staring, and hurried across the street, with Mr. Pitmilly half a step in advance. The door was open, and Janet standing at it, looking out to see what she could see of the ladies in their grand dresses. She gave a shriek when she saw me hurrying across the street; but I brushed past her, and pushed Mr. Pitmilly up the stairs, and took him breathless to the recess, where I threw myself down on the seat, feeling as if I could not have gone another step farther, and waved my hand across to the window. "There! there!" I cried. Ah! there it was—not that senseless mob—not the theatre and the gas, and the people all in a murmur and clang of talking. Never in all these days had I seen that room so clearly. There was a faint tone of light behind, as if it might have been a reflection

---

1 *braw ane* Fine one.

from some of those vulgar lights in the hall, and he sat against it, calm, wrapped in his thoughts, with his face turned to the window. Nobody but must have seen him. Janet could have seen him had I called her upstairs. It was like a picture, all the things I knew, and the same attitude, and the atmosphere, full of quietness, not disturbed by anything. I pulled Mr. Pitmilly's arm before I let him go,—"You see, you see!" I cried. He gave me the most bewildered look, as if he would have liked to cry. He saw nothing! I was sure of that from his eyes. He was an old man, and there was no vision in him. If I had called up Janet, she would have seen it all. "My dear!" he said. "My dear!" waving his hands in a helpless way.

"He has been there all these nights," I cried, "and I thought you could tell me who he was and what he was doing; and that he might have taken me in to that room, and showed me, that I might tell papa. Papa would understand, he would like to hear. Oh, can't you tell me what work he is doing, Mr. Pitmilly? He never lifts his head as long as the light throws a shadow, and then when it is like this he turns round and thinks, and takes a rest!"

Mr. Pitmilly was trembling, whether it was with cold or I know not what. He said, with a shake in his voice, "My dear young lady—my dear—" and then stopped and looked at me as if he were going to cry. "It's peetiful, it's peetiful," he said; and then in another voice, "I am going across there again to bring your Aunt Mary home; do you understand, my poor little thing, my—I am going to bring her home—you will be better when she is here." I was glad when he went away, as he could not see anything: and I sat alone in the dark which was not dark, but quite clear light—a light like nothing I ever saw. How clear it was in that room! not glaring like the gas and the voices, but so quiet, everything so visible, as if it were in another world. I heard a little rustle behind me, and there was Janet, standing staring at me with two big eyes wide open. She was only a little older than I was. I called to her, "Janet, come here, come here, and you will see him,—come here and see him!" impatient that she should be so shy and keep behind. "Oh, my bonnie young leddy!" she said, and burst out crying. I stamped my foot at her, in my indignation that she would not come, and she fled before me with a rustle and swing of haste, as if she were afraid. None of them, none of them! not even a girl like myself, with the sight in her eyes, would understand. I turned back again, and held out my hands to him sitting there, who was the only one that knew. "Oh," I said, "say something to me! I don't know who you are, or what you are: but you're lonely and so am I; and I only—feel for you. Say something to me!" I neither hoped that he would hear, nor expected any answer. How could he hear, with the street between us, and his window shut, and all the murmuring of the voices and the people standing about? But for one moment it seemed to me that there was only him and me in the whole world.

But I gasped with my breath, that had almost gone from me, when I saw him move in his chair! He had heard me, though I knew not how. He rose up, and I rose too, speechless, incapable of anything but this mechanical movement. He seemed to draw me as if I were a puppet moved by his will. He came forward to the window, and stood looking across at me. I was sure that he looked at me. At last he had seen me: at last he had found out that somebody, though only a girl, was watching him, looking for him, believing in him. I was in such trouble and commotion of mind and trembling, that I could not keep on my feet, but dropped kneeling on the window-seat, supporting myself against the window, feeling as if my heart were being drawn out of me. I cannot describe his face. It was all dim, yet there was a light on it: I think it must have been a smile; and as closely as I looked at him he looked at me. His hair was fair, and there was a little quiver about his lips. Then he put his hands upon the window to open it. It was stiff and hard to move; but at last he forced it open with a sound that echoed all along the street. I saw that the people heard it, and several looked up. As for me,

I put my hands together, leaning with my face against the glass, drawn to him as if I could have gone out of myself, my heart out of my bosom, my eyes out of my head. He opened the window with a noise that was heard from the West Port to the Abbey. Could any one doubt that?

And then he leaned forward out of the window, looking out. There was not one in the street but must have seen him. He looked at me first, with a little wave of his hand, as if it were a salutation—yet not exactly that either, for I thought he waved me away; and then he looked up and down in the dim shining of the ending day, first to the east, to the old Abbey towers, and then to the west, along the broad line of the street where so many people were coming and going, but so little noise, all like enchanted folk in an enchanted place. I watched him with such a melting heart, with such a deep satisfaction as words could not say; for nobody could tell me now that he was not there,—nobody could say I was dreaming any more. I watched him as if I could not breathe—my heart in my throat, my eyes upon him. He looked up and down, and then he looked back to me. I was the first, and I was the last, though it was not for long: he did know, he did see, who it was that had recognised him and sympathised with him all the time. I was in a kind of rapture, yet stupor too; my look went with his look, following it as if I were his shadow; and then suddenly he was gone, and I saw him no more.

I dropped back again upon my seat, seeking something to support me, something to lean upon. He had lifted his hand and waved it once again to me. How he went I cannot tell, nor where he went I cannot tell; but in a moment he was away, and the window standing open, and the room fading into stillness and dimness, yet so clear, with all its space, and the great picture in its gilded frame upon the wall. It gave me no pain to see him go away. My heart was so content, and I was so worn-out and satisfied—for what doubt or question could there be about him now? As I was lying back as weak as water, Aunt Mary came in behind me, and flew to me with a little rustle as if she had come on wings, and put her arms round me, and drew my head on to her breast. I had begun to cry a little, with sobs like a child. "You saw him, you saw him!" I said. To lean upon her, and feel her so soft, so kind, gave me a pleasure I cannot describe, and her arms round me, and her voice saying "Honey, my honey!"—as if she were nearly crying too. Lying there I came back to myself, quite sweetly, glad of everything. But I wanted some assurance from them that they had seen him too. I waved my hand to the window that was still standing open, and the room that was stealing away into the faint dark. "This time you saw it all?" I said, getting more eager. "My honey!" said Aunt Mary, giving me a kiss: and Mr. Pitmilly began to walk about the room with short little steps behind, as if he were out of patience. I sat straight up and put away Aunt Mary's arms. "You cannot be so blind, so blind!" I cried. "Oh, not tonight, at least not to-night!" But neither the one nor the other made any reply. I shook myself quite free, and raised myself up. And there, in the middle of the street, stood the baker's boy like a statue, staring up at the open window, with his mouth open and his face full of wonder—breathless, as if he could not believe what he saw. I darted forward, calling to him, and beckoned him to come to me. "Oh, bring him up! bring him, bring him to me!" I cried.

Mr. Pitmilly went out directly, and got the boy by the shoulder. He did not want to come. It was strange to see the little old gentleman, with his beautiful frill and his diamond pin, standing out in the street, with his hand upon the boy's shoulder, and the other boys round, all in a little crowd. And presently they came towards the house, the others all following, gaping and wondering. He came in unwilling, almost resisting, looking as if we meant him some harm. "Come away, my laddie, come and speak to the young lady," Mr. Pitmilly was saying. And Aunt Mary took my hands to keep me back. But I would not be kept back.

"Boy," I cried, "you saw it too: you saw it: tell them you saw it! It is that I want, and no more."

He looked at me as they all did, as if he thought I was mad. "What's she wantin' wi' me?" he said; and then, "I did nae harm, even if I did throw a bit stane[1] at it—and it's nae sin to throw a stane."

"You rascal!" said Mr. Pitmilly, giving him a shake; "have you been throwing stones? You'll kill somebody some of these days with your stones." The old gentleman was confused and troubled, for he did not understand what I wanted, nor anything that had happened. And then Aunt Mary, holding my hands and drawing me close to her, spoke. "Laddie," she said, "answer the young lady, like a good lad. There's no intention of finding fault with you. Answer her, my man, and then Janet will give ye your supper before you go."

"Oh speak, speak!" I cried; "answer them and tell them! you saw that window opened, and the gentleman look out and wave his hand?"

"I saw nae gentleman," he said, with his head down, "except this wee gentleman here."

"Listen, laddie," said Aunt Mary. "I saw ye standing in the middle of the street staring. What were ye looking at?"

"It was naething to make a wark[2] about. It was just yon windy[3] yonder in the library that is nae windy. And it was open—as sure's death. You may laugh if you like. Is that a' she's wantin' wi' me?"

"You are telling a pack of lies, laddie," Mr. Pitmilly said.

"I'm tellin' nae lees—it was standin' open just like ony ither windy. It's as sure's death. I couldna believe it mysel'; but it's true."

"And there it is," I cried, turning round and pointing it out to them with great triumph in my heart. But the light was all

---

1   *bit stane* Small stone.
2   *wark* Problem, issue.
3   *windy* Window.

grey, it had faded, it had changed. The window was just as it had always been, a sombre break upon the wall.

I was treated like an invalid all that evening, and taken upstairs to bed, and Aunt Mary sat up in my room the whole night through. Whenever I opened my eyes she was always sitting there close to me, watching. And there never was in all my life so strange a night. When I would talk in my excitement, she kissed me and hushed me like a child. "Oh, honey, you are not the only one!" she said. "Oh whisht, whisht,[1] bairn! I should never have let you be there!"

"Aunt Mary, Aunt Mary, you have seen him too?"

"Oh whisht, whisht, honey!" Aunt Mary said: her eyes were shining—there were tears in them. "Oh whisht, whisht! Put it out of your mind, and try to sleep. I will not speak another word," she cried.

But I had my arms round her, and my mouth at her ear. "Who is he there?—tell me that and I will ask no more—"

"Oh honey, rest, and try to sleep! It is just—how can I tell you?—a dream, a dream! Did you not hear what Lady Carnbee said?—the women of our blood—"

"What? what? Aunt Mary, oh Aunt Mary—"

"I canna[2] tell you," she cried in her agitation, "I canna tell you! How can I tell you, when I know just what you know and no more? It is a longing all your life after—it is a looking—for what never comes."

"He will come," I cried. "I shall see him tomorrow—that I know, I know!"

She kissed me and cried over me, her cheek hot and wet like mine. "My honey, try if you can sleep—try if you can sleep: and we'll wait to see what tomorrow brings."

"I have no fear," said I; and then I suppose, though it is strange to think of, I must have fallen asleep—I was so worn-out, and young, and not used to lying in my bed awake. From time to

---

1 *whisht* Keep silent.
2 *canna* Can't.

time I opened my eyes, and sometimes jumped up remember-
ing everything: but Aunt Mary was always there to soothe me,
and I lay down again in her shelter like a bird in its nest.

But I would not let them keep me in bed next day. I was in
a kind of fever, not knowing what I did. The window was quite
opaque, without the least glimmer in it, flat and blank like a
piece of wood. Never from the first day had I seen it so little
like a window. "It cannot be wondered at," I said to myself,
"that seeing it like that, and with eyes that are old, not so clear
as mine, they should think what they do." And then I smiled to
myself to think of the evening and the long light, and whether
he would look out again, or only give me a signal with his hand.
I decided I would like that best: not that he should take the
trouble to come forward and open it again, but just a turn of
his head and a wave of his hand. It would be more friendly
and show more confidence,—not as if I wanted that kind of
demonstration every night.

I did not come down in the afternoon, but kept at my own
window upstairs alone, till the tea-party should be over. I could
hear them making a great talk; and I was sure they were all in
the recess staring at the window, and laughing at the silly lassie.
Let them laugh! I felt above all that now. At dinner I was very
restless, hurrying to get it over; and I think Aunt Mary was
restless too. I doubt whether she read her *Times* when it came;
she opened it up so as to shield her, and watched from a corner.
And I settled myself in the recess, with my heart full of expectation. I wanted nothing more than to see him writing at his
table, and to turn his head and give me a little wave of his hand,
just to show that he knew I was there. I sat from half-past seven
o'clock to ten o'clock: and the daylight grew softer and softer,
till at last it was as if it was shining through a pearl, and not a
shadow to be seen. But the window all the time was as black as
night, and there was nothing, nothing there.

Well: but other nights it had been like that: he would not be
there every night only to please me. There are other things in a

man's life, a great learned man like that. I said to myself I was not disappointed. Why should I be disappointed? There had been other nights when he was not there. Aunt Mary watched me, every movement I made, her eyes shining, often wet, with a pity in them that almost made me cry: but I felt as if I were more sorry for her than for myself. And then I flung myself upon her, and asked her, again and again, what it was, and who it was, imploring her to tell me if she knew? and when she had seen him, and what had happened? and what it meant about the women of our blood? She told me that how it was she could not tell, nor when: it was just at the time it had to be; and that we all saw him in our time—"that is," she said, "the ones that are like you and me." What was it that made her and me different from the rest? but she only shook her head and would not tell me. "They say," she said, and then stopped short. "Oh, honey, try and forget all about it—if I had but known you were of that kind! They say—that once there was one that was a Scholar, and liked his books more than any lady's love. Honey, do not look at me like that. To think I should have brought all this on you!"

"He was a Scholar?" I cried.

"And one of us, that must have been a light[1] woman, not like you and me—But may be it was just in innocence; for who can tell? She waved to him and waved to him to come over: and yon ring was the token: but he would not come. But still she sat at her window and waved and waved—till at last her brothers heard of it, that were stirring[2] men; and then—oh, my honey, let us speak of it no more!"

"They killed him!" I cried, carried away. And then I grasped her with my hands, and gave her a shake, and flung away from her. "You tell me that to throw dust in my eyes—when I saw him only last night: and he as living as I am, and as young!"

"My honey, my honey!" Aunt Mary said.

---

1 *light* Frivolous.
2 *stirring* Unstable, active, prone to agitation.

After that I would not speak to her for a long time; but she kept close to me, never leaving me when she could help it, and always with that pity in her eyes. For the next night it was the same; and the third night. That third night I thought I could not bear it any longer. I would have to do something—if only I knew what to do! If it would ever get dark, quite dark, there might be something to be done. I had wild dreams of stealing out of the house and getting a ladder, and mounting up to try if I could not open that window, in the middle of the night—if perhaps I could get the baker's boy to help me; and then my mind got into a whirl, and it was as if I had done it; and I could almost see the boy put the ladder to the window, and hear him cry out that there was nothing there. Oh, how slow it was, the night! and how light it was, and everything so clear—no darkness to cover you, no shadow, whether on one side of the street or on the other side! I could not sleep, though I was forced to go to bed. And in the deep midnight, when it is dark dark in every other place, I slipped very softly downstairs, though there was one board on the landing-place that creaked—and opened the door and stepped out. There was not a soul to be seen, up or down, from the Abbey to the West Port: and the trees stood like ghosts, and the silence was terrible, and everything as clear as day. You don't know what silence is till you find it in the light like that, not morning but night, no sunrising, no shadow, but everything as clear as the day.

It did not make any difference as the slow minutes went on: one o'clock, two o'clock. How strange it was to hear the clocks striking in that dead light when there was nobody to hear them! But it made no difference. The window was quite blank; even the marking of the panes seemed to have melted away. I stole up again after a long time, through the silent house, in the clear light, cold and trembling, with despair in my heart.

I am sure Aunt Mary must have watched and seen me coming back, for after a while I heard faint sounds in the house; and very early, when there had come a little sunshine into the air, she came to my bedside with a cup of tea in her hand; and she, too, was looking like a ghost. "Are you warm, honey—are you comfortable?" she said. "It doesn't matter," said I. I did not feel as if anything mattered; unless if one could get into the dark somewhere—the soft, deep dark that would cover you over and hide you—but I could not tell from what. The dreadful thing was that there was nothing, nothing to look for, nothing to hide from—only the silence and the light.

That day my mother came and took me home. I had not heard she was coming; she arrived quite unexpectedly, and said she had no time to stay, but must start the same evening so as to be in London next day, papa having settled to go abroad. At first I had a wild thought I would not go. But how can a girl say I will not, when her mother has come for her, and there is no reason, no reason in the world, to resist, and no right! I had to go, whatever I might wish or any one might say. Aunt Mary's dear eyes were wet; she went about the house drying them quietly with her handkerchief, but she always said, "It is the best thing for you, honey—the best thing for you!" Oh, how I hated to hear it said that it was the best thing, as if anything mattered, one more than another! The old ladies were all there in the afternoon, Lady Carnbee looking at me from under her black lace, and the diamond lurking, sending out darts from under her finger. She patted me on the shoulder, and told me to be a good bairn. "And never lippen to what you see from the window," she said. "The eye is deceitful as well as the heart." She kept patting me on the shoulder, and I felt again as if that sharp wicked stone stung me. Was that what Aunt Mary meant when she said yon ring was the token? I thought afterwards I saw the mark on my shoulder. You will say why? How can I tell why? If I had known, I should have been contented, and it would not have mattered any more.

I never went back to St. Rule's, and for years of my life I never again looked out of a window when any other window was in sight. You ask me did I ever see him again? I cannot tell: the imagination is a great deceiver, as Lady Carnbee said: and if he stayed there so long, only to punish the race that had wronged him, why should I ever have seen him again? for I had received my share. But who can tell what happens in a heart that often, often, and so long as that, comes back to do its errand? If it was he whom I have seen again, the anger is gone from him, and he means good and no longer harm to the house of the woman that loved him. I have seen his face looking at me from a crowd. There was one time when I came home a widow from India, very sad, with my little children: I am certain I saw him there among all the people coming to welcome their friends. There was nobody to welcome me,—for I was not expected: and very sad was I, without a face I knew: when all at once I saw him, and he waved his hand to me. My heart leaped up again: I had forgotten who he was, but only that it was a face I knew, and I landed almost cheerfully, thinking here was some one who would help me. But he had disappeared, as he did from the window, with that one wave of his hand.

And again I was reminded of it all when old Lady Carnbee died—an old, old woman—and it was found in her will that she had left me that diamond ring. I am afraid of it still. It is locked up in an old sandal-wood box in the lumber-room in the little old country house which belongs to me, but where I never live. If any one would steal it, it would be a relief to my mind. Yet I never knew what Aunt Mary meant when she said, "Yon ring was the token," nor what it could have to do with that strange window in the old College Library of St. Rule's.

In Context

from Sir David Brewster, *Letters on Natural Magic, Addressed to Sir Walter Scott* (1832)

The Scottish scientist and inventor David Brewster (1781–1868) trained for a career in the ministry but early on became captivated by experimental investigations, especially inquiries into light and optics. In his *Letters on Natural Magic, Addressed to Sir Walter Scott*, reprinted often in the nineteenth century (the following text comes from an edition of 1883), Brewster explores the scientific causes of phenomena often interpreted as supernatural. He devotes his second letter to the workings of the eye and to the character of optical illusions, a popular fascination in the Victorian era. In this passage, he discusses the anatomy of the eye and considers what it means for the eye to see what may not be present, and how twilight may play a role in such vision.

from Letter 2

Of all the organs by which we acquire a knowledge of external nature the eye is the most remarkable and the most important. By our other senses the information we obtain is comparatively limited. The touch and the taste extend no further than the surface of our own bodies. The sense of smell is exercised within a very narrow sphere, and that of recognizing sounds is limited to the distance at which we hear the bursting of a meteor and the crash of a thunderbolt. But the eye enjoys a boundless range of observation. It takes cognizance not only of other worlds belonging to the solar system, but of other systems of worlds infinitely removed into the immensity of space; and when aided by the telescope, the invention of human wisdom, it is able to discover the forms, the phenomena, and the movements of bodies whose distance is as inexpressible in language as it is inconceivable in thought.

While the human eye has been admired by ordinary observers for the beauty of its form, the power of its movements, and the variety of its expression, it has excited the wonder of philosophers by the exquisite mechanism of its interior, and its singular adaptation to the variety of purposes which it has to serve. The eyeball is nearly globular, and is about an inch in diameter. It is formed externally by a tough opaque membrane called the *sclerotic* coat, which forms the white of the eye, with the exception of a small circular portion in front called the *cornea*. This portion is perfectly transparent, and so tough in its nature as to afford a powerful resistance to external injury. Immediately within the cornea, and in contact with it, is the *aqueous* humour, a clear fluid, which occupies only a small part of the front of the eye. Within this humour is the *iris*, a circular membrane with a hole in its centre called the pupil. The colour of the eye resides in this membrane, which has the curious property of contracting and expanding so as to diminish or enlarge the pupil,—an effect which human ingenuity has not been able even to imitate. Behind the iris is suspended the *crystalline* lens in a fine transparent capsule or bag of the same form with itself. It is then succeeded by the *vitreous humour*, which resembles the transparent white of an egg, and fills up the rest of the eye. Behind the vitreous humour, there is spread out on the inside of the eyeball a fine delicate membrane, called the *retina*, which is an expansion of the *optic nerve*, entering the back of the eye and communicating with the brain.

A perspective view and horizontal section of the left eye, shown in the annexed figure, will convey a popular[1] idea of its structure. It is, as it were, a small camera obscura,[2] by means of which the pictures of external objects are painted on the retina, and in a way of which we are ignorant, it conveys the impression of them to the brain.

---

1   *popular*   Non-specialist's.

2   *camera obscura*   Precursor to the camera, a device consisting of a dark box with a lens or pinhole on one side, enabling projection of an image of external objects onto one of the device's dark surfaces.

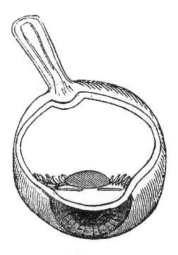

Figure 1.

This wonderful organ may be considered as the sentinel which guards the pass between the worlds of matter and of spirit, and through which all their communications are interchanged. The optic nerve is the channel by which the mind peruses the handwriting of Nature on the retina, and through which it transfers to that material tablet its decisions and its creations. The eye is consequently the principal seat of the supernatural. When the indications of the marvellous are addressed to us through the ear, the mind may be startled without being deceived, and reason may succeed in suggesting some probable source of the illusion by which we have been alarmed: but when the eye in solitude sees before it the forms of life, fresh in their colours and vivid in their outline; when distant or departed friends are suddenly presented to its view; when visible bodies disappear and reappear without any intelligible cause; and when it beholds objects, whether real or imaginary, for whose presence no cause can be assigned, the conviction of supernatural agency becomes under ordinary circumstances unavoidable.

Hence it is not only an amusing but an useful occupation to acquire a knowledge of those causes which are capable of producing so strange a belief, whether it arises from the delusions which the mind practises upon itself, or from the dexterity and science of others. I shall therefore proceed to explain those illusions which have their origin in the eye, whether they are general, or only occasionally exhibited in particular persons, and under particular circumstances. ...

Effects still more remarkable are produced in the eye when it views objects that are difficult to be seen from the small degree of light with which they happen to be illuminated. The imperfect view which we obtain of such objects forces us to fix the eye more steadily upon them; but the more exertion we make to ascertain what they are, the greater difficulties do we encounter to accomplish our object. The eye is actually thrown into a state of the most painful agitation, the object will swell and contract, and partly disappear, and it will again become visible when the eye has recovered from the delirium into which it has been thrown. This phenomenon may be most distinctly seen when the objects in a room are illuminated with the feeble gleam of a fire almost extinguished; but it may be observed in daylight by the sportsman when he endeavours to mark upon the monotonous heath the particular spot where moor-game has alighted. Availing himself of the slightest difference of tint in the adjacent heath, he keeps his eye steadily fixed on it as he advances, but whenever the contrast of illumination is feeble, he will invariably lose sight of his mark and if the retina is capable of taking it up, it is only to lose it a second time.

This illusion is likely to be most efficacious in the dark, when there is just sufficient light to render white objects faintly visible, and to persons who are either timid or credulous must prove a frequent source of alarm. Its influence too is greatly aided by another condition of the eye, into which it is thrown during partial darkness. The pupil expands nearly to the whole width of the iris in order to collect the feeble light which prevails; but it is demonstrable that in this state the eye cannot accommodate itself to see near objects distinctly, so that the forms of persons and things actually become more shadowy and confused when they come within the very distance at which we count upon obtaining the best view of them. These affections[1] of the eye are, we are persuaded, very frequent causes of a particular class of apparitions which are seen at night by the young and the ignorant. The spectres which are conjured up are always *white*, because no other colour can be seen, and they are either formed out of inanimate objects which reflect more light than others around them, or of animals or human beings whose colour or change of place renders them more visible in the dark. When the eye dimly descries an inanimate object whose different parts reflect different degrees of light, its brighter parts may enable the spectator to keep up a continued view of it; but the disappearance and reappearance of its fainter parts, and the change of shape which ensues, will necessarily give it the semblance of a living form, and if it occupies a position which is unapproachable, and where animate objects cannot find their way, the mind will soon transfer to it a supernatural existence. In like manner a human figure shadowed forth in a feeble twilight may undergo similar changes, and after being distinctly seen while it is in a situation favourable for receiving and reflecting light, it may suddenly disappear in a position fully before, and within the reach of, the observer's eye; and if this evanescence takes place in a path or road where there was no side-way by which the figure could escape, it is not easy for an ordinary mind to efface the impression which it cannot fail to receive. Under such circumstances, we never think of distrusting an organ which we have never found to deceive us; and the truth of the maxim that "seeing is believing," is too universally admitted, and too deeply rooted in our nature to admit on any occasion of a single exception.

---

1 *affections* Qualities, inclinations.

In these observations we have supposed that the spectator bears along with him no fears or prejudices, and is a faithful interpreter of the phenomena presented to his senses; but if he is himself a believer in apparitions, and unwilling to receive an ocular demonstration of their reality, it is not difficult to conceive the picture which will be drawn when external objects are distorted and caricatured by the imperfect indications of his senses, and coloured with all the vivid hues of the imagination. ...

from Margaret Oliphant, "Scotland and Her Accusers" (1861)

In an essay published in the September 1861 number of *Blackwood's*, Oliphant took up the subject of Scottish identity, responding to perspectives on Scottish history and culture that troubled her. One was the fervent nationalism of the poet and classical scholar John Stuart Blackie (1809–95), a professor of Greek at the University of Edinburgh whose *Lyric Poems* (1860) had recently been published. Another perspective, more objectionable to Oliphant, was that of the historian Henry Thomas Buckle (1821–62), whose *History of Civilization in England* (vol. 1 1857; vol. 2 1861) disparaged Scotland and its people. In this early section of the essay, she considers common characterizations of Scotland, and their limitations.

… Three pictures side by side present themselves before us, each claiming to be an authentic portrait of the face which we know so well. The first is drawn in light and sketchy outlines, with features caricatured, indeed, but recognisable. Here it is an eager, alert, and energetic figure, which looms red and strong through the traditionary mists; a figure rich in traditionary features, high cheek-boned, red-haired—covetous but enterprising, prompt, shrewd, selfish, clear-sighted, fortunate—always on the outlook for opportunities of personal advantage, generally most successful in seizing them—unscrupulous, but not unkind, ready to lend a hand to another Scot, or even, no Scot being in the way, to any fit follower—always steady, cool, pertinacious; a figure so distinct and well defined that it does credit to the popular imagination. Emotions are few in this development of character, and graces do not exist. It has no enthusiasms, no humour, in its composition. In face of a joke it stares blankly, but in sight of an investment or a promising occupation becomes immediately acute. It goes out upon the world raw-boned (whatever that may be) and hungry, and returns, weighted with money, or covered with decorations, amid sneers and plaudits. Such is the Scotch character, as renowned in contemporary journals and periodical literature. Of this native stuff, all unadorned and unsusceptible of adornment, Generals and Chancellors are made. And when they die, it is recorded of them how, being Scotch, they had but to set out to conquer Fortune, when fortune flew into their arms.

The next portrait is very different. The air trembles with sighs more vulgar but scarce less dreadful than those of the *Inferno*.[1] The heavens are dark above, and the earth is desolate below. Through the murky atmosphere appears a frantic figure in a pulpit, uttering wild denunciations; underneath, a cowed and wretched assemblage sits groaning. A melancholy ascetic sits in grim self-inquisition in the front of the picture, frowning at earth and heaven; for him no sun lights the world, no music breathes, no beauty exists. Neither love nor human kindness can find entrance into his sullen soul; enterprise, activity, and thought are as foreign to him as love and charity. Too timorous to move a step out of that horrific gloom, he sits amusing himself with hideous speculations upon the future damnation of his neighbours; and if a gleam of ghastly comfort ever enters his heart, it is contained in a reflection of that thanksgiving of the Pharisee,[2] that he is not as other men. Black against the pale unwholesome sky he rises grimly, an apparition wonderful to behold. This is the Scotland which, with much elaboration, Mr. Buckle, who professes to be at once the most unimpassioned and profound of historians, has just communicated to the world.

And beside this extraordinary presentment[3] rises another scarcely less extraordinary. The scene again is changed. On the top of the softest wooded height, fair, rich, and serene, a shrill outcry and Babel of tongues startles the tender mists. There,

---

1   *the Inferno*   First book of the fourteenth-century epic Italian poem *The Divine Comedy* by Dante Alighieri (1265–1321) that tells of the poet's journey through Hell.
2   *Pharisee*   I.e., hypocrite.
3   *presentment*   Representation.

all shrill and furious, stands a rampant nationality, grinning desperate in hot spite and malice against her wedded part-ner[1]—living on the recollection of certain passages of arms between them six or seven centuries ago, and, with all the wild tricks of a mountebank,[2] made doubly absurd by the fact that mountebankism is exotic to the soil and never looks natural, thrusting her infuriate fist into the calm, puzzled face of the companion of her days. This is Professor Blackie's idea upon the subject. The three pictures range together all strange and unlike, with nothing common to them but their name. The Scotch are nation of adventurers, bound upon getting all the good things that come within their reach, and not at all over-scrupulous as to the means by which they must obtain them. The Scotch are a nation of the sourest ascetics—ascetics of an asceticism unsoftened even by those gleams of light which made monks and convents tolerable; mean, vulgar, and sullen in their self-mortification. The Scotch are a nation of furious patriots, defying all the world, and especially England, to prove them anything but perfection. You can take your choice, for the field is all before you. Scotland has lived as long a lifetime as most nations, and done such work as she had to do with tolerable effectiveness. What she has done is written in various histories; what she is, does not appear very hard to come at, seeing the doors of her house are open, and travellers come and go without let or hindrance; yet some certain inherent mystery must surely exist in the country of which so many conflicting representa-tions are given to the world. ...

---

1   *her wedded partner*   England, following the Acts of Union (1707).
2   *mountebank*   Itinerant charlatan selling supposed medicines and remedies, often using entertainments to attract a crowd of potential customers; swindler.

from Margaret Oliphant, "The Sisters Brontë," in
Women Novelists of Queen Victoria's Reign (1897)

> For a volume celebrating the long reign of Queen Victoria, Oliphant
> and other women of letters assessed the work of women novelists who
> had written during Victoria's rule and who had already died. Oliphant
> contributed the chapter on the Brontë sisters. In her account of the
> Brontës, she praises the skill with which Charlotte Brontë (1816–55)
> depicts feminine longing and mentions broader debates associated
> with such representation.

… There was however one subject of less absolute realism which
Charlotte Brontë had at her command, having experienced in
her own person and seen her nearest friends under the experience, of that solitude and longing of women, of which she
has made so remarkable an exposition. The long silence of life
without an adventure or a change, the forlorn gaze out at windows which never show any one coming who can rouse the
slightest interest in the mind, the endless years and days which
pass and pass, carrying away the bloom, extinguishing the lights
of youth, bringing a dreary middle age before which the very
soul shrinks, while yet the sufferer feels how strong is the current of life in her own veins, and how capable she is of all the
active duties of existence—this was the essence and soul of the
existence she knew best. Was there no help for it? Must the
women wait and long and see their lives thrown away, and have
no power to save themselves?

The position in itself so tragic is one which can scarcely be
expressed without calling forth an inevitable ridicule, a laugh
at the best, more often a sneer at the women whose desire for
a husband is thus betrayed. Shirley and Caroline Helston[1]
both cried out for that husband with an indignation, a fire and
impatience, a sense of wrong and injury, which stopped the
laugh for the moment. It might be ludicrous but it was horribly

---

1 *Shirley and Caroline Helston*   Characters in Charlotte Brontë's novel *Shirley* (1849).

genuine and true. Note there was nothing sensual about these young women. It was life they wanted; they knew nothing of the grosser thoughts which the world with its jeers attributes to them: of such thoughts they were unconscious in a primitive innocence which perhaps only women understand. They wanted their life, their place in the world, the rightful share of women in the scheme of nature. Why did not it come to them? The old patience in which women have lived for all the centuries fails now and again in a keen moment of energy when some one arises who sees no reason why she should endure this forced inaction, or why she should invent for herself inferior ways of working and give up her birthright, which is to carry on the world.

The reader was horrified with these sentiments from the lips of young women. The women were half ashamed, yet more than half stirred and excited by the outcry, which was true enough if indelicate. All very well to talk of women working for their living, finding new channels for themselves, establishing their independence. How much have we said of all that, endeavouring to persuade ourselves! Charlotte Brontë had the courage of her opinions. It was not education nor a trade that her women wanted. It was not a living but their share in life, a much more legitimate object had that been the way to secure it, or had there been any way to secure it in England. Miss Brontë herself said correct things about the protection which a trade is to a woman, keeping her from a mercenary marriage; but this was not in the least the way of her heroines. They wanted to be happy, no doubt, but above all things they wanted their share in life—to have their position by the side of men, which alone confers a natural equality, to have their shoulder to the wheel, their hands on the reins of common life, to build up the world, and link the generations each to each. ...

This longing which she expressed with so much vehemence and some poetic fervour as the burden of the lives of Shirley and her friends has been the keynote of a great deal that has followed—the revolts and rebellions, the wild notions about marriage, the "Sex Problem,"[1] and a great deal more. From that first point to the prevailing discussion of all the questions involved is a long way; but it is a matter of logical progression, and when once the primary matter is opened, every enlargement of the subject may be taken as a thing to be expected. Charlotte Brontë was in herself the embodiment of all old-fashioned restrictions. She was proper, she was prim, her life was hedged in by all the little rules which bind the primitive woman. But when she left her little recluse behind and rushed into the world of imagination her exposure of the bondage in which she sat with all her sisters was far more daring than if she had been a woman of many experiences and knew what she was speaking of. She did know the longing, the discontent, the universal contradiction and contrariety which is involved in that condition of unfulfilment to which so many grey and undeveloped lives are condemned. For her and her class, which did not speak of it, everything depended upon whether the woman married or did not marry. Their thoughts were thus artificially fixed to one point in the horizon, but their ambition was neither ignoble nor unclean. It was bold, indeed, in proportion to its almost ridiculous innocence, and want of perception of any grosser side. Their share in life, their part in the mutual building of the house, was what they sought. But the seed she thus sowed has come to many growths which would have appalled Charlotte Brontë. Those who took their first inspiration from this cry of hers, have quite forgotten what it was she wanted, which was not emancipation but an extended duty. But while it would be very unjust to blame her for the vagaries that have followed and to which nothing could be less desirable than any building of the house or growth of the race, any responsibility or service— we must still believe that it was she who drew the curtain first aside and opened the gates to imps of evil meaning, polluting and profaning the domestic hearth.

---

1   *the "Sex Problem"*   Broadly, the question of women's place in society, including the question of whether or to what extent marriage should be understood as part of women's fulfillment.

from J.E. [Jane Ellen] Panton, *A Gentlewoman's Home: The Whole Art of Building, Furnishing, and Beautifying the Home* (1896)

The opening of the first free public libraries in Britain from 1850 offered a growing population of readers better access to books, but the long-established image of the private library as a site of privilege and as a pleasurable aspect of a well-appointed home persisted. The English writer Jane Ellen Panton (1847–1923), who also authored poems, novels, and a memoir, created detailed guidebooks on domestic life. In *A Gentlewoman's Home*, Panton devotes much attention to the library, which she suggests may have various identities depending on the gender, age, and activities of its primary occupant and which she says should be carefully furnished and decorated. Through its interior design and through the books it contains—chosen, Panton instructs, because their contents are meaningful to their owner, and not based on rarity or other kinds of value—a library becomes a form of expression. Consideration of the library leads Panton to reflect on whether and to what degree the reading of young people, especially girls, should be restricted.

from Chapter 9, "Libraries"

…The window curtains in this room should be of printed velveteen in blue, lined with dark blue and bound with tufted guimpe.[1] The top lights of the Caldecott windows[2] should be in leaded glass rendered almost opaque. There should be no muslin curtains, and the thick ones should hang simply down the wooden slats between each frame. Five curtains would be required for the side window, and should just touch the window-sill. These would draw easily at night or when sunny, but

---

1 *guimpe* Gimp: that is, a trimming of silk, cotton, or another fabric twisted or braided.
2 *Caldecott windows* For Panton, a style of window reminiscent of the work of the British artist and illustrator Randolph Caldecott (1846–86), with an immovable upper section of stained glass and a clear lower section that could be opened inwards or outwards.

any great sunshine can only be kept out, should we desire to deprive ourselves of God's best gift to man, by outside jalousies,[1] as I have explained so often that I cannot think it necessary to repeat it any more. If deep enough, great blue jars for yellow flowers should be placed upon it, and just in front should stand a good square real writing-table, wide enough for the two ends to serve as tables should it be necessary, so that three people could write notes at once, and chairs should be put one at each end and one in the centre, and on the table should be three flat blotting-books in red leather cases inscribed with the name of the house and owner; but I do not advise pens being left here, though of course there should be three inkstands and plenty of writing-paper and envelopes in a top drawer, but nothing else should be there at all, save, perhaps, a Salviati glass[2] full of flowers, while a big waste-paper basket should not be forgotten, nor should string, scissors, and sealing-wax, in the same drawer as the writing paper. This drawer should be divided into spaces inside by slight wooden partitions.

Beyond the writing-table the shelves that would stretch from there to the dais should be arranged precisely as those which come from the drawing-room door to the window, and then the dais itself would be the subject for treatment. Of course the curtains and windows should be of the same nature here as those in the first one, and the window seat, which must be low and broad always, should be covered in some strong material, such as Eastern saddle-bags, in which blue largely predominates, mixed judiciously with red and yellow; and on the dais itself could be arranged a couple of good chairs and small tables for the day's and week's papers, or even more chairs and tables of course as space permitted, and on one side could be a movable flap for writing. This could let up and down as required, were

---

1   *jalousies*   Blinds or shutters with tilted slats that admit air and light while keeping out precipitation and direct sun.

2   *Salviati glass*   Glass from the Salviati family of glassmakers, who had offices in Venice and London.

space a great object, but if not, it would be much better to place here one of Hewetson's charming screen desks[1] and a light chair before it. It would be a pleasant place to write in, and a wife occupied here would not interfere in the least with a husband's occupations at the other window.

In the centre of the room should be a square library table and some more chairs; the table should be provided with reading stands for heavy books, and with movable and shaded reading lamps, and indeed great care must be taken with the arrangement of light in this room; albeit, I should cling to my idea of a softly diffused general light, resembling sunshine, diffused through the pierced and moulded plaster ceiling, which should be simply coloured real ivory, as should any cornice round the room that may be employed to finish it off. I am specially fond of a coved cornice in a library. If one is used the coving can be filled in with embossed leather or Japanese paper, not the same one by any means that is used on the walls, but something entirely different, or else it can be raised plaster-work. If plaster, this too must be simply tinted ivory, and must not be coloured in any way; albeit, if we are quite sure of ourselves and our taste we may sparingly and most carefully introduce here just the very merest suspicion of gold.

There is yet a small portion in the room to be arranged for before we suggest another scheme of colour, which is after all the most important of all, and that is the long unbroken space of wall from the door into the hall until we reach the dais, and over this we shall have to be very careful. I think we should obtain an admirable corner if we place between the dais and the long piece of wall a really comfortable seat, which however must not be a fixture, but which can be drawn out from the wall for cleaning purposes. The back should be high enough to enable a tall person to rest his or her head against it in comfort, and the arms should be wide, as should be the seat, which should also be

---

1 *Hewetson's charming screen desks* A style of desk from the Hewetson furniture store, a well-known firm located on London's Tottenham Court Road.

low and most comfortable, and then above that shelves could be placed, divided properly by curtains and niches. Here, if we are unable to obtain our diffused light we must have either a hanging lamp from an arm fixed in the corner itself and depending from a chain, or else a cluster of electric lights in Salviati glass receivers. Then the wall beyond should be filled entirely by more shelves, though I should be inclined to break the long line in the centre by a species of pediment enshrining a piece of china. If this were impossible a tall vase should be placed there to make a centre, otherwise the line will be too long and unbroken to be quite successful.

On this side of the wall I should be inclined to have rather a bold innovation, and should leave sufficient space in our woodwork for these panels to be filled in with family portraits. These should be no higher than the "line" at the Royal Academy,[1] i.e., the base of the frame should be no higher than three feet from the floor. At the same time, the centre panel should be a couple of inches lower than those on the sides, or else we shall fall into the error of having once more too much of an unbroken line to contemplate. Land or seascapes could be introduced to advantage instead of the portraits, but the portraits are to be preferred. Other pictures are not required. The ideal library is sacred to books, to writing, to reading, therefore all other matters, including brainless chatter, should be left outside. "All ye who enter here abandon frivolity" should be the unwritten motto sacred to this room at least, if to no other in the house.

There is one thing we have forgotten, and that is the floor covering; and here I should have the silent wood blocks used for the flooring of all too few churches. These no doubt could be stained dark, and so made unobtrusive in colouring. But they must not be polished, and the rugs used must be large and square and thick to deaden sound. Indeed noise must be "taboo," here, as indeed it ought to be in the world at large, but never will

---

1   *the Royal Academy*   The Royal Academy of Arts in London, an institution dedicated to the visual arts, and the site of frequent exhibitions.

be, I am afraid. I relegate in my own house all newspapers to some other spot, any other spot than the library, because of the fearful rustling their leaves make, and because people will discuss politics and the questions of the day remorselessly, if their favourite and maybe rival journals are within their reach in what should most emphatically be a veritable temple of the most profound silence.

One word more before we leave the oaken scheme and speak of yet another. Remember all chairs and tables should be of the same old wood, and that nowhere must they be unduly heavy; moreover, if possible, we should procure one of those immensely useful bookcases which revolve, and which are now universal, but of which only two specimens were at one time in England, and I possessed one, given me with a delightful volume of contraband poetry from America, where they were first born and thought of, many, many years ago. These can be made of oak, I know, and one of these could stand five or six feet in front, or at one side of the cosy seat of which I have already written.

If the house should be in any way surrounded by trees, and so darkened in a manner I for one cannot bear, for I have a standing quarrel with all trees near enough to a dwelling house to keep away my beloved air and light, then a most beautiful effect can be obtained by a judicious arrangement of ivory enamelled shelves, red and gold leather paper, red and gold old Derby china,[1] red lustre tiles for the hearth, and either blue or yellow plain curtains. In this case the library should bedowered with a noble collection of admirable books in calf and gold tooling. Admirable, by the way, because of their contents merely, and because they are tried friends and true companions, and not because of their age (for though age of course is always a claim on one's esteem, it is not invariably or necessarily on one's affections), nor because they are unique in themselves or merely first

---

1 *Derby china* China from the Crown Derby Porcelain Company (Royal Crown Derby from 1890) based in Derby, England.

editions. These qualities give them every claim on the British Museum and on public libraries belonging to the nation, for there they will be ensured against probable fires and possible thefts and destruction, but should never be considered by the private individual for one moment, who should buy his books to read and read them, thus enjoying one of the pleasures which once acquired never fail us, and render us unassailable by any after woes.

At the same time a book should never for one moment be allowed to remain torn or shabby in a private library, or indeed for the matter of that in any public one. If a book be worth buying it is worthy of a decent dress, and therefore should be kept in one, without any doubt at all. A great many people I know abuse circulating libraries, and consider them foes indeed of those who gain their living by their pens, but I always look upon them with the deepest gratitude, for one uses them to sift the wheat from the chaff, and having once read the book by the aid of these ever useful institutions we can tell if it is worth buying, or merely serves to pass away pleasantly a passing hour. If it be worth buying it should be bought, Oh British public! and kept and properly clad and housed, and far rather would I have a good library than an enormous stock of wine or jewels or any other superfluity. No one is as good a companion as a book is; nothing makes us at once so immediately independent of our circumstances and our surroundings.

Forgive this small sermon, dear readers, but I so often hear in reply to the question, "What are you reading?" "Oh, only a novel," that I cannot help expressing here, in my library, my extreme wonder at the "only" which invariably forms part of the reply. Only a novel; only, perhaps, the life experience of some man or woman; only the fruits of toil and labour; only a thrilling story which has made us forget our aches and pains, our troubles, our disasters. Ah! once more let me record my own indebtedness to the producers of "only a novel," only an amusing book, and once more let me beg for these same writers a shrine in every house where they can be worthily entertained and properly appreciated. There are libraries beautifully furnished and decorated, yet which make one's heart sink into one's shoes when one enters them, because of the dreariness of the contents of their shelves, where "standard authors" jostle translations from the classics, and where commentaries which are never opened lean against volumes of dry-as-dust theories, long since exploded and dead as one wishes the books were; and while we are thinking out our schemes of decoration and adornment of the room, let us yet remember that after all its truest ornaments are the books, which should be the true and real jewels in the casket.

Everyone has his or her own particular "hundred books," his or her favourites, and everyone who tells the honest truth is always a little bit shy of confessing to the real facts about them; but I would ask everyone not to be swayed too much by popular prejudice, which sometimes right is often enough very, very wrong; to rely on his or her own judgment; and while owning that age is the only absolute test of reality, to give the young eager generation a chance, and if the books it produces please and amuse, to buy them, and so encourage those who all too often never put out their best because they cannot afford to wait, and because the ordinary Englishman would rather do anything almost than openly and honestly purchase a book.

Well, perhaps if his library be made more seductive he may presently begin to learn how to buy his books himself; therefore will I propose yet another scheme of decoration, which this time can be carried out in Chippendale[1] mahogany and pink and blue. ...

I should certainly advocate a sofa as well as the window-seat in the deep comfortable Chippendale style, for I am a great believer in being able to rest, but of course a great deal must depend on the individual tastes of whoever is to inhabit the

---

1   *Chippendale* Style of furniture associated with the English designer and woodworker Thomas Chippendale (1718–79).

room. For some libraries are held sacred to the master of the house, and here he interviews his tenants or his business-men, or allows the latter to interview him. Here he reads the girls lectures on their frivolities and their expenditure, and here he rows the boys and utterly forgets that he was once every bit as bad if not worse than his offspring, when he too in those long dead days was young and most eminently foolish. In such a room as this our prettinesses would maybe be out of place, but I should still introduce them, for then his womenfolk would feel they had a right to be with him, while in face of such suggestions Paterfamilias[1] would wax less stern than he would otherwise be prepared to be. Still, if the house-master is much at home, if he be a country gentleman and has all the tastes and duties inseparable from this position he must have a somewhat severe library and keep it to himself, or should have what indeed would be preferable: a business-room set apart entirely for business, where he could do exactly as he wished and see anyone, even his coachman or farm bailiff, neither of whom should ever come beyond the servants' arch, and who would both be out of place in a library situated where we have placed ours in our present plan. Of course, if the master has an occupation that takes him out all day, there is no trouble then about the library as regards general visitors; it can be kept for him on Sundays, he can use it all the evening if he does not care for billiards and is too tired or too misanthropic for the drawing-room; in that case he will be very glad of the sofa, and under any conditions I think it would be wiser to have one.

Never under any circumstances allow the shelves to reach to the ceiling; never collect immense stores of rubbish in the shape of either silly or unreadable books, and never put an embargo on the contents of your library as far as the younger members of the family are concerned. Of course, I suppose, all libraries must contain books they should not read, but why, I honestly do not

---

1 *Paterfamilias*   Head of the family (Latin: literally, father of the family).

know. I do know what I read long before I was twelve, and I do know also that it never did me any harm, for what might have done so I naturally could not understand, and simply took as a matter of course. While I equally well remember papers and books being spoken of as "not fit for the children," which the children immediately looked out for and possessed themselves of, only to wonder why they weren't fit, for they didn't seem half as bloodthirsty as several of our own books, nor as wildly improbable as the "Arabian Nights,"[1] which was one of the first books I remember possessing as my "very own." If a book is not fit for the children it isn't fit for us. The "young person" who is popularly supposed to do so much harm to the cause of the British drama, should do as much harm as she likes to the contents of our libraries; but then one has to determine where the harm comes in. I should give my daughters "Tess of the D'Urbervilles" to read, while I should most certainly draw the line at "Dodo," "The Heavenly Twins," *et hoc genus omne.*[2]

Anyhow, whatever line is taken do not forbid the books to the children. Place what you object them to read on the highest shelves, and don't have any library steps, and do not speak about them, but discuss the books you do want them to read before them but not *at* them, and you will find you won't have much trouble. But also thank the advance of the century for the fact that there are so many good books nowadays that if they are properly read and enjoyed there is no time left for the bad ones; and always begin early with the children's reading, and don't bore them. They may not care for Scott nowadays, but they will

---

1 *Arabian Nights* Collection of stories (also known as *The Thousand and One Nights*) drawn from various sources, mostly Middle Eastern and Indian. Compiled in Arabic, the stories were made available in the nineteenth century in numerous English translations.

2 *Tess of the D'Urbervilles* Novel by Thomas Hardy (1840–1928) published in book form in 1892; *Dodo* 1893 novel by E.F. [Edward Frederic] Benson (1867–1940). It included controversial depictions of fashionable society; *The Heavenly Twins* 1893 novel by Sarah Grand, pseudonym of Frances Elizabeth Bellenden McFall née Clark (1854–1943). It critiqued the inequity of women in marriage and detailed the perils of syphilis, published in 1893; *et hoc genus omne* Latin: and all of this kind.

adore Thackeray;[1] they can't help doing so. They may turn from Dickens (albeit I hope they won't), but they will eagerly read the younger men, who are so many and so good that one hesitates to name one name, albeit no one can forget "Vice Versa,"[2] and the many admirably humourous volumes which have emanated from the same pen; while a healthy love of books, aye, books as books, not as literature, will help all who cultivate it to pass through the worst times of their lives better than they could otherwise have done, for, as I say to myself a hundred times a day, where should I be were it not for the heaps of books one can get, and the hundreds of people who are all engaged in writing, as it appears to me, simply for my edification?

What wonder then that I want the library to be very carefully and beautifully finished and filled, that I should desire the eye to be pleased by colour and form, while the senses are soothed by sweet scents from flowers, by sunshine, by warm breezes, and cool and occasional shade, and above all by a sense of complete stillness and silence which should pervade this room, even more than any other room in the house? This must be ensured by heavily curtained doors, the doors themselves being of such substance that they shall absolutely perform their business in life, which is to keep out sound and cold, by thick rugs laid on soundless floors and by cultivating a habit of silence therein. Once give this room over to exciting gabble, as opposed to real conversation, its purpose will most certainly vanish; it may be a library by name, it will certainly never be one by nature any more.

---

1   *Scott*   Sir Walter Scott, Scottish author noted for his ballads and for developing the historical novel (1771–1832);   *Thackeray*   William Makepeace Thackeray, English novelist (1811–63).

2   *Dickens*   English novelist Charles Dickens (1812–79);   *Vice Versa*   Comic novel of a father and son trading places. Written by F. Anstey, pseudonym of Thomas Anstey Guthrie (1856–1934), it was published in 1882.

from E.J. [Edward John] Tilt, *On the Preservation of the Health of Women at the Critical Periods of Life* (1851)

> As the number of female readers and the supply of reading materials directed towards them increased across the nineteenth century, discussion intensified of the dangers reading might pose for women and girls. One contributor to that conversation was the physician E.J. Tilt (1815–93), who argued that their physiology made women and girls uniquely susceptible to developing nervous disorders in consequence of reading, with novels posing special peril.

from Chapter 1, "On the Right Management of Young Women before the First Appearance of Menstruation"

... Novels and romances, speaking generally, should be spurned, as capable of calling forth emotions of the same morbid description which, when habitually indulged in, exert a disastrous influence on the nervous system, sufficient to explain that frequency of hysteria and nervous diseases which we find among women of the higher classes. "Si votre fille lit des romans à dix ans, elle aura des vapeurs à vingt."[1] It may be contended that many of these works contain excellent principles and admirable precepts of morality; but what do girls care about moral axioms, which are almost always obscured in the brilliancy of fiction? They seek for the stirring adventure, the extravagant romance, the victorious hero, as if there were not sufficient romance in real life to excite the young imagination, without stimulating this faculty by creations, evoking heroes for them to set up as gods of their idolatry, with whom their fancy may suggest they could live for ever in regions of boundless and unfading bliss. ...

---

1   *Si votre ... à vingt*   French: If your daughter reads novels at 10, she will have the vapors at 20; "the vapors" in Victorian usage referred to vaguely defined nervous disorders often associated with femininity: fainting spells, hysteria, melancholy.

from G. Stanley Hall, *Adolescence: Its Psychology and Its
Relations to Physiology, Anthropology, Sociology, Sex,
Crime, Religion and Education*, vol. 2 (1904)

> Grenville Stanley Hall (1846–1924), an influential American in the
> young discipline of psychology, published the first significant study
> of adolescence. Adolescence itself, as a distinct stage in human devel-
> opment between childhood and adulthood, was a new conception,
> formulated in Victorian times, and Hall's account includes explora-
> tion of the reading habits of young people and the role of reading in
> the formation of the self.

from Chapter 16, "Intellectual Development and Education"

... Interest in story-telling rises till twelve or thirteen, and
thereafter falls off perhaps rather suddenly, partly because
youth is now more interested in receiving than in giving. As in
the drawing curve we saw a characteristic age when the child
loses pleasure in creating as its power of appreciating pictures
rapidly arises, so now as the reading curve rises auditory recep-
tivity makes way for the visual method shown in the rise of
the reading curve with augmented zest for book-method of
acquisition. Darkness or twilight enhances the story interest in
children, for it eliminates the distraction of sense and encourages the imagination to unfold its pinions, but the youthful
fancy is less bat-like and can take its boldest flights in broad
daylight. A camp-fire, or an open hearth with tales of animals,
ghosts, heroism, and adventure, can teach virtue, and vocabulary, style, and substance in their native unity.

The pubescent reading passion is partly the cause and partly
an effect of the new zest in and docility to the adult world and
also of the act that the receptive are now and here so immea-
surably in advance of the creative powers. Now the individual
transcends his own experience and learns to profit by that of
others. There is now evolved a penumbral region in the soul

more or less beyond the reach of all school methods, a world of glimpses and hints, and the work here is that of the prospector and not of the careful miner. It is the age of skipping and sampling, of pressing the keys lightly. What is acquired is not examinable but only suggestive. Perhaps nothing read now fails to leave its mark. It can not be orally reproduced at call, but on emergency it is at hand for use. As Augustine[1] said of God, so the child might say of most of his mental content in these psychic areas, "If you ask me, I do not know; but if you do not ask me, I know very well"—a case analogous to the typical girl who exclaimed to her teacher, "I can and do understand this perfectly if only you won't explain it." That is why examinations in English, if not impossible ... are very liable to be harmful, and recitations and critical notes an impertinence, and always in danger of causing arrest of this exquisite romantic function in which literature comes in the closest *rapport* to life, keeping the heart warm, reinforcing all its good motives, preforming choices, and universalizing its sympathies. ...

The reading passion may rage with great intensity when the soul takes its first long flight into the world of books, and ninety percent of all Conradi's[2] cases showed it. Of these, thirty-two per cent read to have the feelings stirred and the desire of knowledge was a far less frequent motive. Some read to pass idle time, others to appear learned or to acquire a style or a vocabulary. Romance led. Some specialized, and with some the appetite was omnivorous. Some preferred books about or addressed to children, some fairy tales, and some sought only those for adults. The night is often invaded and some become "perfectly wild" over exciting adventures or the dangers and hardships of true lovers, laughing and crying as the story took turns from grave to gay, and a few read several books a week. Some were forbid-

---

1 *Augustine* St. Augustine of Hippo (354–430 CE), a Christian theologian whose writings were influential in the formation of the early Catholic Church.

2 *Conradi* Edward Conradi (1869–1944), a psychologist and student of Hall's who focused on language and speech development.

den and read by stealth alone, or with books hidden in their desks or under school books. Some few live thus for years in an atmosphere highly charged with romance, and burn out their fires wickedly early with a sudden and extreme expansiveness that makes life about them uninteresting and unreal, and that reacts to commonplace later. ...

from Margaret Oliphant, *The Autobiography and Letters of Mrs. M.O.W. Oliphant* (1899)

> Oliphant's *Autobiography* (which was not published until after her death) was written at different stages of her life, in the form of occasional entries resembling those of a diary. In the entry excerpted here (written 8 February 1885), Oliphant recalls the experience of having her first book published (in 1849), and describes her work habits as a writer, reflecting on their connection to her girlhood.

... And then Mr. Colburn[1] kindly—I thought most kindly, and thanked him *avec effusion*—gave me £150 for "Margaret Maitland." I remember walking along the street with delightful elation, thinking that, after all, I was worth something—and not to be hustled about. I remember, too, getting the first review of my book in the twilight of a wintry dark afternoon and reading it by the firelight—always half-amused at the thought that it was *me* who was being thus discussed in the newspapers. It was the *Athenaeum*,[2] and it was on the whole favourable. Of course this event preceded by a couple of months the transaction with Mr. Colburn. I think the book was in its third edition before he offered me that £150. I remember no reviews except that one of the *Athenaeum*, nor any particular effect which my success produced in me, except that sense of elation. I cannot think why the book succeeded so well. When I read it over some years after, I felt nothing but shame at its foolish little polemics and opinions. I suppose there must have been some breath of youth and sincerity in it which touched people, and there had been no Scotch stories for a long time. Lord Jeffrey,[3] then an old man and very near his end, sent me a letter of sweet praise, which filled my mother with rapture and myself

---

1   *Mr. Colburn*   Publisher Henry Colburn (1784–1855).

2   *Athenaeum*   Literary magazine published from 1828 to 1921.

3   *Lord Jeffrey*   Francis Jeffrey (1773–1850), Scottish founder and early editor of the *Edinburgh Review*; he was active in political life and was eventually made a judge.

with an abashed gratitude. I was very young. Oddly enough, it has always remained a matter of doubt with me whether the book was published in 1849 or 1850. I thought the former; but Geraldine Macpherson, whom I met in London for the first time a day or two before it was published, declared it to be 1850, from the fact that *that* was the year of her marriage. If a woman remembers any date, it must be the date of her marriage! so I don't doubt Geddie was right. Anyhow, if it was 1850, I was then only twenty-two, and in some things very young for my age, as in others perhaps older than my years. I was wonderfully little moved by the business altogether. I had a great pleasure in writing, but the success and the three editions had no particular effect on my mind. For one thing, I saw very few people. We had no society. My father had a horror of strangers, and would never see any one who came to the house, which was a continual wet blanket to my mother's cordial, hospitable nature; but she had given up struggling long before my time, and I grew up without any idea of the pleasures and companions of youth. I did not know them, and therefore did not miss them; but I daresay this helped to make me—not indifferent, rather unconscious, of what might in other circumstances have "turned my head." My head was as steady as a rock. I had nobody to praise me except my mother and Frank, and their applause—well, it was delightful, it was everything in the world—it was life,—but it did not count. They were part of me, and I of them, and we were all in it. After a while it came to be the custom that I should every night "read what I had written" to them before I went to bed. They were very critical sometimes, and I felt I was reading whether my little audience was with me or not, which put a good deal of excitement into the performance. But that was all the excitement I had.

I began another book called "Caleb Field," about the Plague in London, the very night I had finished "Margaret Maitland."

I had been reading Defoe,[1] and got the subject into my head. It came to one volume only, and I took a great deal of trouble about a Nonconformist[2] minister who spoke in antitheses very carefully constructed. I don't think it attracted much notice, but I don't remember. Other matters, events even of our uneventful life, took so much more importance in life than these books— nay, it must be a kind of affectation to say that, for the writing ran through everything. But then it was also subordinate to everything, to be pushed aside for any little necessity. I had no table even to myself, much less a room to work in, but sat at the corner of the family table with my writing-book, with everything going on as if I had been making a shirt instead of writing a book. Our rooms in those days were sadly wanting in artistic arrangement. The table was in the middle of the room, the centre round which everybody sat with the candles or the lamp upon it. My mother sat always at needle-work of some kind, and talked to whomever might be present, and I took my share in the conversation, going on all the same with my story, the little groups of imaginary persons, these other talks evolving themselves quite undisturbed. It would put me out now to have some one sitting at the same table talking while I worked—at least I would think it put me out, with that sort of conventionalism which grows upon one. But up to this date, 1888, I have never been shut up in a separate room, or hedged off with any observances. My study, all the study I have ever attained to, is the little second drawing-room where all the (feminine) life of the house goes on; and I don't think I have ever had two hours undisturbed (except at night, when everybody is in bed) during my whole literary life. Miss Austen,[3] I believe, wrote in the same way, and very much for the same reason; but at her period the natural flow of life took another form. Her family were half ashamed to have it known that she was not just a young lady

---

1 *Defoe* Novelist Daniel Defoe (1660–1731).
2 *Nonconformist* I.e., Puritan.
3 *Miss Austen* Novelist Jane Austen (1775–1817).

like the others, doing her embroidery. Mine were quite pleased to magnify me, and to be proud of my work, but always with a hidden sense that it was an admirable joke, and no idea that any special facilities or retirement was necessary. My mother, I believe, would have felt her pride and rapture much checked, almost humiliated, if she had conceived that I stood in need of any artificial aids of that or any other description. That would at once have made the work unnatural to her eyes, and also to mine. I think the first time I ever secluded myself for my work was years after it had become my profession and sole dependence—when I was living after my widowhood in a relation's house, and withdrew with my book and my inkstand from the family drawing-room out of a little conscious ill-temper which made me feel guilty, notwithstanding that the retirement was so very justifiable! But I did not feel it to be so, neither did the companions from whom I withdrew. ...

Images of Scottish Street Scenes and Interiors

The setting of "The Library Window" is the fictional Scottish town of St. Rule's, the name of which alludes to Saint Regulus (also known as Saint Rule), who in a legend with political significance for Scotland brought relics of Saint Andrew from Greece to the Scottish town of St. Andrews (and in one case, the nearby town of Dundee).

Arts Divinity Reading Room Library, University of St. Andrews, 1890s

Bell Street, St. Andrews, from the north, 1895

Market Street, St. Andrews, 1896

Castle Street, Dundee, 1876

North Street, St. Andrews, 1887

BLACKWOOD'S

𝕰𝖉𝖎𝖓𝖇𝖚𝖗𝖌𝖍

MAGAZINE.

VOL. CLIX.

JANUARY—JUNE 1896.

WILLIAM BLACKWOOD & SONS, EDINBURGH;

AND

37 PATERNOSTER ROW, LONDON.

1896.

"The Library Window" was first published in the January 1896 issue of *Blackwood's Edinburgh Magazine*.

BLACKWOOD'S
EDINBURGH MAGAZINE.

No. DCCCCLXIII.   JANUARY 1896.   Vol. CLIX.

THE LIBRARY WINDOW.

A STORY OF THE SEEN AND THE UNSEEN.

I.

I WAS not aware at first of the many discussions which had gone on about that window. It was almost opposite one of the windows of the large old-fashioned drawing-room of the house in which I spent that summer, which was of so much importance in my life. Our house and the library were on opposite sides of the broad High Street of St Rule's, which is a fine street, wide and ample, and very quiet, as strangers think who come from noisier places; but in a summer evening there is much coming and going, and the stillness is full of sound—the sound of footsteps and pleasant voices, softened by the summer air. There are even exceptional moments when it is noisy: the time of the fair, and on Saturday nights sometimes, and when there are excursion trains. Then even the softest sunny air of the evening will not smooth the harsh tones and the stumbling steps; but at these unlovely moments we shut the windows, and even I, who am so fond of that deep recess where I can take refuge from all that is going on inside, and make myself a spectator of all the varied story out of doors, withdraw from my watch-tower. To tell the truth, there never was very much going on inside. The house belonged to my aunt, to whom (she says, Thank God!) nothing ever happens. I believe that many things have happened to her in her time; but that was all over at the period of which I am speaking, and she was old, and very quiet. Her life went on in a routine never broken. She

The first page of "The Library Window" as it appeared in
Blackwood's Edinburgh Magazine

From the Publisher

A name never says it all, but the word "Broadview" expresses a good deal of the philosophy behind our company. We are open to a broad range of academic approaches and political viewpoints. We pay attention to the broad impact book publishing and book printing has in the wider world; for some years now we have used 100% recycled paper for most titles. Our publishing program is internationally oriented and broad-ranging. Our individual titles often appeal to a broad readership too; many are of interest as much to general readers as to academics and students.

Founded in 1985, Broadview remains a fully independent company owned by its shareholders—not an imprint or subsidiary of a larger multinational.

For the most accurate information on our books (including information on pricing, editions, and formats) please visit our website at www.broadviewpress.com. Our print books and ebooks are also available for sale on our site.

broadview press
www.broadviewpress.com

The interior of this book is printed on 100% recycled paper.